Alliances

Alliances

An Executive Guide to Designing Successful Strategic Partnerships

Ard-Pieter de Man

Registered office
John Wiley & Sons Ltd, The Atrium, Southern Gate, Chichester, West Sussex,
PO19 8SQ, United Kingdom

For details of our global editorial offices, for customer services and for information
about how to apply for permission to reuse the copyright material in this book please
see our website at www.wiley.com.

Wiley publishes in a variety of print and electronic formats and by print-on-demand.
Some material included with standard print versions of this book may not be included
in e-books or in print-on-demand. If this book refers to media such as a CD or DVD
that is not included in the version you purchased, you may download this material
at http://booksupport.wiley.com. For more information about Wiley products, visit
www.wiley.com.

Designations used by companies to distinguish their products are often claimed as
trademarks. All brand names and product names used in this book are trade names,
service marks, trademarks or registered trademarks of their respective owners. The
publisher is not associated with any product or vendor mentioned in this book.

Library of Congress Cataloging-in-Publication Data

Man, Adrianus Pieter de
    Alliances : an executive guide to designing successful strategic partnerships /
Ard-Pieter de Man.
        pages cm
    Includes index.
      ISBN 978-1-118-48639-9 (hardback)
    1. Strategic alliances (Business)   I. Title.
    HD69.S8.M32 2014
    658'.046—dc23   2013039719

A catalogue record for this book is available from the British Library.

ISBN 978-1-118-48639-9 (hardback) ISBN 978-1-118-48632-0 (ebk)
ISBN 978-1-118-48636-8 (ebk)

Cover design/image: Dan Jubb/iStock

Set in 9.5/13 pt Melior LT Std by Toppan Best-set Premedia Limited, Hong Kong
Printed in Great Britain by TJ International Ltd, Padstow, Cornwall, UK

Contents

Foreword   vii

Introduction   ix

Acknowledgments   xiii

1 Strategic alliances: The control–trust dilemma   1

2 The Alliance Design Framework   21

3 Turning suppliers into allies   51

4 Contractual alliances: The customization of alliance design   71

5 The virtual joint venture model: Air France/KLM, Delta Airlines,
   and Alitalia   101

6 Equity alliances and joint ventures   121

7 Multi-partner alliances: The more the merrier?   145

8 Managing the dynamics: Mutual adjustment and
   continuous negotiation   167

9 Designing and implementing strategic alliances:
   Art, science, and craft   181

10 Open alliances: Towards the third generation of collaboration   195

Appendix   Financial models behind alliances   207

Index   215

Foreword

Strategic alliances are particularly important in today's highly competitive and increasingly complex global markets. Alliances are used to share costs, conduct collaborative research, mitigate risk, grow product pipelines, expand geographic boundaries and profit from the blending of industries which continue at an accelerated pace. One of the recurrent challenges with strategic alliances is how to design and implement the correct governance platform and supportive organizational structure. Developing, implementing and maintaining a suitable alliance form is a key factor for strategic alliance success. Over the years this issue has been an important element in the meetings, summits and publications of the leading organization dedicated to the practice of alliance management, the Association of Strategic Alliance Professionals (ASAP).

In this book, Ard-Pieter de Man investigates a number of areas that active practitioners of alliance management focus on to achieve desired results from a strategic relationship. Overall development of the partnership agreement, the overarching governance structure and the ongoing tactical execution and essential measurement tools are considered. These elements, and the challenges they bring, are clearly evidenced in any type of agreement. The area of collaboration governance by itself is a particularly sensitive issue as partnerships cross company boundaries, cultures and hierarchies.

As a long-time practicing professional and contributor in the area of strategic alliance management, I have been highly familiarized by the work and teachings of Ard-Pieter de Man on this topic. As I endeavored to develop a global alliance management team at a world-renowned drug development organization and help build the ASAP proposition, I have come to respect his perspective on this emergent and growing business requirement.

One particular effort Ard-Pieter de Man has put forward in concert with other highly respected alliance experts, (a research project called "It's in the DNA") is a fine outline of how alignment of cultural norms can affect alliance success. Without the development of a strong base in this regard, a critical success factor is left wanting and the overall success of the alliance could be put at risk. In this book, the important themes of culture, norms and values are integrated with aspects of formal structures and governance. This gives a full-blown account of how alliances should be designed while incorporating this essential, but many times undervalued, piece of the partnership equation.

This book will introduce you to in-depth case studies, useful checklists and strong issue resolution techniques that are supported by years of Ard-Pieter de Man's ongoing research and active consulting practice. These important concepts outline why alliance management is seen as important by the global business community and how it continues to evolve as new partnership applications develop.

The detailed case studies focus on some of the world's leading alliances. They form the backbone of an extensive overview of different alliance governance forms, which will help managers navigate the many different choices they face. Unique characteristics of the book also include the integration of the "hard" and "soft" side of alliances, the first ever discussion of financial models in alliances and the role of change management in alliances.

As Ard-Pieter de Man has continued his examination of this profession, I have become increasingly appreciative of his dedication to the study of the business contributions that the practice of strategic alliance management brings forward. His representation around the most current thinking, ongoing development and important financial nuances on this subject is absolutely additive to an organizational bottom line. I would strongly recommend this as a read for any individual – practitioner or decision maker – who holds strategic alliances as a component of their business development plans.

Jack W. Pearson
Acting President & CEO
Board Vice Chair/Chairman-Elect
Association of Strategic Alliance Professionals
Cary, North Carolina
2013

Introduction

Collaboration between organizations is an increasingly common way of organizing. Strategic alliances have become a standard organization form over the past decade. The majority of organizations, whether private or public, are embedded in networks of partners. Still, finding the right form for alliances is difficult. New alliance forms have emerged over the past years and they have broadened the arsenal of possibilities that companies have at their disposal. Even though many different forms of alliances exist, companies usually are aware of only one or two models which they tend to apply over and over again. In addition, mistakes in designing alliances are not uncommon. Many alliance failures are explained by the choice for a design that does not fit with the alliance objectives. In contrast, the most successful alliances build on creative alliance governance structures. This book presents an overview of the most relevant alliance forms and provides guidelines about when and how to apply them.

The book aims to help managers navigate through the many choices they face when entering the alliance arena. The various chapters deal with questions like: should I choose a joint venture or a contractual alliance? When should I opt for an alliance over a merger or an acquisition? Which elements should I put in the contract and which should I leave out? How do I deal with change in alliances? What alliance governance models exist? Case studies into some of the world's leading and most innovative alliances provide answers to these questions. Many if not all sectors use alliances and therefore the book includes cases from retail, pharma, IT, the financial industry, and many more industries. Companies like to compare themselves to their direct peers and competitors. This book shows that different industries sometimes have surprising insights in alliances that have a very broad applicability.

Academics form another audience for this book. Alliances are an important field of research in the area of management. The academic literature has focused on only some elements of alliance design. An integrated view of alliance governance is absent and as a consequence only a few insights have been generated that are of practical use. Still the literature has come up with some fundamental ideas. By translating these into practice I hope to show that research can help to provide answers to managerial challenges. I also hope this book will help to generate new research agendas. Rather than focusing on one or two areas of alliance design, academics should now focus on building a configurational theory of alliances that shows how all the pieces should fit together. Doing so will increase the practical relevance of research. The dynamics of alliances are another largely unexplored area that deserves much more attention. Change management in alliances is a topic of considerable importance.

Outline of the book

The first chapter of the book describes the core challenges of designing alliances and the general principles behind alliance design. This chapter analyzes two views on alliance design: the control view and the trust view. Chapter 2 presents the Alliance Design Framework. The Alliance Design Framework describes all elements of alliance design in detail. This chapter can be read as an extensive checklist that contains all aspects that a good alliance design should incorporate. It will be useful for anyone designing an alliance to keep this chapter close at hand.

The core of the book is formed by Chapters 3 to 7, which analyze the most important alliance forms and their specific characteristics. They are all based on case studies that highlight how the Alliance Design Framework is operationalized in that specific case. For each alliance form, the different subforms that emerged in practice are analyzed. Figure I.1 gives an overview of all these forms.

Chapter 3 focuses on collaboration in supply chains and client–supplier relationships. The trend of moving from a traditional purchasing mentality focusing on cost towards a mentality focusing on risk sharing and innovation is common in an increasing number of client–supplier relationships. Chapter 4 focuses on the most frequently used form of alliances: contractual alliances between two partners. This chapter describes four models to structure contractual alliances: the lone ranger, specialization, joint teams, and peer-to-peer models. Chapter 5 focuses on the virtual joint venture. Virtual joint ventures are relatively rare due to their complexity, but they provide very interesting lessons that are valuable for many other alliances. Equity alliances are the topic of Chapter 6. The joint venture is the most common form of equity alliance. The chapter shows

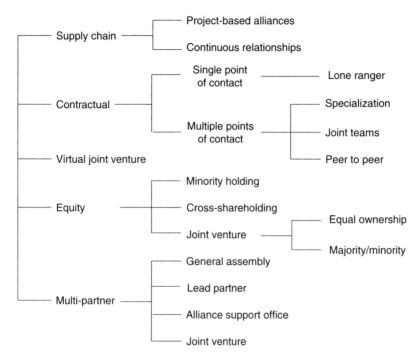

FIGURE I.1: Alliance forms

the specific success factors of such alliance forms. Chapter 7 highlights the organization of multi-partner alliances. Bilateral alliances are difficult to design and manage; multi-partner alliances even more so. Still, four effective structures for multi-partner alliances exist. Multi-partner alliances may use a general assembly, a lead partner, an alliance support office, or a joint venture to govern the collaboration.

The next two chapters draw some lessons across these five different alliance forms. Chapter 8 goes into more detail about managing the dynamics of alliances. A recurrent theme in the cases is that designing alliances is not a one-time activity. Instead alliance designs must be adapted regularly over the alliance lifespan. The chapter outlines the mechanisms behind change management in alliances. Chapter 9 is a practical guide to developing alliance structures. It lists the steps in the design process that need to be followed. In many consulting assignments this process has proven to be useful. The final Chapter 10 looks ahead. New alliance forms continue to emerge. However, many alliances still try to combine traditional hierarchy with horizontal coordination in a model of "vertical horizontalism." Open alliances appear to become the third generation of alliances and dispense with such hierarchical thinking. Chapter 10 speculates on what open alliances may look like and which challenges and opportunities they face.

Acknowledgments

Some years ago Stichting Management Studies in the Netherlands asked me to execute a study on alliance governance. Together with Nadine Roijakkers I explored the ins and outs of this topic. That study provided a first start for the exploration of the theme of alliance design in this book. I am particularly grateful to all those people in companies who helped me execute the case studies. Time is a scarce resource and without the participation of the companies it would not have been possible to write this book and to advance our understanding of alliances. Over the years I have been involved with many companies and alliances as a consultant. Many of the lessons learnt during those consulting assignments are now part of this book and I would like to express my gratitude to all those organizations that collaborated with me on their alliance adventures. Finally, via my membership of the Board of Directors of the Association of Strategic Alliance Professionals (ASAP) I got access to many of the world's leading alliance managers and to a plethora of alliance ideas and resources. The many conversations, presentations, and best practices shared via ASAP have sharpened my thinking on alliances enormously.

Ard-Pieter de Man

CHAPTER 1

Strategic alliances: The control–trust dilemma

The airlines Air France/KLM, Delta and Alitalia jointly operate an alliance with gross revenues of $10 billion. The alliance is based on an extensive contract that stipulates precisely the costs and revenues that are shared, which activities are part of the alliance and which are not and the responsibilities of the partners. A well-defined contract is not the only source of the alliance's success. The organizations involved have a long history of collaboration between them, have invested in personal relationships and have implemented a governance structure to manage the turbulence expected in the business of airlines. The alliance partners recognized that the contract could not foresee all future possibilities and, hence, developed a governance structure to guide and initiate change within the alliance.

Even more flexible was German supermarket METRO's coalition involving approximately 50 partners that aimed to build the supermarket of the future. The coalition's legal backbone is a very short memorandum of understanding. Still, the partners to METRO's Future Store Initiative were able to create one of the industry's strongest engines for innovation. The secret? No complex contracts were necessary because METRO selected partners that they knew and trusted. In addition, METRO created a compelling vision for the alliance with clear benefits for all. Consequently, partners were highly motivated to contribute and dispensed with the need for a myriad of complex control mechanisms.

In September 2009, Danone, the French food and beverage company, announced that it would sell its 51 percent stake in its joint venture (JV) with Wahaha, its Chinese counterpart. This sale ended a successful $2 billion joint venture and a prolonged struggle between the companies. Danone accused Wahaha of breaching their agreement by copying the joint venture in other parts of China and keeping all of the profits. Wahaha claimed that Danone invested in its Chinese competitors, despite the fact that their collaboration was exclusive. For two years, the companies fought each other in court and engaged in extensive mudslinging before reaching what they called "an amicable settlement."[1]

In 2012, BP announced that it intended to sell its 50 percent stake in TNK–BP,[2] its joint venture with AAR, an investment vehicle owned by three Russian businessmen. The sale would result in BP losing one-third of its production, reserves and profits. The reason behind the proposed sale was a series of conflicts, among others over an attempt by BP to set up a joint venture with the Russian gas company Gazprom. According to AAR, this attempt represented a breach of their confidential shareholder agreement, which stipulated that such a deal should have been concluded via TNK–BP. The Gazprom deal fell through and TNK–BP's British chief fled the country in fear of his safety. The dispute did not end there. The relationship soured and another deal by BP with the Russian state-owned oil company Rosneft to explore oil in the Arctic was contested in a Swedish court and halted. In the meantime, the joint venture became ungovernable after one of the Russian businessmen resigned from its board. During and after difficult negotiations involving Russian President Vladimir Putin in early 2013, the joint venture was sold to Rosneft for €40 billion. The secret shareholder agreement and the less than transparent Russian oil sector make it difficult to judge which party was wrong or right; regardless, significant interests were clearly at stake and the conflict did not help anyone's business.

These four examples are of high-profile alliances. The last two show that even financially successful alliances may falter. More importantly, the examples show that owning a majority or 50 percent of the shares does not mean that a company is in control of its joint venture. The behavior of the partners (do they or do they not adhere to the terms of the contract?) and other contractual provisions (did Wahaha have the right to imitate the joint venture? Was the collaboration between BP and AAR exclusive?) are also very relevant elements of the joint venture structure. In fact, in these cases, these elements completely overrode the shareholding arrangements. The lesson is that the formal elements in the design of an alliance are not sufficient to ensure good governance; the predictability of the partner's behavior must also be considered. METRO built on this insight by aligning itself only with trusted partners. Air France/KLM recognized that alliances were more than contracts and, for that reason, invested in personal relationships. A good alliance design takes into account all such hard and soft elements.

However, balancing the hard and soft elements is a challenge. Because partners do not always behave in the manner desired, control mechanisms must be implemented. Too many control mechanisms make the alliance inflexible and smother creativity. Too few control mechanisms may undermine the clarity of the direction of the alliance and open up space for partners to behave in a manner that benefits their own interests, which damages the alliance. These cases show that alliances with many control mechanisms can be successful (the airlines) but may also fail (TNK–BP). Few control mechanisms and high reliance on trust (the Future Store Initiative) may result in success but leave the partners vulnerable to opportunistic behavior by their collaborators. Therefore, the key dilemma in designing alliances is balancing trust with control. Given specific circumstances, what is the right equilibrium between these two? Designing successful alliances requires answers to this question.

Why is alliance design relevant?

Alliance design is relevant because alliances have become a standard to organize businesses. An alliance represents a collaboration between at least two independent organizations aiming to achieve a competitive advantage that each cannot achieve on its own. An alliance is characterized by joint goals, involves some form of sharing of revenue, costs and risk between the partners, provides for joint decision making and is based on open-ended or incomplete agreements.[3] These open-ended agreements are an important characteristic of alliances. Standard purchasing contracts are "closed": company A delivers to company B a fixed number of products at a certain price. In alliances, closed contracts do not exist, and alliance contracts are open ended: they do not specify what each partner must do in every conceivable situation, simply because doing so is not possible or is too expensive.

Implied in this definition of alliances is that many forms of alliances exist. A basic distinction is between equity alliances and contractual alliances. Equity alliances involve a shareholding arrangement, which can be a minority share of one company in another, a cross-shareholding or a joint venture, which is a separate legal entity in which two or more companies hold shares. However, most alliances are contractual and the diversity of contractual alliances is probably as significant as the number of alliances itself. In fact, this diversity shows the strengths of alliances and one of the major reasons for their popularity: each agreement can be perfectly customized to the specific needs of the partners. Simultaneously, typical alliance forms have emerged in practice, the most important of which are discussed in this book.

The increased importance of alliances has been documented extensively. In 2007, companies entered into 12 new alliances, and by 2011 that number had risen to 18. The total number of alliances has increased to such an extent that, in 2011, companies reported that one-third of their market value depended on them.[4] The 2012 IBM CEO study found that almost 70 percent of CEOs partnered extensively.[5] For the 21st century organization, having a smooth-running internal organization is no longer sufficient. Its external relationships also need to be effectively organized.

The reasons for the increase in alliances are the usual suspects. The speed of technological development has two effects. First, a company may no longer want to commit resources to only one technology because it runs the risk of betting on the wrong horse. Spreading risk through alliances makes more sense. Second, the existence of numerous technologies makes keeping track of all of them impossible, even for the largest organizations. Gaining access to these technologies through alliance partners enables companies to learn from others and, if necessary, integrate those technologies into their products. Increased competition is another reason for entering into alliances. By combining resources, companies may be able to face greater competition. Competition also forces companies to be world class in only a few products or services, and complementary products and services may be obtained through alliances. Customer demand is another driver of alliances. Customers are not primarily interested in the individual products offered by large IT companies such as SAP, Oracle, Microsoft, HP, IBM and Cisco. Instead, they want those products to work together in coherent solutions. For that reason, these companies have established alliances that ensure that their products are compatible. Alliances do not stop there. They also enable companies to jointly bring these products to market. Internationalization is also a driving force for alliances. Demand arises in a variety of markets across the globe, and entering markets on one's own is not always possible or desirable. Local partners are often instrumental to gaining a foothold in a new country. Finally, the alliance revolution has dynamics of its own. Companies develop new techniques for alliance management; they learn from one another and, in so doing, discover new opportunities for alliances.

Creating and maintaining alliances

Alliances help companies to realize numerous goals such as efficiency increases, access to new markets, hedging risks related to innovation, standardization and gaining market power. However, each of these opportunities requires a different form of alliance organization based on the specific goal of the alliance. The alliance lifecycle approach shown in Figure 1.1 ensures that alliances fit with a company's strategy and shows where alliance design fits in the overall alliance process.

Organizations need to define how alliances can help realize their business strategy. They need to clarify the areas of their strategy for which they want to use alliances over other mechanisms such as mergers, acquisitions or internal investments. Next, organizations need to determine the desired alliance portfolio. How many alliances are needed, in what areas and what resources will be committed to them? What are the most desirable alliance structures for the company? Are loose, short-term alliances called for or are long-term arrangements with a high level of integration between the organizations preferred? Based on these decisions, the partner selection process begins by seeking potential partners and selecting them. This process leads to a deal and an alliance business plan. This process also involves setting the vision, mission and strategy for each particular alliance. The partner selection phase usually ends with a contract. The alliance design brings all of the elements together; based on the

FIGURE 1.1: The alliance lifecycle

goal of the alliance and the business plan, a structure and governance process is developed that should be implemented in the next phase. After implementation, the alliance becomes operational and moves into the phase of day-to-day management. Day-to-day management does not imply that the alliance structuring is complete. Because of the open-ended nature of alliance contracts, all aspects of an alliance's operations must be regularly evaluated. The outcome may be that the alliance needs to change. A new alliance structure may be necessary to support further growth or to wind down after its objectives are achieved or the benefits fail to materialize. Both of these outcomes are relevant inputs for refining the business strategy.

Of course, this process is messier in practice. For example, in the partner selection phase, partners usually discuss the alliance design at a high level. Alliance design permeates the alliance lifecycle. Companies need to be aware of all of the possibilities for alliances in the early strategy-setting phases. The choice of partner may also affect the alliance design. For example, that companies entering into a second alliance with the same partner write contracts that are substantially different from their first alliance contract is a well-established fact.[6] This practice is rooted in the fact that companies get to know one another and are able to fine-tune contracts more to the specific partner situation that they face. In later phases of the alliance lifecycle, changes in alliance structures are very common; therefore, an existing alliance design requires regular monitoring and maintenance. Thus, alliance design is integral to all alliance-related activities.

Control versus trust

Following from the definition of alliances, alliances face a number of specific challenges that a good alliance design must overcome. These challenges, which make alliance design different from the design of internal organization structures, are as follows:

- Absence of hierarchy. Companies have a chief executive officer (CEO) who ultimately has full control, whereas alliances are comprised of at least two companies that have to make decisions together. No single authority sits above these companies. Instead, the companies mutually depend on one another when decisions have to be made.

- Dynamics. Of course, organizations operate in a changing world and dynamics always affect any form of organization regardless of whether it is an alliance. However, the key point is that changes in the business environment will affect partners in an alliance differently. One partner may gain, whereas the other may lose, which may create tension in an alliance. A solid alliance design is able to cope with such tensions.

- Open-ended contracts.[7] Because of the space inherent in open-ended contracts, mechanisms need to be devised to manage the gaps. Joint decision making is imperative. However, lying behind that is also an attitude to compromise, to be flexible and to live and let live. A good alliance design fosters such an attitude in both partners and makes partner behavior predictable. The open-ended nature of an alliance contract is both an opportunity and a threat. The opportunity is that it enables the partners to deal with the dynamics in a much more flexible way than when a contract is set in stone. The Future Store Initiative is a great example of this opportunity. Its open design greatly enhanced creativity. The threat lies in the fact that partners' needs and interests are seldom perfectly aligned. At any point in time, one partner in an alliance may see an opportunity to advance its interest at the expense of its partner. The Danone–Wahaha break-up is a case in point.

- Temporal nature. Alliances tend to be temporary. Figure 1.2 shows the average alliance lifetime in three industries. In each of these industries,

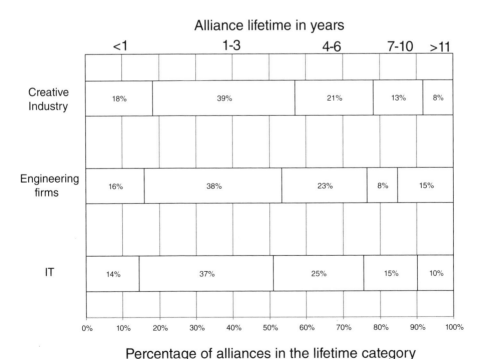

Alliance lifetime in years

	<1	1-3	4-6	7-10	>11
Creative Industry	18%	39%	21%	13%	8%
Engineering firms	16%	38%	23%	8%	15%
IT	14%	37%	25%	15%	10%

Percentage of alliances in the lifetime category

FIGURE 1.2: The average lifetime of alliances (2012)[8]

more than half of the alliances did not exist for more than three years, and three-quarters of the alliances did not make it past a six-year lifetime. Because alliances can be disbanded when they no longer serve their purpose, they can become self-defeating: they may be set up to benefit from a temporary opportunity, but the temporary nature of the opportunity may cause companies to avoid committing the required resources. In addition, a fear of the alliance being disbanded may prevent companies from entering into them altogether. For example, that certain customers are hurt by the end of an alliance or that certain patients no longer receive treatment in the case of health care organizations are real threats. However, good exit provisions can usually remedy such situations and need to be incorporated in the design of an alliance.

- Company differences. Companies' differences in structures and cultures need to be bridged in an alliance. Eliminating these differences is usually not feasible, but processes can be implemented to manage them. In the alliance between Sara Lee/DE and Philips, the corporate structures were an obstacle. Sara Lee/DE's organizational structure was based on geography, whereas Philips had product divisions. The companies implemented specific mechanisms that worked around the obstacles. The horizontal collaboration between the partners therefore did not suffer from the vertical pressures inside each of the partners.

These alliance-specific elements must be taken into account when designing an alliance. A variety of mechanisms can be implemented to address these elements. Think about decision-making procedures, conflict resolution mechanisms and the use of communication structures. The next chapter discusses the building blocks of alliance design in greater detail. These building blocks are not standard: each can be implemented in a variety of ways. Each alliance has its own unique structure, which is why some alliance managers claim that "if you have seen one alliance, you have seen one alliance." Even though this statement is true, concluding from it that nothing more can be learned from studying individual alliances is a mistake. This statement clearly does not carry that message. Although each alliance is unique, many common characteristics exist among alliances to allow us to learn from them.

For example, to address the specific characteristics previously mentioned, companies can adopt one of two basic approaches when designing their alliances: the control view and the trust view. Table 1.1 summarizes the two views by reviewing the assumptions behind each view, how they define the key challenge for alliance design and their effect on the prescriptions provided for how alliances should be designed.

TABLE 1.1: The control and the trust approach to alliance design

	Control	Trust
Alliance assumption	• Partners look out for their own self-interests • Conflicts of interest are likely to arise	• Partners benefit from a common interest • Joint growth and development ensure long-term alignment
Alliance design challenge	• Prevent opportunism	• Build social capital
View on alliance design	• Target driven • Value appropriation • Rule based; detailed contracts • Extrinsic motivation • Strong senior management control	• Vision driven • Value creation • Principle based; norms and values • Intrinsic motivation • Senior management as coach

The control view:[9] taming opportunism

The control view makes the assumption that partners in an alliance join the alliance because of their self-interest. Therefore, they will see the alliance as a vehicle to promote their own good, without much regard for their partner's interests. The most important challenge in designing alliances is to create safeguards against opportunistic behavior. This view of alliances was epitomized by a controller of a pharmaceutical company, who described his job in an internal alliance conference as: "I am here to protect us from our partners."[10]

Opportunism in alliances may come in different forms. Often, such actions are small, such as investing slightly less time than the partner does, thus shifting some of the burden to the partner. Sometimes such actions are significant, as in the case of Danone and Wahaha. This view of alliances underlines American writer Ambrose Bierce's definition of an alliance in international politics from his notorious *Devil's Dictionary* as "the union of two thieves who have their hands so deeply inserted in each other's pockets that they cannot separately plunder a third." The possibility that a partner will engage in opportunistic behavior and free-riding based on self-interest defines the control view of strategic alliances.

When designing an alliance, this view leads to an emphasis on using formal mechanisms in alliance design. The first element is defining commonly agreed on targets with a partner to ensure that both partners are on the same page regarding what they want to achieve. Making these targets measurable is the first safeguard against conflicts of interest. Clear definitions of targets is important, and an extensive planning and control system that measures deviations from the plan, reports progress and highlights areas for improvement directly follows the target-setting process. Targets may also be set for the inputs that both partners have to deliver to the alliance to ensure that investments are reasonably shared.

The focus on targets immediately raises the question of how the benefits will be shared once a target is achieved. Control-based alliances tend to have detailed value appropriation mechanisms in place, clarifying exactly which revenues and costs belong to whom. This clarification is achieved by the use of many detailed rules to govern the alliance. Elaborate contracts are implemented to cover as many eventualities as possible. An alliance may be open ended by definition, but the control view sees incomplete contracts as a negative. The contractual space needs to be reduced as much as possible to ensure that – in case of a conflict – the solution to that conflict is completely clear. Senior management up to the board level needs to deal with any remaining space during the course of the lifetime of the alliance. Therefore, senior management is closely connected to the alliance and provides it with active guidance. If necessary, they will even intervene in alliance operations to ensure that the company's interests are well looked after.

To stimulate both sides to collaborate, their targets are connected to bonuses and pay-offs based on alliance performance. Thus, control thinking extends to the individuals that comprise the alliance. People are rewarded when they behave in accordance with alliance targets. In short, alliances highly rely on extrinsic motivation: sticks and carrots guide the alliance in the right direction, not the personal responsibility that someone feels to contribute to the alliance. Structures and systems are in the lead.

The trust view:[11] building social capital

Whereas the control view departs from the self-interest of partners to join an alliance, the starting point for the trust view is common interest. Although two sides of the same coin, the implications for alliance design are profound. The shift in focus from conflict prevention to joint growth entails a completely different view on alliance design. As long as partners are able to identify new opportunities for growth and development, partners' interests will be aligned and the collaboration should be stable. To continuously identify these new opportunities, companies must get to know each other, be willing to share their ideas and insights openly and foster a dynamic culture in the alliance. Doing so requires a high level of social capital; that is, people need to know and trust one another. In the trust view, the challenge is to design an alliance that fosters the social bonds between organizations that are needed to build that social capital.

One way to build these bonds is by developing a joint vision for the alliance. Rather than setting narrow targets, the concept is that companies discuss a broader set of issues when creating a joint vision than when limiting themselves to merely setting targets. Developing the vision for an alliance demands that organizations exchange their views on long-term developments in their market and how the alliance fits into those views. These discussions enhance mutual understanding and provide greater certainty to a partner's intentions, thus reducing the chance that a partner takes unexpected actions.

The emphasis on growth and development also leads to an emphasis on value creation. By learning and innovating, an alliance can continue to add value to its partners. The well-known distinction between sharing and growing the pie applies. In the control view, the emphasis is on sharing the pie; in the trust view, the emphasis is on growing the pie. If the partners can ensure that the pie continues to grow, a natural incentive exists for partners to stay in the alliance and to avoid behaving opportunistically and killing the goose that lays the golden eggs. Sufficient value is created for everybody to earn a living.

Because too many rules stifle innovation and creativity, trust-based alliances do not define detailed regulations for what should happen under certain circumstances. Instead, they focus on behavior, such as how the partners should behave when something happens that requires their joint attention. In the design of alliances, such an approach leads to an emphasis on norms and values that support mutual adjustment. An increasing number of alliances implement codes of conduct to that effect. Instead of detailed rules, the concept is that an alliance is more flexible when it is based on certain principles that dictate how partners deal with one another, rather than attempting to cover every possible option in a lengthy contract.

This type of thinking also has an effect on the level of the individuals working in alliances. Instead of attempting to align their behavior using targets and bonuses, the trust approach attempts to create a psychological contract with an individual. Through an appealing vision of what the alliance can mean in its market, employees are positively motivated to contribute. Fun, recognition and meaningful work tie the partner companies together through its employees. The

Future Store Initiative had such an appealing vision: building a supermarket of the future that made room for a variety of new ideas and experiments generated energy in the partnering companies and their employees. The project was fun to work on.

If an alliance succeeds in building social capital in this way, elaborate planning and control processes are not needed. When both sides to an alliance automatically do what is in their joint and individual interests, the alliance should run smoothly. Senior management involvement can be limited to a coaching role. For example, they can help remove barriers to the alliance or think along with alliance managers about next steps.

In short, the trust approach builds on the informal elements of alliance design. It is able to do so given the emphasis on growth and development that should guarantee that the alliance is not only beneficial to the partners at its inception, but also continues to add value over time.

Balancing control and trust

Obviously, the previous description is somewhat black and white in nature. Many shades of gray exist in between. However, that all alliances end up in the middle is certainly not true. In fact, some alliances clearly depart from one perspective and have completely different alliance designs than when the opposite point of departure is taken. A clear difference exists between, for example, the KLM–NWA alliance discussed later in this book in which the control view is predominant, and the primarily trust-based Future Store Initiative.

Both alliance types are successful. Control is not necessarily better than trust or vice versa. Some people have an instinctive preference for one or the other. Accountants and lawyers tend to like the control approach; entrepreneurs usually have a preference for the trust approach. However, the real issue is to find the right design in the right situation. Thinking that everyone will always be intrinsically motivated to contribute to an alliance is as equally naïve as believing that having a good contract in place will in itself ensure the success of the alliance. The point is to custom design an alliance.

Control and trust may strengthen each other. A discussion about all of the issues that may call for greater control can help strengthen the understanding between the partners. Clarity on each other's perspective regarding the alliance may help build trust.[12] Trust may make it easier to share concerns and, as a result, formal rules may be agreed on to alleviate these concerns. In this way, trust may strengthen control. The concepts of control and trust may be intuitively clear but their practical application is less straightforward.

Each approach has its limits. Although having a high level of trust may sound ideal, the downside may be that the attention paid to the goals of the alliance may diminish when a partnership becomes too intimate. Groupthink may lead alliance partners to ignore or downplay changes in the environment, putting the alliance at risk. A formal control mechanism ensures that alliance partners ask the right questions about their business and help maintain their focus on the goals. In contrast, placing too much emphasis on control may undermine employees' identification with the alliance and the mutual adjustments necessary for effective alliance operations. Processes, procedures and contracts do not make an alliance. People need to be willing to invest in the alliance, which requires that they form a psychological bond with it. When people identify with the goals of the alliance, the alliance will operate more smoothly.

The cases presented later in this book show that defining the conditions that determine whether control or trust is called for is possible. For now, each approach clearly has its limits. An overly heavy emphasis on control will reduce flexibility and creativity in an alliance. It may induce people to focus on the rules instead of the goals. Moreover, the costs of governing the alliance will be high. In contrast, significant emphasis on trust may lead to a loss of focus and lower operational efficiency, and may provide no explicit mechanism to correct free riding and opportunism. In an alliance that aims to create economies of scale, trust may be ineffective. In alliances aimed at innovation, control will be counterproductive. Therefore, one of the most fundamental questions that needs to be answered when designing an alliance is: What is the right balance between control and trust given the specific aims this alliance seeks to achieve?

Common mistakes

Many things can go wrong when designing strategic alliances. Some mistakes prove difficult to eradicate. Table 1.2 provides an overview of the mistakes that occur frequently in practice. Each of these mistakes is reviewed.

Lumping lust

The first mistake listed occurs frequently in partnerships with public organizations and is not uncommon in the private sector. Some organizations lump

TABLE 1.2: Common mistakes in designing alliances

- Lumping lust: adding goals to an alliance, leading to a loss of direction
- 51 percent fever: the belief that a majority gives control
- Set in stone: keeping to an agreement that is past its sell-by date
- Inbox indigestion: communicating through emails and letters, instead of at face-to-face meetings
- Lack of a joint design: leaving the work of designing the alliance to one of the partners, to a third party or to deal-makers
- JV junkies: having a preference for joint ventures even if not the optimal form
- Expertise arrogance: believing that one knows better, even in the area of one's partner's expertise
- Equity addiction: using equity stakes to create commitment
- Internal incentives: forgetting to adapt internal incentives to fit the alliance
- Shaky steering committees: nominating people to the alliance steering committee or alliance board who do not have a stake in the alliance
- Committee confusion: creating a plethora of committees to deal with any conceivable problem
- A mess for less: selecting a lower cost governance structure or a faster process, resulting in a structure that does not meet the alliance's need
- Myopic management: focusing on a governance structure that works well today but is not future-proof

together many different goals into a single alliance. For public sector organizations, doing so may sometimes be logical because they have a broader responsibility to society and may want to achieve several, possibly contradictory, goals through a single alliance. Because aligning goals on a single issue is often difficult enough, adding different goals makes coming to an agreement almost impossible. Even if agreement is possible, the different goals make governing the alliance difficult because each goal may require a particular balance between control and trust. Therefore, the preferred option is for the same partners to create several independent alliances than a single large alliance with a variety of goals.

51 percent fever

Another common mistake is the notion that a 51 percent stake in a joint venture or having the majority of votes in an alliance gives an organization more influence. This notion ignores the simple fact that it takes two to tango in an alliance. When one partner consistently overrides the other, the other partner will sooner or later start free riding or become unhappy, which may eventually lead to the dissolution of the alliance. Moreover, the 51 percent fever may not be as relevant from another perspective. In the NUMMI joint venture between General Motors and Toyota, GM owned the majority. However, Toyota was not focused on control but on learning about the American car market:[13] that knowledge proved more valuable than GM's 1 percent advantage. An alliance manager once said, "when the other side demands 51 percent, the alliance will likely be very profitable for us, because that party will give up much knowledge for it to get to that 51 percent." This is not to say that there may be no reason for one partner to have more shares or greater voting rights than others. For example, one partner may have to invest more in the alliance than the other or may be able to avoid tax issues through a higher stake. However, when gaining control is the main reason to demand 51 percent, the alliance is likely to be unstable.

Set in stone

A further mistake is to believe that all agreements are set in stone and that such a situation is correct. The dynamics of alliances imply that any agreement needs to be adapted sooner or later. Holding on to agreements that were developed in different market circumstances may significantly damage an alliance's development. In addition, holding on to an agreement that is clearly detrimental to one of the partners does not make sense, for the same reason as previously explained. The partner will begin to view the alliance negatively and act accordingly. Obviously, starting legal procedures will not remedy the situation. Agreements are necessary and provide a basic framework; however, more important to adhering to a contract is thinking about how changing an agreement will be managed. Contracts may diverge substantially from reality. For example, in the KLM–NWA relationship, the operational integration went far beyond the initial legal agreement.

Inbox indigestion

This is an intriguing phenomenon that reflects the notion that communication with a partner is best carried out by sending emails instead of engaging in face-to-face meetings. Amid the pressure of day-to-day work, this phenomenon may easily occur but usually leads to misunderstandings. Although saying that good communication is a key success factor for alliances is a cliché, the statement is no less true. In face-to-face meetings or phone calls, issues get clarified and resolved much quicker. Experience shows that, in practice, good communication is difficult to realize, despite the fact that everybody recognizes its significance.

Lack of a joint design

Leaving the design of the alliance to the partner, a third party or non-operational individuals is another mistake. The development of an alliance design should always be done by a group of people that includes individuals who will ultimately have to work with the design, for three reasons: knowledge, relationship and speed. Knowledge pertains to the fact that the person who will be responsible for the alliance will need to know why it was structured as it was. That person will likely be knowledgeable about the business of the alliance. Therefore, he or she can bring operational knowledge to the design team, reducing the risk that a design will not work in practice. Second, joint design of the alliance helps develop the relationship between the partners in the alliance. The process that the managers have to go through increases their understanding of each other's business and of each other as individuals. The third and final advantage is speed. When the people in the alliance also help to design it, the speed of implementation will increase because they know what the alliance has to do from day one. Handover from the design team to the implementation team is not needed. Separating people who "make the deal" from those who have to execute it is, without a doubt, one of the worst and most expensive mistakes made in practice, and one of the most common. Frequently, lawyers, business developers or purchasing managers make the deal and then toss it over the wall to alliance managers, which is the perfect recipe for delay, misunderstanding and contracts that are out of touch with reality.

JV junkies

Organizations with little experience in alliances always have difficulty understanding how contractual alliances work. Therefore, they frequently prefer the clarity of joint ventures because at least they understand that they have a stake in something. This choice of a joint venture is a mistake for a number of reasons. First, joint ventures are not usually as clear-cut as they seem to be and that joint ventures are simple is an assumption that is not supported in practice. As a rule, joint ventures require agreements that are as detailed as contractual alliances. Second, joint ventures involve extra costs in terms of investment in shares, reporting requirements and managerial oversight. Contractual alliances also have costs but are usually less expensive during use. Third, setting up a joint venture is time consuming. Particularly in fast-moving markets, the time needed to incorporate the joint venture is time that the partners may not be able to afford to lose. Disbanding joint ventures is also difficult. Contracts are easily disbanded when both partners agree; joint ventures do not fall into this category because they contain assets that need to be disposed of and people who need to be let go. Although joint ventures may have clear benefits in certain circumstances, they should not be the default choice.

Expertise arrogance

This phenomenon causes a partner to make decisions regarding, or to meddle with, the other partner's expertise. Although consensus decision making is a good practice in alliance management, it should not be extended to the other partner's competences. For example, in an alliance between home appliance producer Philips and coffee producer Sara Lee/DE, the understanding is that Philips decides on the machine, whereas Sara Lee/DE focuses on producing the right coffee mélanges. Clearly, the results would be suboptimal if they behaved otherwise.

Equity addiction

Chapter 6 discusses solid reasons for engaging in equity deals. Gaining extra commitment from a partner is not one of them. If a deal needs to be sealed by an equity investment for only this reason, the business plan is probably not solid enough to solicit automatic commitment. Equity stakes should not be used solely to create commitment. The vision and a sound business plan should be sufficient for that. If a feeling exists that cross-equity stakes are necessary only to increase commitment, the business plan may not be compelling enough.

Internal incentives

By their nature, alliances affect the internal organizations of the partners involved. This aspect of alliances is often overlooked, particularly with respect to governance and target setting processes through which numerous difficulties may arise. For example, a conflict of interest may arise if managers of a company are rewarded based on their sales performance yet the alliance aims to increase the margin of both companies. In that case, managers will dedicate their resources to increasing sales instead of investing in high margin alliance projects. Alternatively, alliance managers from one company may have monthly targets but managers from the other company may be evaluated based on annual targets. Such a situation leads to completely different dynamics. The best approach is to align the internal targets of the managers involved with those of the alliance. Doing so is not easy because bonus plans and compensation structures within companies tend to be rigid.

Shaky steering committees

The composition of the highest committee in the alliance, the alliance steering committee or alliance board, requires careful attention. Frequently, individuals are nominated for a position on that committee because of their hierarchical status. Alternatively, sometimes individuals on that committee do not have real power to push through decisions in their own organizations. A useful steering committee should include individuals with business and budget responsibility in the areas relevant to the alliance. Although a neutral third person representing the alliance interest may be helpful, a link to the business is a necessity for a steering committee to be effective.

Committee confusion

Committees and working groups in alliances are important design elements. Common problems with these elements include too many committees, making coordination across them impossible; unclear scoping of committees, leading to either overlap or things falling between the cracks; and using ceremonial committees that have no real say in the alliance but are there to please stakeholders. Another problem may occur over time. When an alliance runs into problems, the partners may feel the need to add a committee to solve that problem. Doing so may lead to committee creep and a growing number of committees. Broadening the scope of an existing committee or reviewing and redesigning the committee structure altogether may be a better approach. However, before doing so, the first step is a review of the alliance's strategy and goals to determine whether they are still valid. This approach prevents reorganization without focus on the goals.

A mess for less

Some companies are tempted to reduce costs when designing their alliances in one of two ways. They may opt for a cheaper structure, such as a supply relationship, when a more complex structure would work better. The clearest example is the manner in which American car companies used to work with their suppliers versus Toyota's alliances with its suppliers. Research shows that the more expensive governance structure that Toyota implements with its partners generates more value in the long run, in contrast to the purchasing attitude that American car companies had in the 1990s.[14] Focusing on cost savings instead of value generation is an important pitfall. Another way to cut costs is to create shortcuts in the partnering and alliance design process, which usually leads to badly implemented deals.

Myopic management

Alliances are inherently dynamic, which is why a good alliance design should facilitate change. However, at the outset of an alliance, the natural inclination of many managers is to organize for the current situation. Such short sightedness may lead to a variety of provisions in an alliance that may work well today but may be irrelevant tomorrow. Therefore, a solid alliance structure involves a clear process for changing and adapting the alliance to new circumstances that were not foreseen at the outset.

Notes

1 *New York Times*. 2009. Danone Exits China Venture after Years of Legal Dispute, 30 September.
2 *The Economist*. 2012. Twilight for BP in Russia?, 9 June, 58–59.
3 Gomes-Casseres, B. 1996. *The Alliance Revolution*, Cambridge, MA, Harvard University Press; Williamson, O.E. 1985. *The Economic Institutions of Capitalism*, New York, The Free Press.
4 Duysters, G., A.P. de Man, D. Luvison and A. Krijnen. 2012. *The State of Alliance Management: Past, Present, Future*, Canton, MA, The Association of Strategic Alliance Professionals.
5 IBM. 2012. *Leading Through Connections*, IBM Institute for Business Value.
6 Ryall, M.D. and R.C. Sampson. 2009. Formal contracts in the presence of relational enforcement mechanisms: evidence from technology development projects, *Management Science*, 55, 6, 906–925.
7 Williamson, O.E. 1975. *Markets and Hierarchies: Analysis and Antitrust Implications*, New York, The Free Press.
8 These figures are based on unpublished research conducted with Alexander Alexiev, Marc Bahlmann and Brian Tjemkes, all at VU University.
9 The theoretical background of this discussion is derived from transaction cost theory, agency theory and industrial organization. For more information, see: Bain, J.S. 1968. *Industrial Organization*, John Wiley; Eisenhardt, K.M. 1989. Agency theory: an assessment and review, *Academy of Management Review*, 14, 1, 57–74; Jensen, M.C. and W. Meckling. 1976. Theory of the firm: managerial behavior, agency costs, and capital structure, *Journal of Financial Economics*, 3, October, 305–360; Williamson, O.E. 1975. *Markets and Hierarchies: Analysis and Antitrust Implications*, New York, The Free Press; Williamson, O.E. 1985. *The Economic Institutions of Capitalism*, New York, The Free Press.

10   Thanks to Dave Luvison of DeVry University for sharing this quote with me.

11   Sumantra Ghoshal primarily developed the theoretical background of this discussion. For further reading, see: Bartlett, C.A. and S. Ghoshal. 1993. Beyond the M-Form: toward a managerial theory of the firm, *Strategic Management Journal*, 14, 23–46; Ghoshal, S., C. Bartlett and P. Moran. 1999. A new manifesto for management, *Sloan Management Review*, 40, 3, 9–19; Ghoshal, S. and H. Bruch. 2003. Going beyond motivation to the power of volition, *MIT Sloan Management Review*, 44, 3, 51–57; Ghoshal, S. and P. Moran. 1996. Bad for practice: a critique of transaction theory, *Academy of Management Review*, 21, 1, 13–47; Nahapiet, J. and S. Ghoshal. 1998. Social capital, intellectual capital and the organizational advantage, *Academy of Management Review*, 23, 2, 242–266. Stewardship theory also provided some elements for this discussion, specifically Davis, J.H., F.D. Schoorman and L. Donaldson. 1997. Toward a stewardship theory of management, *Academy of Management Review*, 22, 1, 20–47.

12   Vosselman, J. and J. van der Meer-Kooistra. 2009. Accounting for control and trust building in interfirm transactional relationships, *Accounting, Organizations and Society*, 34, 267–283.

13   Gomes-Casseres, B. 2009. Nummi: What Toyota learned and GM didn't, *HBR Blog Network*, September 1, http://blogs.hbr.org/now-new-next/2009/09/nummi-what-toyota-learned.html.

14   Dyer, J.H. 2000. *Collaborative Advantage*, Oxford, Oxford University Press.

CHAPTER 2

The Alliance Design Framework

The three requirements of alliance design

The decision to base an alliance on control or trust is abstract. Control and trust need to be made concrete. This chapter describes all of the practical building blocks of alliance design. Depending on the alliance, these building blocks can be combined to create levels of control and trust that fit the strategy that the alliance aims to realize. The variety in alliance designs is almost infinite; however, the building blocks tend to be the same. What matters is the manner in which the building blocks are combined to meet specific needs. A solid alliance design should achieve the following three objectives (Figure 2.1).

- Enable value creation. A good alliance design ensures that the alliance is able to create value, meaning that it should focus and align the partners. Without focus and alignment, value creation becomes impossible. Next, the alliance should ensure optimal resource allocation throughout its work. Investments should flow to the right activities. Finally, the alliance should be effective and efficient. Additional layers and procedures over and above what is strictly necessary should not exist, and decisions need to be made at the lowest possible level to ensure optimal horizontal coordination.

- Protect partners' interests. All partners in an alliance should be able to make a return on their investment. Therefore, alliances should have a business

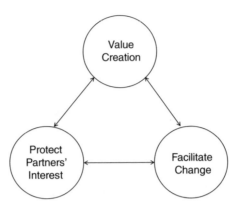

FIGURE 2.1: The three aims of alliance design

and a financial model that benefits all parties involved. Clear guidelines for value appropriation, in other words, who gets what piece of the pie, are fundamental for such models.[1] Similarly, risk mitigation strategies and clear accountabilities are important elements to protecting partners' interests.

- Facilitate change. One of the dangers of alliance management is to see alliances as static. The truth is that markets change, partners change, and strategies change. For alliances to be able to cope with these changes is more important than creating a good alliance design at the outset. Managing change requires clear and fast decision-making procedures together with effective conflict resolution mechanisms. The faster and the smoother an alliance can adapt to change, the more value it will create for its partners in the long run.

These three elements are not mutually independent. Alliances that create value will find it easier to satisfy the interests of all partners. When the partners are certain that their interests are protected, they may share more knowledge and improve value creation. The easier it is to change an alliance and to adapt it to changing circumstances, the greater the chance that it will continue to create value and, hence, serve the interests of its partners.

The building blocks: an overview

Some of the alliance building blocks are formal, such as contracts and decision-making procedures. Other building blocks, such as leadership and commitment, are less formal. In general, control-based alliances emphasize the formal ele-

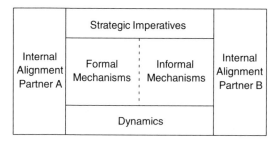

FIGURE 2.2: The Alliance Design Framework

ments, whereas a trust-based design emphasizes the informal elements. Trust-based alliances also use formal elements such as contracts. The length and detail of these contracts are limited in trust-based alliances: more is left to decide on at a later point in time. Similarly, control-based alliances pay attention to the personal relationships between both partners' managers. In contrast to trust-based alliances, they refrain from relying too much on these relationships and probably do not invest in them to the extent necessary in a trust-based alliance. The cases in this book demonstrate how companies use the building blocks of alliance design to create the desired level of control and trust.

Figure 2.2 depicts the Alliance Design Framework. The Alliance Design Framework summarizes the building blocks of alliance design. They are:

- Strategic imperatives: The vision, mission, strategy, and value proposition of an alliance as the starting point for alliance design;

- Formal mechanisms: The explicit elements of alliance design, such as the legal model and the financial model;

- Informal mechanisms: The intangible elements of alliance design, such as trust, leadership, and commitment;

- Internal alignment: Alliance design must take into account the link to partners' internal organizations given that company policies and regulations may be at odds with alliance agreements. As internal alignment needs to occur on both sides of an alliance it is included in the Alliance Design Framework for partner A and partner B. Obviously, for an alliance with more than two partners, all partners should pay attention to internal alignment;

- Dynamics: A design adaptable to external changes given that alliances occur in dynamic business environments; Chapter 8 addresses the issue of dynamics in detail; the current chapter focuses on the original design.

All of these alliance elements, excepting dynamics, are discussed in greater detail below. Companies may adopt many different mechanisms to develop the right alliance design. Naturally, not all elements are necessary in all alliances. Companies need to select and combine the elements they need to develop custom-made alliance designs for each alliance.

Strategic imperatives

Without a clear view of the strategic rationale behind an alliance, developing a fitting alliance design is impossible. In essence, the elements of alliance strategy are no different from those of a business strategy. The traditional triumvirate of vision, mission, and strategy is relevant for alliances as well (see Table 2.1). However, the process of developing an alliance strategy is different because the needs of all partners must also be taken into account. The major difficulty in developing a sound strategic rationale for alliances is that the alliance needs to be aligned with the partners' strategies. For that reason, discussing the partners' vision of the market and how the alliance will be distinctive in that market is important. If partners cannot agree on a similar vision on the future state of affairs in their market, the chances are limited that a sound alliance strategy can be developed.

For example, airline alliances may be based on the vision that, in the end, three alliance groups will dominate intercontinental air travel. If partners agree on this vision, their strategy will be to increase the integration between the airlines in an alliance group: a more integrated group will be more effective in compet-

TABLE 2.1: Strategic rationale

Vision, mission, strategy	• How do partners perceive the market and the distinctive alliance role in it?
	• A vision describes the view that the partners have of the business environment and how the alliance will distinguish itself in that environment.
	• An alliance's mission, as a statement of why the alliance exists, directs, legitimizes, and motivates the parties involved.
	• An alliance strategy translates the vision and mission into activities to realize its goals.
Value propositions	• What value does the alliance create for clients and for each of the alliance partners?
Scope	• Which products, services, technologies, geographies, activities, and timeframes are involved? What will be the division of labor?

ing against the other two groups. A group may also discuss how it distinguishes itself from other groups. One group may aim for a quality image whereas another may pursue a low-cost strategy. In contrast, if partners cannot agree on their vision that three groups will dominate intercontinental air travel, a strategy of further integration does not make much sense. Because the joint vision is decisive for many operational choices, it should be explicitly discussed.

An alliance's mission summarizes the role that an alliance wants to fulfill. A mission may be written down in a lengthy statement full of long-running sentences, which is not likely to inspire anyone. Shorter statements have more strength. For example, take the slogan of the Disney–Siemens alliance for hearing aids for children: "Helping children discover the magic of better hearing." The alliance created a kit for children with hearing problems that contained all of the supplies that such a child may need (among others, an instruction book and a battery tester). The kit also contained a comic book created by Disney on Mickey Mouse (after all, Mickey has the world's most famous ears) and his rabbit friend Bunny, who has hearing loss. The goal was to help children cope with their hearing loss. The slogan served all of the purposes that a mission should serve:[2] it points the alliance in a certain direction, it shows the outside world the valuable activity that the alliance is performing, and it motivates the people involved to do their best (who would not want to help children with hearing problems?).

The collaboration between the North Yorkshire Fire Service and McCain also had an inspiring mission: reduce the number of chip pan fires. Chip pan fires are a major concern for UK fire brigades. Annually, dozens of people are severely injured when frying chips because the boiling oil catches fire or causes severe burns. McCain developed a safe product that it wanted to introduce into the market: oven chips. Together, the organizations developed a program involving joint education at schools to warn children about the dangers of chip pans. The children also received a coupon for oven chips. Fifty fire engines carried the partnership message and the McCain logo. The result was a 24 percent decline in chip pan fires. McCain sold 15 percent more oven chips in the Yorkshire area than in any other area in the UK, showing that commerce and increased safety went hand in hand.

The alliance strategy translates the vision and mission into actions and goals. However, over the past few years, the notion of developing an alliance strategy was replaced by a focus on the alliance's value proposition. A value proposition represents the set of needs that an alliance can meet for its customers and parents that alternative options cannot.[3] A value proposition defines the measurable results that the alliance intends to achieve. The customer value proposition describes the benefits that the alliance will generate for customers. If at all possible, the value proposition should be measurable by making explicit the cost savings, benefits or additional revenues that a customer will gain from the alliance's offerings. Some alliances are far removed from customers, such as R&D alliances. Such alliances may have difficulty developing measurable value propositions, although numbers of projects realized or technologies tested may resolve the issue. Otherwise, a clear view of the qualitative benefits of the alliance should be developed.

In addition to the customer value proposition, an alliance must develop value propositions for the partners involved.[4] What each partner could gain from joining the alliance must be clear. Partners may generate different types of value from the same alliance. In the same alliance, one partner may benefit from cost savings, whereas the other partner may primarily benefit from learning. Rarely will partners experience exactly the same benefits, or benefits of equal value, from the same alliance. Such a result is not a problem as long as both partners understand their own and their partner's benefits. Hence, a bilateral alliance has three value propositions: one for the customer and one for each partner.

A final element of the strategic rationale is to define the scope of the alliance. Which products, services, technologies, geographies, activities, and timeframes are involved? Clarity about the scope of an alliance is an important step to operationalizing the collaboration. Many misunderstandings are avoided by clearly describing the elements that an alliance includes and excludes. Most alliances have a narrowly defined scope. For example, Air France/KLM and Delta Airlines identified the scope of their alliance as all passenger traffic across the North Atlantic and India. Philips and Sara Lee/DE defined the scope of their alliances in the coffee market by limiting their work to the "packaged coffee" market – coffee packaged in small pods for a single person. Despite – or because of – their narrow scope, both alliances developed into sizeable businesses. The scope of an alliance also helps determine who contributes what. The division of labor between the partners follows from the scope and determines the activities each partner executes.[5]

A clearly defined scope gives clarity to the individuals involved. It also implies that partners are allowed to seek other companies with which to team up regarding anything out of the scope. Elements in the scope of the alliance may or may not be exclusive. Many IT companies engage in alliances with several system integrators without any exclusivity. Therefore, each new client project in which they engage raises the question of which alliance partner to collaborate with.

Scope with respect to time determines how long an alliance will last. Partners may decide to enter an alliance for a limited time or indefinitely. Even after an alliance has ended, contractual provisions may remain valid for a number of years. For example, after an alliance ends, an agreement may exist that one of the partners will not be active in a certain market for one or two years or that clients of the alliance will continue to be served.

The scope of an alliance is likely to change over time. For Air France/Delta, the forerunner of this alliance was an agreement between Northwest Airlines and KLM that primarily focused on freight. Over time, passenger transport became more important and grew to be the dominant element in the alliance. Similarly, the Philips–Sara Lee/DE alliance expanded its scope to include tea when packaged coffee turned out to be extremely successful. Scope changes require careful attention. They may change the playing field, other partners may be affected, or antitrust regulations may be violated. Because alliances may grow naturally and in a step-by-step fashion in a certain direction, a scope change may take place in practice without those involved directly noticing that it occurred.

Formal building blocks

The next building block in the Alliance Design Framework is formal elements. Table 2.2 lists the most important of these. Formal elements normally find their way into contracts, but contracts do not need to cover all elements from Table 2.2. Alliance partners have to judge on a case-by-case basis which elements are sufficiently significant to warrant inclusion in a contract.

Financial model

Because alliances may have widely varying objectives, the financial models behind alliances are very diverse. Developing the right financial model is essential for achieving alliance success. No matter how important trust is in a relationship, if one of the partners is not satisfied with the financial results, the alliance will not have a long life. For an overview of the financial models, Figure 2.3 presents the most important elements. The appendix discusses all of these elements in much greater detail; the role of equity stakes is discussed in Chapter 6.

Based on the strategy, the alliance will have a cost, revenue, or profit focus. A cost focus exists when the main aim of the alliance is to save money through collaboration. One example is the Future Store Initiative in which many

TABLE 2.2: Formal building blocks of alliances

Financial model	• Sharing of cost, revenues, profits • Cash flow projections • Property rights
Legal structure	• Legal form of the alliance
Organization structure	• Executive committee, alliance managers, working groups, project teams • Staffing • Communication structure • Team charters
Decision making	• Decision-making method • People involved • Mandates • Conflict resolution/escalation procedures, subsidiarity principle • RACI (Responsible/Accountable/Consulted/Informed) scheme
Planning and control	• Scorecards • Planning cycle • Reporting cycle • Sanctions, liability/indemnity, incentives, audits • Risk management • Alliance health check
Competition clauses	• Exclusivity • Non-compete clauses • Confidentiality • Change of control
Exit agreement	• Provisions around alliance dissolution • Reasons for exiting • Term of notice • Exit fee

companies gathered to jointly develop a new IT standard around RFID (Radio-Frequency IDentification). By joining forces, they shared the expenses for this standard. A revenue focus exists when companies collaborate around joint sales and marketing efforts. By jointly entering the market, they may combine their products or may make use of each other's sales force to increase their earnings. Many IT alliances use this model. Alliances with a profit focus include both the cost and the revenue side. In that case, companies focus more on improving margins, as in the Air France/KLM–Delta alliance.

Essentially, one of three financial models may underpin an alliance. In the pooling model, partners pool their revenues, costs, or profits and divide them according to a predetermined sharing arrangement. All joint ventures operate using a pooling model and so do some contractual alliances like the Air France/KLM–Delta alliance. In the second main model each partner pays for its own costs and generates its own revenues from the alliance. This model is very

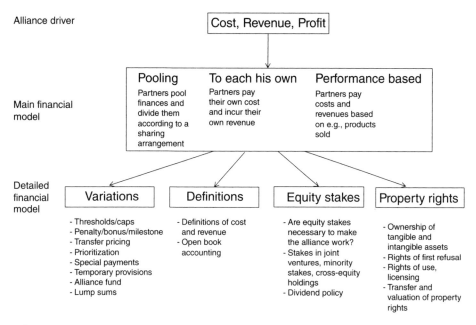

FIGURE 2.3: Elements of financial models

frequently used, such as by marketing and sales alliances in the IT industry. The benefit may lie in the fact that companies jointly go to market and, hence, are able to attract new customers. In the third main model, financials are related to a performance measure. For example, in the Novartis–Orion alliance, sales of an Orion drug generated by Novartis determine the amount of money that flows to Orion. The main mechanisms are not mutually exclusive because combinations of them can be found.

The main financial models are rarely sufficient to create a coherent financial structure. Many variations are possible, as listed in Figure 2.3. Companies also need to be aware of the definitions of costs and revenues. Companies differ in their definition of what constitutes a sale, when an asset is depreciated, or what is included in the total cost of goods sold. Such differences must be addressed. The use of equity stakes is another method of tightening a financial structure. Chapter 6 goes into detail about when they should and should not be applied. Finally, a correct assignment of property rights may help balance the financial model. The appendix provides a detailed overview of all of these issues and variations.

TABLE 2.3: Financial deal structure of the Bayer–Millennium alliance[6]

- Millennium receives a license fee for genomic technology and know-how
- Millennium receives an annual payment to build/maintain a research lab
- Millennium receives a performance fee for delivered drug targets
- Millennium receives royalties on products originating from the program
- Bayer receives an exclusive license on Millennium know-how and patent rights related to use of the delivered targets and to commercialize compounds
- If a target fails, Millennium has an option for a non-exclusive license for that target on knowledge and patent rights generated by Bayer
- Bayer invests $97 million in Millennium equity; Millennium will make a maximum of $368 million from this deal
- Each partner contributes approximately 200 people to the alliance that they pay for themselves

Financial models may consist of a mix of the elements previously discussed. Table 2.3 shows an example of an alliance between Bayer and Millennium for drug development, in which Millennium researches – simply put – target structures involved in creating a disease and against which a drug should be directed. A target that is found represents valuable information because a drug can then be developed to work on that target. Millennium was responsible for discovering drug targets, the next development phase was carried out jointly, and Bayer had responsibility for the final phases of the development process. Table 2.3 provides an overview of the financial deal structure of the partnership. Many of the elements mentioned previously were combined to create a financial model for this alliance.

A final element of the financial model of alliances is to project the alliance cash flows. Obviously, when cash flows out of the alliance, the partners need to be sure they can finance those outflows. More surprisingly, alliance growth may cause a cash flow problem. For example, if additional investments need to be made in production capacity, the partners need to have the means to do so. In particular, smaller companies may not always have such means.

Legal structure

Legal agreements around alliances may take various forms. First, legal documentation is often used before agreeing on the alliance. In the partner selection and alliance design phase, documents such as non-disclosure agreements (NDAs) may stipulate the information exchanged between partners that is confidential and cannot be disclosed to third parties. Partners may also sign a letter of intent (LoI) or a memorandum of understanding (MoU). The contents of these documents vary widely, but they tend to focus on non-legally binding intentions and principles rather than on legally binding issues. For example, they may include a timeline to getting to a final agreement and a commitment to make resources available. They may also contain a first version of the scope of the alliance. Binding aspects of LoIs or MoUs may include a non-sue clause that states that if the process does not lead to an alliance, the potential partners will not sue one another for damages.

Once partners come to an agreement, the basic choice for the legal structure of an alliance is between a contractual alliance and a joint venture. In the latter case, a separate legal entity is created. The various forms of these legal entities differ across countries. However, the best-known ones are public or limited companies, of which each country has its own version. In these legal structures, partners become shareholders. Other forms that occur under different names in different countries are foundations and cooperatives. The choice of legal form depends highly on local circumstances and often on fiscal considerations. Therefore, legal and fiscal council should always be involved in the selection of the legal form.

From a management perspective, the question is whether a joint venture is necessary at all. The vast majority of alliances are contractual agreements, which provide enormous flexibility because they enable partners to agree on anything they want. Such flexibility enables the partners to write agreements that fit precisely with their goals. When the partners apply a control perspective, contracts tend to become lengthy and detailed. A trust perspective tends to result in shorter contracts.

The value attached to a contract also differs by country. Verbal agreements may exist in some subcultures that build on very strong personal relationships. The Japanese may use contracts, but they believe that the relationship with the partner is much more important than getting the legal document signed. Such cultural differences need to be understood. The systems of corporate law vary across countries and courts uphold agreements in many different ways.

Decision making

Because alliances are open-ended agreements with contractual space, important decisions will need to be taken at various times during the alliance's lifecycle. For that reason, the decision-making process is one of the most important elements of alliance design. A first topic in this regard is the decision-making methods that the partners will use. A variety of methods exist, including the following:

- The preferred method in most alliances is consensus. Only when all partners agree to a proposed decision is the decision enacted.

- Consent is a decision-making method that enables a decision to be made only when no party has a reasonable objection. Basically, a decision is considered made when nobody is against it (with consensus, partners are in favor of a decision; with consent, they are not against it).

- Voting in all of its varieties is also possible. Partners may vote by normal majority or qualified majority on some issues. An example of the latter is requiring 70 percent of votes for investments larger than $1 million. Blocking votes may also be used. For example, if in the last example one partner has 31 percent of the votes, that partner can block a large investment but cannot block decisions made on other issues. The right to veto can also be defined. If voting is used, the next question is how to divide the votes among the partners. Again, different systems are possible: one man one vote gives each partner one vote, or votes may be allocated based on partner size, the investments made, or the number of clients brought into the alliance. The allocation of voting rights may change over time and the initial agreement needs to stipulate when and how voting rights are reallocated.

- Expertise-based decision making or reserved powers limit specific partners or alliance committees from the right to make certain decisions. Expertise-based decision making occurred in the Senseo alliance between Philips and Sara Lee/DE. Philips made all of the decisions for the alliance regarding the coffee-making machine, whereas DE decided on the blends of coffee to be developed. This approach enabled each partner to make decisions based on its area of strength.

- Core group decision making enables a core group of partners in larger alliances, such as airline alliances with 20 or more partners, to make the key decisions that the others follow. This structure may not necessarily be contractually confirmed but often emerges in practice. In the Star Alliance, Lufthansa and United Airlines are clearly more important than the other members, as are British Airways and American Airlines in the oneworld Alliance. Sometimes, core companies may exchange equity to strengthen their bond, leading to an equity core.[7]

- Lead partner. A final method is to let the lead partner in the alliance make the decisions. For example, many joint ventures in the oil industry have a majority shareholder that has all of the rights to make decisions. One reason for this structure is the absolute necessity of clarity of control for safety reasons. Partners that mingle in each other's safety procedures likely create suboptimal results.

The person making the decision is as important as the method of decision making. Decision makers require knowledge about the things on which they have to decide. They also need a mandate to commit their organization to a decision. In many alliances, these conditions are not fulfilled: the people knowing the most do not have the right to make the decisions. These alliances violate the subsidiarity principle that states that decisions should be taken at the lowest possible level; in other words, higher governance bodies in an alliance should not do anything that can be taken care of at a lower level. A decision matrix or RACI scheme may be helpful in clarifying the decision-making process by listing the decision points and showing who is responsible, accountable, consulted, and informed regarding decisions. A decision matrix or RACI scheme may change over the life of an alliance. An alliance that moves from R&D to a marketing and sales perspective over time should include marketing and sales executives at the appropriate time, who may even replace the R&D executives altogether.

If the normal decision-making process does not lead to a solution to an issue, partners have a conflict. Conflicts may occur at a low level in the alliance. In that case, an alliance should stipulate escalation procedures, which delineate to whom conflicts should be escalated. When problems occur in a working group, that working group may escalate to the alliance steering committee. If the alliance steering committee is not able to solve the issue, they may bring it to the CEO level. Escalation should occur quickly enough not to burden relationships on an operational level; it should also be slow enough to avoid the lower levels passing on all of their responsibilities to a higher level. A best practice around escalation is to have the alliance team create a joint problem document that describes the issue before it moves to senior management. Such a document ensures that the alliance team reviewed the issue from all perspectives. It also increases the chance that the steering committee will give them a relevant answer to their question.

When companies cannot resolve their conflicts internally, external conflict resolution mechanisms come into play. Partners need to agree upfront on whether and how they will use arbitration, mediation, one or more wise men, or the court of law to settle their disputes.

Organization structure

Alliance organization structures may be developed from several elements. In general, alliances include an executive committee, alliance managers, working groups, and project teams. In practice, executive committees may be found under several names, such as alliance executive council, steering group, or alliance board. The main tasks of the executive committee are to review, approve, amend, or reject strategies proposed by the alliance managers, monitor progress and results, make key decisions on resource allocation, and serve as the last resort for conflict resolution.[8] As such, the committee is the highest governance body in the alliance. In joint ventures, this committee may include the non-executive members of the board. In countries with a two-tiered board system, the supervisory board of the joint venture will act as the alliance executive committee. Partners with several alliances between them may determine whether using the same executive committee for all or some of those alliances is possible. This depends largely on the question of whether the same executive committee has the knowledge and mandate to govern all of the alliances.

Both partners in the alliance usually nominate the alliance managers. The managers' tasks vary depending on the alliance, but in general include the following at a minimum:

- ensuring external coordination with the partner(s);

- ensuring internal coordination within their own organization;

- maintaining an overview of all relevant issues in an alliance;

- signaling when actions are needed; and

- preparing meetings of the steering committee.

The managers may also be responsible for contract management and reporting. They may support individual projects or deals made by the alliance. Normally, their formal powers are limited and a minority of alliance managers have an actual mandate to change things within their organization. The setup may differ in joint ventures because the CEO of a joint venture often plays the role of alliance manager and is responsible for all of the joint venture's activities. The type of alliance manager necessary and his or her mandate and targets depend heavily on the specific alliance.

Working groups and project teams represent the operational level of the alliance. They consist of representatives of both partners and execute the various alliance projects, whether research projects, production, service delivery, or joint sales. Some alliances may create a separate group to handle the operational tasks. Such a management company or alliance support office occurs in large alliances that have many issues to organize. For example, Star Alliance created a separate organization with dozens of people to support the implementation of the alliance's policies throughout its more than 20 members. They do not make the decisions in the alliance but are purely operational.

When designing these structures, all of their elements should fit together. Overlap between committees needs to be avoided but they must be sufficiently complementary to prevent anything from falling through the cracks – both vertically (from the executive committee to the governance bodies below it) and horizontally (such as between working groups). One way to ensure such a structure is to ask each team to develop an alliance team charter.[9] Quintiles Corporation has a fixed format and process for developing team charters that describe the team's goals, work processes, and methods (decision making, accountability). The charter clarifies roles, deadlines, and manners for dealing with cultural differences and the like. Having a team develop this charter achieves clarity about what it should do and how its work relates to other groups in the alliance.

The communication structure is part of the organization structure as well. Clarity about who communicates with whom is an important prerequisite for success, even if the concept seems like an open door. The problem is that companies have different organizational structures and sizes; therefore, figuring out who is whose counterpart in the alliance takes time. The notion of peer-to-peer mapping has been developed to tackle this problem.[10] On each level of the alliance, counterparts are identified and prepared for their role. The peer-to-peer map ensures that a minimum (not a maximum) of communication takes place between the right people.

Broader communication between the organizations may be established using different mechanisms such as organizing partner events. Alliances are also increasing their use of social media. For example, Oracle uses social media to reach more than 20,000 partners (of all shapes and sizes that contribute 40 percent of Oracle's revenue). A dedicated partner blog gets information out to a vast network, as do Facebook, YouTube, LinkedIn, and Twitter. Events are promoted, problem solving between partners occurs, and news spreads rapidly.[11] A final element is the use of linking-pins: individuals who have a role in different parts of the alliance organization. For example, the alliance manager may also have a role in a working group. Linking-pins are a means to ensure that information flows rapidly and correctly through the alliance. The KLM–Northwest alliance made extensive use of linking-pins and this model is successfully incorporated in the successor to this alliance.

Planning and control

In an alliance, the planning and control processes are tied to its strategy. An alliance between Solvay and Quintiles concerning the development of new drugs used the strategy map process to translate the strategy into measurable targets.[12] Aligning interests, as ensured by the process of developing the strategy map, is more valuable than any short cut taken by directly specifying a scorecard. Although the use of a scorecard for alliances can be very valuable in attaining alignment, many alliances face problems when the scorecard is not linked correctly to their strategy or when the background of why some targets are chosen over others is lost on the alliance staff. Joint development of a strategy map helps alleviate some of those problems.

Most alliances have a planning cycle in place with annual business plans and budgets, along with a reporting cycle to monitor progress. The planning cycle is no different from that used by companies, except for one important element: it needs to fit into the planning cycle of two companies. The content and the pacing of the cycle can create problems. Companies may want to measure different things or at different time intervals. In the Senseo alliance, the annual planning cycle of Philips and Sara Lee/DE differed, with one company closing its books at the end of the year and the other at the end of the first quarter. To accommodate for this difference, the alliance executed two business planning cycles.

Sanctions and incentives may be used to keep an alliance on track. Sanctions and liability for non-performance or falling behind schedule and incentives for overperformance and increasing speed may be part of the planning and control system. Audits of product quality, financials, registration of hours, and the like may be necessary to ascertain whether certain targets were met. Again, the correct extent of using audits depends on the specific situation because over-reliance on audits is a major pitfall. Not all people respond to incentives in the same way and sometimes the incentives themselves lead people to focus on the wrong elements in the alliance.

Regarding risk management, Eli Lilly uses, among others, a system similar to that depicted in Figure 2.4. The system rates the effect of alliance-related events

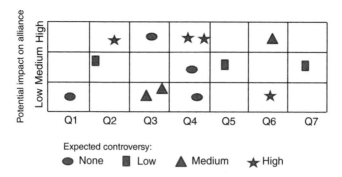

FIGURE 2.4: Effect of controversy of key events/discussions on alliances (indicative).[13]

as low, medium, or high, and estimates the expected controversy around that event on a similar scale. By plotting the events on a timeline, possible risks are identified ahead of time.

The keystone to alliance planning and control is the annual alliance diagnostic or health check.[14] This health check is a survey sent out to those involved in the alliance that measures its overall health and usually includes measurements of strategic, organizational, cultural, and operational elements. This form of joint evaluation has proven so helpful and effective that 92 percent of companies used it in 2011, an increase from 42 percent in 2002.[15] The reasons for this increase are easy to identify. First, maintaining alignment between two different companies is a daunting task and regular measurement and discussions of alliance health help to maintain alignment. Second, alliances usually operate in dynamic business environments. An alliance health check helps maintain a fit between the alliance and its business environment. Therefore, regular diagnostics form the cornerstone of alliance planning and control.

Competition clauses

Alliances should contribute to their partners' competitive advantage. They are used to address competition. Therefore, competitive implications need to be discussed, with specific attention to possible competition between the partners. Will the partnership be exclusive or are partners allowed to enter into similar partnerships with other organizations? Exclusivity is not always necessary or desirable. It is desirable when the goal of an alliance cannot be attained without it. For example, if an alliance is based on the premise that economies of scale have to be reached, then the partners must engage in all of their business through the alliance. Exclusivity can also ensure partner commitment. On the downside, exclusivity may remove the incentive to improve: if a company realizes that its partner may engage in business with another entity, it will always feel pressure to deliver to the best of its ability.

Agreements can also be created that dictate how companies will compete after the alliance ends. Will the companies compete with each other after the alliance ends? Alternatively, will the companies agree to a non-compete clause that states that they will not compete in each other's territories or the alliance's territory for a number of years? Is knowledge and information exchanged and generated in the alliance confidential or can it be shared with others? If one of the partners is taken over by the competitor of the other partner, will the alliance be disbanded automatically? Or, does such a change of control not affect the collaboration?

All of these questions regarding who can collaborate with whom under which conditions require attention. Sometimes, as in the Future Store Initiative, the answers to these questions are relatively straightforward: competitors can join the alliance on non-exclusive terms. In other alliances, the deals are more complex. A discussion on these issues is also affected by anti-trust regulations that may not allow too many restrictions on competition.

Exit agreement

Alliances are temporary, implying that companies need to think through what will happen when the alliance ends. Consider the case of a biotech company that partnered with a large pharma company. They set up a joint venture to develop the biotech's IP (intellectual property) into a product that could be brought to market. The biotech company contributed its IP to the joint venture. For various reasons, the joint venture went bankrupt. The biotech company expected the IP to be returned, but the original alliance agreement stated nothing regarding this issue. A judge ruled that because the joint venture was co-owned, the IP was jointly owned as well. A better exit clause in the contract stating that the IP would return to the biotech firm in the case of bankruptcy would have prevented this leakage of knowledge to the partner. Exit clauses may deal with a variety of similar issues. Provisions around alliance dissolution may also address what to do with clients that the alliance served. Will they continue to be served by both partners? Who owns the assets? Which company will serve which geographic market? Who bears the dissolution costs?

The reasons and timing for exiting alliances may be listed as well. Should a partner that wants to exit give notice to the other partners? If so, how far in advance? Is a takeover a reason for exiting? If a partner wants to exit, can it take back part of its contributed assets? Or, should it pay an exit fee to the other partners? Partners may also agree on a lockup period that determines the minimum runtime of the alliance. Clear exit provisions not only help reduce uncertainty in an alliance, but can also save the partners significant legal costs. In the absence of exit provisions, lawyers will have a feast.

Informal building blocks

Although the formal elements of alliance governance may form the backbone of an alliance, the alliance will not come alive without paying attention to informal aspects. Informal aspects constitute the next element in the Alliance Design Framework (see Table 2.4). They improve the communication that is central to alliance success. In particular, because of the open-ended nature of alliances, companies need to rely on more than formalities. Coping with change and uncertainty demands a psychological contract between the partners. Viewed from the opposite perspective, informal elements may undermine the formal elements. A business plan may be brilliant, but if the two alliance managers involved do not like each other, chances are that the plan will remain just that: a plan.

The first informal element is general norms and values that underpin alliances. Table 2.5 provides a list of 10 norms and values that are important in guiding the behavior of individuals in alliances. In their absence, collaboration becomes difficult. Alliances require organizations to be emphatic and to see things not

TABLE 2.4: Informal building blocks of alliance design

Norms and values	Assumptions that guide behavior in alliances in general
Code of conduct	Statement of behavior required in a specific alliance
Leadership	Alliance leaders need to have the right skills for their alliance
Personal relationships and team building	Meetings, informal events, and the like help build personal relationships
Bridge cultural differences	Organizational and international culture scans shed light on differences and how to cope with them
Trust, commitment, reputation	When both partners trust each other, different alliance designs are possible than when trust is lower
Informal communication	Sounding out ideas and proposals informally with the partner; managing expectations

TABLE 2.5: Alliance norms and values[16]

Norms and values	Definition
Empathy	Seeing things from the partner's perspective
Flexibility	The attitude that an agreement is a starting point and is to be modified as circumstances change
Conflict harmonization	Spirit of mutual accommodation; extent to which parties are confrontational or seek consensus
Solidarity	Belief that success comes from working cooperatively instead of competing against one another
Mutuality	Attitude that each party's success is a function of everyone's success; one cannot prosper at the expense of one's partner
Restraint of use of power	Forbearance from taking advantage of one's bargaining position in an exchange
Spirit of commitment	Staying in the alliance for the longer run; the opposite of opportunism
Trustworthy behavior	Refrain from consciously damaging a partner
Proactive	Initiate activities in the alliance rather than wait for the partner to take the first step
Strategic outlook	Viewing alliances as strategic rather than operational

only from their side, for example. This list also teaches something about the people that should be involved in alliances. Specialists in mergers and acquisitions (M&A), as well as purchasing professionals, tend not to be good alliance managers. Behavior that is highly effective in M&A situations or in purchasing organizations is completely counterproductive in alliances.

The elements mentioned in Table 2.5 can be very abstract for people working in an alliance. Therefore, an increasing number of companies develop concrete codes of conduct that explain the behavior required in an alliance. An example is the Behavioral Principles defined in the Abbott–Reata alliance (see Table 2.6). The two parties entered into a 50/50 cost and revenue sharing alliance to develop and commercialize drug candidates for inflammatory diseases. As part of the alliance launch process, they developed these principles. Note that the first letters of the principles put together form the words "Get Facts," indicating the importance of not assuming anything about either the drug research or the partner's intentions, but always discussing issues openly.

The partners of an alliance need to develop the code of conduct jointly. Discussions on the code of conduct are instrumental in creating the mindset that alliances require. Communicating the code is the next step. Alliance members may receive a short brochure that describes the goals on one side and the code

TABLE 2.6: Abbott–Reata Behavioral Principles[17]

Go deeper. When in disagreement, ask questions to understand your partner's perspective and explain yours. Talk about underlying interests, not just positions.
Enthusiastically celebrate. Celebrate achievements together.
Talk before email. Pick up the phone and regularly reach out to your colleagues and partners.
Focus on the "how". Clarify how we will collaborate, communicate, and make decisions before moving on to what needs to be done and decided.
Assume positive intent. Always assume the best intent from your partner.
Consult and collaborate. When in doubt, consult. Assume collaboration unless explicitly agreed otherwise. Respect your partner's expertise.
Take extra time to step in. Intervene on unhealthy interactions in a timely manner.
Share. Make it a habit to share information with your partner.

of conduct on the other. The code may also be hung up in places with a lot of traffic, such as the coffee corner.

No matter how valuable the experience may be of developing a code of conduct, in the end the words have to be brought to life. The leadership of an alliance is responsible for engaging in exemplary behavior in accordance with the espoused principles. Leadership can also make or break the formal governance structure. According to Steve Steinhilber, Cisco's Vice-President of Strategic Alliances, good alliance leadership has the following seven characteristics:[18]

- Cross-functional experience. Experience across different business functions helps an alliance manager understand how all of the diverse elements of an alliance fit together.

- Ability to synthesize quickly. An alliance manager must be able to make complex issues intelligible.

- Multimode communication skills. Written and verbal skills must be excellent and the alliance manager must be comfortable communicating across all hierarchical levels.

- Strategically relevant knowledge. Such knowledge is necessary to understand how to align companies in a changing market environment.

- Global experience and sensitivity. Many alliances operate across borders; hence, alliance managers need to appreciate the differences between countries.

- Ability to work in unstructured and ambiguous environments. Alliances operate in these conditions; hence, alliance managers need to be disciplined and focused to avoid getting lost.

- Emotional balance and self-confidence. Alliance managers need to be able to handle disappointment and give credit to others.

Alliance leaders play a pivotal role in the success of the alliance. Therefore, one of the most critical incidents in an alliance is a change of leadership. Succession issues are often badly handled. If an alliance manager changes, will he have personal chemistry with his counterpart in the partner? Will the alliance team accept him? In modern corporations in the West, the endless churn of managers poses many threats to the survival of an alliance. Japanese companies tend to enjoy the advantage of more stable alliance leadership. The possibility of leadership change underlines the importance of building relationships that go beyond individuals and that reach deeper in the organizations involved. Companies need to develop critical mass in their own organization and ensure that they have multiple points of contact in the partner organization to protect an alliance from changes in management at either partner company.

Alliance leaders are responsible for alliance teams. Broad literature exists on teams and that literature is not repeated here. Specific to alliances is the fact that team members have different organizational backgrounds. To get those people to communicate effectively requires close attention. With better communication among individuals, tensions in an alliance become easier to resolve and the formal governance structure becomes less burdened by escalations. Team members may also work in different locations. Some practices that have demonstrated effectiveness in alliances are the following:

- Colocation. By putting people from both partners together in one location, they get to know one another, communicate more easily with one another, and learn to see things from others' perspectives.

- Teambuilding activities. Teambuilding does not necessarily have to involve outdoorsy types of activities, such as whitewater rafting. Making time available for an informal event during an alliance team meeting may be just as effective. One trick is to organize alliance team meetings that start in the afternoon and end the next morning. Such meetings provide opportunities for having drinks and dinner together.

- Personnel exchanges and internships. Exchanging staff members between partners, even if only for a short period, helps individuals better understand one another. Knowing how a partner organization works and, even better, knowing why it works in that way is sure to facilitate collaboration. Problems, details, and processes not previously understood will stand in a different light after spending time on the other side.

These practices also help to bridge cultural differences, which can be either organizational or national. Even within the same national culture, firms' organizational cultures differ. The extent to which a culture is hierarchical, risk taking or risk averse, and slow or fast moving affects alliances. National cultural differences are usually easier to spot than organizational cultural differences. Many culture management approaches are available in the market that help companies manage cultural differences. Using such approaches in an alliance setting is another step to creating mutual understanding. Cultural differences should not be eradicated because they provide learning opportunities. Understanding cultural differences and why they exist usually goes a long way to avoiding the irritation that they may cause.

Cultural differences may also affect an alliance at the operational level. For example, consider the numerous international airline alliances. On-board service depends heavily on the country of origin of the carrier. Food and beverages are important to Italian or Japanese travelers, and they frown on the offerings of American airlines. A simple thing such as touching a passenger to help him put his seat in an upright position can be interpreted as helping in the USA and an invasion of privacy or a downright insult in other countries. Cultural differences seriously affect alliance success rates. One study showed that domestic alliances have a success rate of 57 percent, whereas international alliances did not even achieve 49 percent.[19]

Trust, commitment, and reputation are important relational aspects of alliances as well. Trust is the belief that a partner makes an effort to behave in accordance with the agreements made, is honest in negotiations that precede the agreements, and does not take advantage of another when the opportunity presents itself.[20] Trust is a success factor for alliances, although alliances with a low level of trust may still be effective. Co-opetition alliances in which competitors collaborate do not exhibit high trust levels but still successfully bring products to market. In the KLM–NWA alliance, the partners sued each other, but operationally the alliance continued to be highly profitable.

Trust is interpreted differently across organizations, countries, and individuals. Therefore, building on trust right from the start of a relationship is difficult. Trust usually builds over time as partners keep to their promises and show actual (rather than merely verbal) commitment. Hence, in many cases, trust is more a consequence of collaboration than a prerequisite, and a high level of trust emerges when interactions go well and success is attained. In addition, a lack of trust is usually not a failure factor in itself. A basic level of trust exists at the outset of alliances that may be eroded because one or both partners do not behave according to expectations, possibly because they are untrustworthy. However, more often the cause lies in unclear agreements, bad communication, or ineffective alliance implementation.

The implication is not that trust is not important in alliances. On the contrary; trust can make alliances more efficient and effective. An important efficiency gain is that a high level of trust lessens the need for control. Double control mechanisms can be abolished when partners trust each other. Effectiveness increases in high trust situations because trust stimulates knowledge and information sharing. These aspects usually lead to the discovery of new opportunities for the alliance. Once trust exists in a relationship, it will be of immense value.

Developing trust is not easily organized. The best motto is to keep to one's commitment. Sometimes a partner is trusted because of certain characteristics such as his competence or consistent behavior, or because he belongs to a certain cultural or ethnic group.[21] As an illustration of the latter, in the world's premier horticultural cluster in the Netherlands, growers of flowers, plants, and vegetables team up in cooperatives to innovate and bring their produce to market. These alliances have a low level of formalization, but are rooted in the fact that all partners hail from the same region. They are neighbors, family, or active in the same sports clubs. Being one of the locals underpins the trust in these cooperatives.

An important precondition for trust to work in the long run is that it must be mutual. If one partner trusts the other one, but this trust is not reciprocated or – worse – it is reciprocated by distrustful behavior, the damage to the trusting partner may be substantial. However, the distrustful partner will also suffer a dent in his reputation. Once this behavior is known, that partner may be excluded from future alliances.

Once a good reputation is established, it is valuable to both the company with the reputation and to its partners. The partners may be quite confident that the reputable partner will not behave opportunistically because doing so may damage its reputation. That reputation is valuable because it helps attract the best partners in the industry. For this reason, companies set up partners of choice or premier partner programs[22] that aim to establish the reputation of a company as reliable. Pharmaceutical company Eli Lilly has been successful with such programs. Eli Lilly's partners rank it as one of the best companies to work with.[23] However, the company was not always viewed as favorably. In 1999, only half of its partners stated that they would recommend Eli Lilly as a good partner to other organizations. By investing in top-notch alliance management, this figure rose to 90 percent in 2003.[24] Eli Lilly's good reputation means that partners with an interesting technology put it high on their list of partners to work with, giving Eli Lilly first pick and, hence, an advantage over its competitors.

IBM aims to create the image of being a reputable partner by publishing its Business Partner Charter. This charter includes six guiding principles that define what a partner may expect of IBM (see Table 2.7). As a counterpoint, IBM also lists the minimum standards of business conduct to which partners must adhere. These standards include financial integrity, fair competition, and respect for diversity. Although many of these elements are general, they form the basis of building trustworthy partnerships.

The triumvirate of trust, commitment, and reputation affect the design and effectiveness of alliances. The better these elements are developed, the fewer control mechanisms are needed, the more flexibly the organization can be organized, the fewer doubts that value is shared evenly, and the easier it is to change the alliance to stay current with changing business environments. The importance of trust, commitment, and reputation reinforces why partner selection is an important control mechanism in alliances: if selecting the right, trusted partner is possible, completely different alliance designs are possible than when a partner is selected without knowing how it will behave. Companies may not always have the option to choose a known and trusted partner. In such cases, a control-based alliance design is more likely.

A final informal element is the use of informal communication. Similar to many of the previous points, consciously designing informal communication into an alliance is not easy. However, companies can stimulate awareness over the fact that informal communication improves the functioning of an alliance. They may stress, for example, that informal communication may help to manage a

TABLE 2.7: Six guiding principles of IBM[25]

- IBM business partners are vital to IBM's business.
- Our relationship is a collaboration of equals.
- We invest in IBM business partners' success.
- We strive to provide the industry's best business partner experience in all respects.
- We work with our business partners to seize the opportunities presented by a smarter planet.
- We ground our relationships in the core values of IBM.

partner's expectations. Sounding out ideas and proposals informally with the partner will help prevent unpleasant surprises.

Internal alignment

Internal alignment is the fourth element of the Alliance Design Framework. One of the most important mistakes in developing an alliance design rests on the assumption that when the relationship between the partners is agreed on, the alliance design is finished. In reality, many problems in alliances are not so much caused by tensions in the alliance relationship as they are by tensions in each of the individual partners[26] or tensions caused by the fact that the companies' operating procedures are aimed at optimizing the internal, vertical organization. Therefore, they conflict with the horizontal alliance requirements. Consequently, "40 percent of my job is selling to the alliance partner and 60 percent is actually selling alliances to the rest of my own company," according to an alliance manager in an American telecom company. To ensure that an alliance runs effectively, companies may need to align their internal organization to the alliance, which requires investing in the elements listed in Table 2.8.

Without a doubt, the most difficult issue is the alignment of internal targets and bonuses to the requirements of the alliance. Companies have their own systems for individual performance management that are often at odds with what an alliance needs. Sometimes such alignment is not even desirable; after all, the tail should not start to wag the dog. Alliances are derived from company strategy and not the other way around. However, companies at least need to be aware that internal targets may harm an alliance and they need to understand that targets are not normally aligned.

TABLE 2.8: Elements of internal alignment

Align targets/bonuses	Adapt internal targets and bonuses to the requirements of the alliance
Obtain internal commitment	Executive sponsor buy-in from business units and other relevant departments
Pre-governance meetings	Internal meetings at the partner to ensure that everyone within the organization is aligned before a governance meeting takes place
Develop an alliance culture	Ensure company staff behave in an alliance-friendly manner

An American software company planned to enter the European market through partners. It hired sales managers that were responsible for direct selling and for selling together with partners. However, the company put them on the monthly sales target system they used for the American market, in which direct selling was the standard. None of the partnerships that the company set up in Europe worked, which made sense given the bonus system implemented.

Partnerships require at least one year to get off the ground. A sales manager must invest a significant amount of time to develop a strong relationship with a partner, and that time cannot be devoted to direct selling. Consequently, the sales manager will miss earning a bonus for at least 12 consecutive months, until the alliance gets off the ground. Therefore, no sales manager would invest in partnerships under such a scenario. The result was that the company's growth in Europe was stalled. If investments in partnerships had been made, after a year or so the company would have been able to sell with and sell through its partner sales force, effectively multiplying its sales strength many times over. However, the bonus system was so deeply ingrained in this organization that it was unable and unwilling to change it. After attempting partnerships for a number of years, it disbanded the partnerships and increased its investment in direct selling.

Adapting bonus and rewards systems is difficult because career paths, planning and control mechanisms, and review procedures are all tied to them. If targets and bonuses cannot be aligned perfectly with an alliance, a second best option is to make them depend partly on alliance success. For example, a business unit manager may have as one of her targets to generate at least a certain amount of sales via an alliance.

Obtaining buy-in for a new alliance within each of the partners is another important mechanism to align the organizations with the alliance. An executive sponsor is necessary to signal to the rest of the organization that the alliance is important. However, such signaling is not sufficient, and support from other managers who may have to work with the alliance is also required. Some companies have guidelines that state that a minimum number of board members or executive vice presidents should support the alliance for it to go ahead, which is sensible. No matter how good an alliance may look on paper, if key executives do not support it, it will not get off the ground.

Because alliances often cut across different departments in an organization, during the lifetime of the alliance, differences in viewpoints about it may arise throughout the organization. Internal meetings are necessary to ensure that everyone within the organization behaves in line with the alliance and sends out similar signals to the partner. In particular, before a meeting with the partner, an internal meeting can help avoid the embarrassment in the presence of your partner of finding out that no agreement exists within your organization about what is the right direction to take when going forward.

The final and most far-reaching action of a company is to work on its organizational culture and make it more susceptible to alliances. Processes may be adapted to partner needs; a coherent language and positive stories about alliance successes may be circulated throughout the company; partner logos may be made visible; and employees may be taught to see things from the partner's perspective. All off these elements contribute to building an organizational culture that is receptive to alliances.[27] An alliance-friendly culture is particularly valuable when dealing with changes in the alliance that will inevitably occur.

Trust and control in the Alliance Design Framework

The Alliance Design Framework developed in this chapter enables companies to realize a balance between trust and control that fits with their specific alliance. In general, alliances based on trust will emphasize informal elements, whereas control-based alliance will focus on the formal elements. However, this issue is not simply black or white. Trust-based alliances require formal elements, and control-based alliances need to pay attention to informal elements. When trust-based alliances apply formal elements, they tend not to be very elaborate. For example, contracts will be shorter than in control-based alliances. The next chapters show how companies combine the building blocks from the Alliance Design Framework to create the level of control and trust required by their specific circumstance.

Notes

1 Dekker, H.C. 2004. Control of inter-organizational relationships: evidence on appropriation concerns and coordination requirements, *Accounting, Organizations and Society*, 29(1), 27–49; Gulati, R. and H. Singh. 1998. The architecture of cooperation: managing coordination costs and appropriation concerns in strategic alliances, *Administrative Science Quarterly*, 43, 781–814; Tjemkes, B.V. 2008. *Growing and Sharing the Pie*, PhD thesis, Radboud Universiteit, Nijmegen.
2 De Wit, B. and R. Meyer. 1999. *Strategy Synthesis*, London, Thomson Business Press.
3 Porter, M.E. and M.R. Kramer. 2006. Strategy and society: the link between competitive advantage and corporate social responsibility, *Harvard Business Review*, December, 78–90.

4   ASAP. 2012. *The ASAP Handbook of Alliance Management: A practitioner's guide*, Canton, MA, Association of Strategic Alliance Professionals.

5   Albers, S. 2010. Configurations of alliance governance systems, *Schmalenbach Business Review*, 62, July, 204–233.

6   Ziegelbauer, K. and R. Farquhar. 2004. Strategic alliance management: lessons learned from the Bayer–Millennium collaboration, *Drug Discovery Today*, 9(20), 864–868.

7   Gomes-Casseres, B. and J. Bamford. 2001. The corporation is dead . . . long live the constellation, in: A.P. de Man, G.M. Duysters and A. Vasudevan, *The Allianced Enterprise*, London, Imperial College Press.

8   This definition of the function of executive committees was suggested by Shuman, J. and J. Twombly. 2009. *Alliance Governance – Helpful or Hurtful?*, Boston, MA, The Rhythm of Business, p. 5.

9   Mylenski, T. 2012. *Implementing an alliance team charter*, Durham, NC, Quintiles, white paper.

10 ASAP, 2012, *The ASAP Handbook of Alliance Management: A practitioner's guide*, Canton, MA, Association of Strategic Alliance Professionals.

11 Fouts, R. and T. Bova. 2010. *Case Study: Using social media to deepen partner relationships, an inside look at the Oracle Partner Network*, Gartner, Dataquest Note G00175794, 9 June.

12 Kaplan, R.S., D.P. Norton and B. Rugelsjoen. 2010. Managing alliances with the balanced scorecard, *Harvard Business Review*, January/February, 114–120.

13 Adapted from: Thompson, D.S., S.E. Twait and K.R. Fill. 2011. Measuring alliance management: quantify your value by showing how you mitigate risk and solve problems, *Strategic Alliance Magazine*, Quarter 3, pp. 22–25/53.

14 Futrell, D., M. Slugay and C.H. Stephens. 2001. Becoming a premier partner: measuring, managing and changing partner capabilities at Eli Lilly and company, *Journal of Commercial Biotechnology*, 8, 1, 5–13; Nevin, M. 2006. *Three stages of alliance maturity*, White Paper, Alliance Best Practice, www.alliancebestpractice.com.

15 Duysters, G., A.P. de Man, D. Luvison and A. Krijnen. 2012. *The State of Alliance Management: Past, Present and Future*, Eindhoven, Brabant Centre for Entrepreneurship/Canton MA, Association of Strategic Alliance Professionals.

16 Cannon, J.P., R.S. Achrol and G.T. Gundlach. 2000. Contracts, norms, and plural form governance, *Journal of the Academy of Marketing Science*, 28, 2, 180–194; De Man, A.P. and D. Luvison. 2010. *Alliance culture: It's in the DNA!*, White Paper, Association of Strategic Alliance Professionals.

17 Vantage Partners. 2012. *Planning for and Implementing a New Alliance Launch Process for a New Worldwide Collaboration*, www.vantagepartners.com.

18 Steinhilber, S. 2008. *Strategic Alliances*, Boston (MA), Harvard Business Press.

19 De Man, A.P., G.M. Duysters and I. Neyens. 2009. *The Third State of Alliance Management*, Needham MA, Association of Strategic Alliance Professionals.

20 Cummings, L.L. and P. Bromiley. 1996. The organizational trust inventory (OTI): development and validation, in: R. Kramer and T.R. Tyler (eds.), *Trust in Organizations: Frontiers of theory and research*, Thousand Oaks, CA, Sage, pp. 302–330.

21 McAllister, D.J. 1995. Affect- and cognition-based trust as foundations for interpersonal cooperation in organizations, *Academy of Management Journal*, 38, 1, 24–59.

22 Futrell, D., M. Slugay and C.H. Stephens. 2001. Becoming a premier partner: measuring, managing and changing partner capabilities at Eli Lilly and company, *Journal of Commercial Biotechnology*, 8, 1, 5–13.

23 IBM. 2004. *Bio Partnering Survey*, February.

24 De Man, A.P. 2006. *Alliantiebesturing*, Assen, Van Gorcum.

25 This table is based on the December 2012 version found at https://www-304.ibm.com/ partnerworld/wps/servlet/ContentHandler/pw_com_jnw_code_conduct.

26 Draulans, J., A.P. de Man and H.W. Volberda. 2003. Building alliance capability: management techniques for superior alliance performance, *Long Range Planning*, 36, 2, April, 151–166.

27 De Man, A.P. and D. Luvison. 2010. *Alliance Culture: It's all in the DNA!*, White Paper, Canton, MA, Association of Strategic Alliance Professionals.

CHAPTER 3

Turning suppliers into allies

Can suppliers become alliance partners? In many ways, the collaboration between clients and suppliers is different from alliances between equals. The most obvious difference is that the money flows only in one direction in client–supplier relationships. Moreover, a procurement procedure usually selects suppliers according to a procurement procedure, whereas in alliances partners select each other. From the start, a procurement procedure introduces inequality into the collaboration. However, inequality does not mean that intensive collaboration is impossible. In fact, a growing trend is the introduction of alliance-like mechanisms in client–supplier relationships. Practice shows that the benefits of more amicable collaboration in such relationships could be substantial, provided that a number of conditions are met. This chapter explores these conditions.

The causes behind the increasing number of client–supplier alliances are not much different than the general causes behind the increased attention for alliances in general. In client–supplier relationships, the complexity has increased such that simple purchasing contracts are inadequate. Rapidly changing business environments require clients and suppliers to adapt to new demands. Contracts between them need to reflect the need for change. Writing complete contracts to procure more complex goods and services becomes increasingly difficult.

The traditional purchasing mindset builds on win–lose thinking: the higher the price paid for a good, the more the buyer loses and the supplier gains. The lower the price, the better for the buyer and the worse for the supplier. Even though the purchasing literature identified various ways to procure goods,[1] in practice an antagonistic approach remains dominant in which the seller attempts to obtain as high a price as possible and the buyer attempts to negotiate the price down. Because of the changing market circumstances, short-term and one-time cost savings become less important than innovation and flexibility. Traditional thinking no longer applies in an increasing number of client–supplier relationships. The search is on for relationships that benefit both sides of the deal.

Two basic types of alliances exist between clients and suppliers. The first are long-term alliances in which partners engage in repeated transactions over time. These alliances may be bilateral but also may involve multiple partners and multiple phases along a supply chain.[2] The second form is the project alliance in which companies collaborate on a single project. In complex projects, developing a detailed blueprint of the final product is difficult. To allow for flexibility in project execution, an alliance may be the solution.

The two types of alliances reflect two different alliance designs. The goals achievable through these designs can be quite different. Client–supplier partnerships might aim to lower costs, increase speed, improve innovation, and grow revenue. Therefore, the diversity of these alliances is high, making developing general guidelines on how to manage them difficult. The examples provided are meant to be sources of inspiration for thinking about what can be done in collaboration with clients or suppliers.

Long-term client–supplier partnerships

Many long-term relationships exist between clients and suppliers, but not all of them are alliances. Even purchases by a client of goods from the same supplier for more than 10 years do not imply an alliance between them. In accordance with the definition of an alliance, an alliance requires joint goals, involves some form of sharing of revenue, cost, and risk between the partners, provides for joint decision making, and is based on open-ended or incomplete agreements. Traditional outsourcing contracts do not meet these qualifications. However, more recent outsourcing deals in the IT sector have become so complex and have incorporated such far-reaching new financial mechanisms, such as pay per use, that they quite closely resemble full-blown partnerships.

The well-known case of Toyota's collaboration with its suppliers reveals more far-reaching partnerships.[3] Toyota's relationships have some of the following characteristics that incentivize suppliers to continually innovate and improve their performance:

- Value generated by a supplier because of the knowledge received from Toyota may initially be appropriated 100 percent by that supplier and should only be shared with Toyota over time. This scenario is markedly different from many traditional client–supplier relationships in which any cost saving is immediately transferred to the client, giving the supplier no strong incentive to save costs.

- Toyota guarantees long-term business to any supplier in its network. Therefore, supplier selection is a crucial capability for Toyota, and suppliers need to meet very demanding criteria. However, once in the network, suppliers are assured of at least some Toyota business for a longer term. Again, this scenario is markedly different from traditional supply relationships in which suppliers have to bid for business on a regular basis. Once more this changes a supplier's incentives. A Toyota supplier can make larger investments in quality and innovation because he is sure to earn back these investments. A supplier on a short-term contract has no incentive to make such investments.

- Suppliers engage in a learning race.[4] Big investments in knowledge sharing are made to help suppliers improve. Toyota makes its knowledge available to its supplier network, and suppliers can use Toyota consultants free of charge for a limited period. Suppliers are also required to share their knowledge with other Toyota suppliers: no proprietary knowledge exists in the Toyota supplier network. An extensive system of teams and working groups is in place to ensure suppliers share knowledge. Suppliers that learn fastest are best positioned to obtain new business.

- Sanctions are implemented to keep the pressure on. Toyota may ultimately remove business from a supplier that does not meet its requirements or exclude the supplier from new business.

The results of these measures are lower cost, higher quality, and quicker response times. Changing the incentives for suppliers is a necessary condition to creating a partnership with them. However, creating a partnership is not sufficient: suppliers also need support through knowledge exchange. Toyota demands continuous improvement from suppliers and facilitates achievement of such improvements. Doing so creates trust and augments knowledge sharing.

In the end, many suppliers identify with the Toyota network and collaborate for a common good. This system is not specifically rooted in a supposedly collaborative Japanese culture. A study of the origins of the system shows that, in fact, economic difficulties and a lack of access to cutting-edge production technology in Japan after World War II were the starting points for the development of the system.[5] Elements of the system were transferred outside of Japan as well. Although not a precondition for the system to work, the Japanese culture may have eased its implementation.

Toyota works with individual suppliers embedded in a large network and gives them some direct tangible incentives in the form of cost savings and knowledge. The model can also work in a multi-partner alliance in which the incentives are not as immediate as in the Toyota case. For example, in the Rolls-Royce Global Physical Logistics alliance, Rolls-Royce collaborates with its main logistics providers.[6] Rolls-Royce is a world-leading provider of power systems and services for use on land, at sea, and in the air. The company has a broad customer base comprised of airlines, corporate and utility aircraft and helicopter operators, armed forces, and energy customers in nearly 120 countries.

Inside Rolls-Royce, the Global Physical Logistics department handles the logistics for direct materials (in other words, materials that end up in original equipment manufacturers' (OEM) products), spare parts, and finished OEM products. To maintain its position in the engine-making business, Rolls-Royce sought to improve its performance in maintenance and spare parts. Because the engine business is global and spare parts may be needed instantly anywhere in the world, logistics is a challenge. Therefore, Rolls-Royce cooperates closely with its preferred logistics suppliers through the GPL alliance. The GPL alliance came into existence in 2004 and initially included, in addition to Rolls-Royce, TNT Logistics (currently named CEVA Logistics), KLM Cargo Aerospace Logistics in a joint bid with second-tier partner Kuehne + Nagel Ltd (KN), and Daher Sawley Ltd. KLM and KN switched positions in 2006, with KN becoming the contractual supplier and KLM becoming the second-tier partner.

Early in 2000, Rolls-Royce had no formal logistics group. Instead, a standalone purchasing group that primarily focused on cost effectiveness managed the supply chain. A new logistics group was set up that started to consider several options for further implementing the logistics function within Rolls-Royce. The company could have decided to manage the execution of this logistics function by itself through a large network of local service providers. Alternatively, it could have followed its competitors by employing a single lead logistics partner (fourth-party logistics or 4PL) to manage that network on its behalf. However,

Rolls-Royce found itself unable to resource the management of a large (diverse) subcontractor network. Furthermore, the company could not find a single fourth-party logistics company that possessed all of the capabilities it needed on a global scale. In addition, Rolls-Royce was not particularly keen on the added costs and commercial hazards of working with a single 4PL. Therefore, the new logistics group started to create a new collaboration-based model and began negotiations with several logistics partners to be part of a new alliance.

The goal of this alliance was to serve an increasingly global market with increasing customer expectations for delivery assurance, speed, responsiveness, and cost. Because no one company had all of the required capabilities, Rolls-Royce selected partners that were able to deliver capabilities in three areas: road transport, international freight forwarding, and packaging (at a later stage, Rolls-Royce made the decision to outsource warehousing). After a careful partner selection process that considered several other partners, Rolls-Royce selected the three core partners for the alliance: CEVA, KLM with KN as its second tier, and Daher. Rolls-Royce sought partners with overlapping yet complementary capabilities. The overlap was deemed necessary in case, for whatever reason, one of the partners must leave the alliance. In that case, the other partners should be able to fill the gap left by that partner on a temporary basis but for a sufficiently long enough time to allow the alliance to find a new partner to plug the gap.

For the partners, the new way of working was quite different than before. Normally, the partners coordinated bilaterally with Rolls-Royce to deliver their services. Because Rolls-Royce believed that better coordination between partners delivers major benefits in terms of cost saving and speed, the partners were also asked to coordinate among one another. Because downtime of planes was very expensive, pre-planning and scheduling of maintenance activities could deliver substantial cost savings. By coordinating partners were expected to better decide which of them could get a spare part at the right place, at the right time, and at the lowest cost. The greater the integration of the collaboration, the faster that engines could be repaired or maintained and the lower the costs of doing so.

Based on studies of other industries in which similar endeavors were undertaken, Rolls-Royce identified a strong business case for supply chain savings of nearly 20 percent per year. In addition to cost savings, Rolls-Royce wanted better quality and higher speed and expected supply chain response time to be reduced significantly. Since the inception of the alliance, Rolls-Royce and its partners have consistently realized significant cost savings and service improvements. For example, CEVA's inbound collection service for gas turbine materials in the UK is on time for more than 99.87 percent of the cases every year. Furthermore, KN achieved significant cost reductions whereas the rest of the market increased its prices.

The partners' incentive to participate was that they are better positioned to potentially receive more business from Rolls-Royce. Partners do not have a preferred status and needed to be competitive with non-partners. However, they benefit in two ways from the alliance. First, they have more intimate knowledge of Rolls-Royce's requirements and are better able to pitch for new Rolls-Royce business. Second, the alliance implemented a joint risk–reward scheme that improves partners' margins.

The alliance governance model is structured on three levels: the executive level, the alliance management level, and the project management level. Each partner appointed one person at each of these levels as the alliance representative. On the executive level, an alliance board was formed that is chaired by Rolls-Royce. The board meets every six months and approves and commits activities and resources. The alliance management group meets monthly to monitor the progress of activities and to identify new opportunities to propose to the board. The operational project management group meets at least monthly and more frequently when required. The project teams are responsible for implementation of alliance projects.

The Toyota and Rolls-Royce cases show that a shift in mindset is needed to make changes happen. An important change was to refocus negotiations from price to margin. As long as clients and suppliers primarily bicker over prices, they remain stuck in a win–lose situation. With the revenue of the supplier being the cost of the client a change in price benefits one party and harms the other party. However, if the organizations refocus on margin, they may identify cost savings or new revenue streams that benefit both client and supplier. The corollary of this concept is that clients and suppliers have to be transparent about their cost prices. Open book accounting is a sine qua non for these alliances to get off the ground.

A related shift in mindset is from a focus on transaction to a focus on relationship. Judging each transaction between a customer and a supplier on its own merits makes seeing the real gains in margin difficult. A focus on the long-term relationship creates new opportunities for cost savings and growth. An extra investment made today may easily earn itself back over a number of years. In the case of Rolls-Royce, today's investment in partnerships pays back over time for both the company and its partners.

The most significant shift that is occurring and that is necessary for successful collaboration between clients and suppliers is changing the attitude in procurement and purchasing departments. Often, these departments are viewed as the arch enemy of alliances because most people working there were trained in short-term, win–lose thinking. This mindset works very well for the vast majority of products and services but is harmful for alliances. Because all supply alliances (and many other alliances) incorporate buyer–seller relationships, they at least need approval from procurement officers. The process of contracting alliances varies from traditional purchasing relationships. The more alliance capable a procurement office is and the greater its understanding of when to use alliances as a procurement tactic, the more likely that a company may benefit from collaboration.

Project alliances

The second major group of client–supplier relationships is project alliances. Project alliances have emerged primarily in the construction industry as a way to manage complex and risky projects. Therefore, much of the thinking around project alliances is based on construction projects, although other applications exist, such as in digital media projects.[7] Large infrastructural projects are good candidates for alliance contracting. Thus, not surprisingly, governments have taken an interest. For example, the Australian government's Department of Infrastructure and Transport published an extensive 168-page guide to alliance contracting.[8] This guide lists a number of conditions that must be met before a project alliance can be considered. Because these conditions provide interesting insight into the dos and don'ts of project alliances, Table 3.1 provides an excerpt.

Apart from the minimum size necessary for an alliance, the second threshold states that adequate staffing resources should be available for an alliance. This lesson learned is based on the experience that many alliances are understaffed. Moreover, even if the operation level has adequate resources, senior management involvement may be inadequate. The open-ended nature of alliance contracts makes this involvement a prerequisite for success. Only senior management has the mandate to agree on contractual changes. Their involvement is necessary to assure internal alignment, as discussed in the Alliance Development Framework in Chapter 2.

The other characteristics deal with risk, time pressure, and contributions to the alliance. Risk sharing is at the heart of most project alliances. Time pressure is

TABLE 3.1: Project characteristics most suited to alliances (Commonwealth of Australia, excerpt)[9]

... before any detailed comparison to other project delivery models is made, it is necessary to understand the "threshold issues" that should be satisfied before an alliance is considered as an appropriate option. These threshold issues include:

- Project value: The policy provides that alliancing is generally not appropriate for simple procurement projects valued under $50 million.* This is due to the high initial start-up management costs (for both Owners and NOPs[†]) associated with both procurement and delivery of alliance contracts.
- Resourcing: To successfully deliver an alliance project, the Owner will require sufficient internal resources, including senior executives, who can effectively represent and manage its interests in relation to external parties and the alliance contract. As a minimum, the number of internal resources available to procure and deliver an alliance contract can be expected to be equivalent to, if not of higher capability than, those normally made available to procure and deliver a traditional contract. The internal resourcing requirements for alliancing should be considered as part of the Business Case.

After taking into account these threshold issues, an alliance may be considered as a suitable project delivery method when the relevant project has one or more of the following characteristics:

- the project has risks that cannot be adequately defined or dimensioned in the Business Case nor during subsequent work prior to tendering;
- the cost of transferring risks is prohibitive in the prevailing market conditions;
- the project needs to start as early as possible before the risks can be fully identified and/or project scope can be finalized, and the Owner is prepared to take the commercial risk of a suboptimal price outcome;
- the Owner has superior knowledge, skills, preference and capacity to influence or participate in the development and delivery of the project (including for example, in the development of the design solution and construction method); and/or
- a collective approach to assessing and managing risk will produce a better outcome; for example, where the preservation of safety to the public/project is best served through the collaborative process of an alliance.

---

* One Australian dollar is approximately equal to one US dollar (March 2013).
† The owner is the entity that eventually owns the asset and is responsible for procurement; NOPs are non-owner participants, such as all other partners in the alliance like building contractors.

mentioned because traditional procurement procedures may be very lengthy. For example, they involve the development of detailed specifications of the object that needs to be built. In alliances, the detailed specifications are usually completed after the contract has been awarded, saving on significant time. Contributions from the client to the alliance in terms of capabilities to influence the outcome are necessary because an alliance is not needed without such contributions. If the client cannot influence the results, no collaboration is needed and the supplier or contractor will achieve the same results working on his own. ProRail is an example of a successful method to set up project alliances that illustrates these principles.

ProRail's project alliances[10]

A significant challenge in developing large infrastructure projects is to get them done on time and within budget. This challenge exists because of the risks that such projects face. Many unexpected things can happen. By collaborating, companies may manage those risks more effectively. In order to ensure collaboration, the incentives of a principal and his building contractor need to be aligned. ProRail, the Dutch government-owned company charged with building and maintaining railways, faced the question of how to achieve this alignment and turn a big project into a win–win situation for ProRail and contractors. An alliance provided the answer.

To understand the alliance mechanism, it is relevant to review how risks are shared between ProRail and contractors. One risk for a project is the discovery of unexpected obstacles in the soil, for instance an old bomb from World War II. If no alliance exists between ProRail and a contractor, the standard procedure would be that ProRail carries the entire risk of this. It would pay for the cost of removal and it would carry the costs of the project's delay. The costs of project delay, however, can be reduced with the help of the contractor. For example, by being inventive and redeploying some of their personnel and material to work on something else, idle time is reduced. In ProRail's alliance mechanism incentives are introduced to make it attractive for a contractor to do so.

To better manage such unforeseen risks, ProRail began experimenting with a new contracting mechanism, centered on an alliance fund. In a risk analysis all major project risks are allocated to ProRail or the contractor or designated to be best managed by both of them together. ProRail put a price on all jointly managed risks in a project and created a fund based on the total value of these risks. If one of those risks materializes, the contractor's additional work is paid out of that fund. In the case of the bomb, the alliance fund carries the costs associated with project delay, with a maximum of a delay of 90 days. The additional costs of project delay above 90 days are paid by ProRail and are not paid for out of the alliance fund. The logic behind this is that the contractor can influence the costs of delay, for example, by redeploying staff. At the end of the project, ProRail and the contractor share what remains in the fund on a 50–50 basis. This method considerably changes the incentives. A contractor only makes a margin of a couple of percentage points on his normal revenue, but the alliance fund's margin is 50 percent. If he reduces the cost of delay, no money flows out of the alliance fund and his profits increase.

Consequently, to make the alliance fund as large as possible is in the interest of the contractor, and he can help grow the fund in two ways. First, the contractor can work with ProRail to minimize the costs once risks have materialized. For example, if ProRail is responsible for obtaining a building permit but the permit threatens to be a month late, in the old situation the contractor sat and waited until the permit was issued. ProRail paid the costs for waiting. In an alliance the waiting period is paid out of the alliance fund and eats into the contractor's margin. Therefore he starts looking for other ways to use his personnel and equipment during the month he waits for the permit, such as by having them work on another stretch of the railway or by helping ProRail in obtaining the permit on time.

The second way that the contractor can keep the alliance fund filled is to suggest ideas for improving the design. A cost saving suggested by a contractor is added to the alliance fund. For example, if the idea is to construct a flyover in a different way that would result in a net €1 million cost saving, that amount is added to the alliance fund. If the contractor had not suggested the cost saving, he would have received revenue of €1 million, but would only earn €50,000 profit assuming a 5 percent margin. By saving the building costs and adding the money to the alliance fund, he instead receives €500,000 net at the completion of the project, as long as no other costs or benefits flow through the alliance fund. This represents a 10-fold increase in his margin. The alliance can decide about such issues as long as the suggested improvements lie within its scope and the improvement meets all specifications.

The alliance fund mechanism is not only based on risks. In addition to the risk sharing mechanism defined above, other elements can also fill or deplete the fund. Such additional elements are:

- Design costs. The alliance is responsible for the detailed design of the project. By combining the expertise of ProRail and that of the contractor the design costs are lowered.

- Organization costs. Costs related to organization, project management, and project staff decrease because of better collaboration.

- Optimizations of the detailed design. Optimizations occur when the alliance identifies improvements in the project design that lead to lower construction costs. Cost savings are added to the alliance fund.

The basic mechanism is simple, but the execution is much more complex. First, a new contracting process needed to be designed that met the requirements of the European Union. The European Union demands transparent contracting rules by government-owned organizations. ProRail designed the next process. Instead of asking contractors to quote one contracting price, it asked bidders for a contracting price and their estimate of the alliance sum based on a risk analysis. For the contracting price, contractors quote the lean construction costs for building the project. This quote is based on a reference design including the contractor's risks, but not including the cost of risks that are allocated to the alliance. In the alliance sum, they estimate the cost of project management, design, and the prices of all of the risks and foreseen chances that are allocated to the alliance. Therefore the basis for the two estimates (contracting price and alliance sum) are a reference design of the project and a definition of the alliance scope. The reference design is the starting point for creating the detailed design, for which the alliance is responsible after the project is awarded to one of the contractors. In the end two contracts are written. One is the construction contract which comprises the building activities and the risks that are carried by the contractor. The other is the alliance contract which defines scope, risks, and rules for the alliance.

An initial issue that needs to be resolved in the contracting phase is which risks are part of the alliance and which risks should be borne by either ProRail or the contractor. The solution was that risks that either party could influence are paid for by that party and are not included in the alliance fund. For example, a breakdown in a contractor's machines is a typical risk of his business that he can influence through maintenance, proper education of personnel, and the like. Therefore, that risk does not fall within the scope of the alliance and is not paid for by the alliance fund.

Only risks that both partners can influence are priced and that amount is added to the alliance fund. This form of risk sharing is a core strength of the alliance. One example of risk sharing relates to the design risk. The alliance is responsible for creating the detailed design. A detailed design requires the design knowledge and practical experience of the building contractor. It also requires ProRail's knowledge about design and project requirements. In addition, ProRail has the mandate to agree to changes in the original design when such changes lead to an improvement. The combination of the knowledge of the partners reduces the risk that the detailed design underestimates the amount of material that needs to be used for construction. Such risk mitigation is an important source of value for the alliance, because it reduces the number of unexpected setbacks and their associated costs. A maximum is defined for some risks; for example, the first million euros are paid out of the alliance fund and ProRail pays the rest.

Of course, a contractor may have an incentive to increase his contracting price. For example, if he charges a high price for concrete in his budget but the concrete turns out to be cheaper, he keeps 100 percent of those savings, which is even better than the 50 percent that the alliance fund would deliver. Two ways exist to address this issue. First, several contractors are asked to bid on a project to create pressure among them to not charge too high a price. This is the traditional effect of market competition. The alliance contracting process still exploits this effect. Second, ProRail awards the project based on the split between the contracting price and the alliance sum. If two contractors offer the same overall price for the same quality, but one has 90 percent of the price in the contracting price and 10 percent in the alliance sum and the other offers an 80/20 split, the latter has an advantage over the former. Thus pressure exists to increase the alliance sum and make the contracting price as lean as possible.

What happens when the alliance fund has a deficit? If a risk exists that the alliance fund will run a deficit the contractors will probably increase their offering price for the project. In addition, for some risks it is impossible to quote a price. The financial consequences of such unlimited risks are so high that it is not reasonable to expect a contractor to pay for them. Letting a contractor go bankrupt because of depletion of the alliance fund that he has to compensate is not in anyone's interest. Therefore, the risk for the contractor needs to be limited in some way. At the same time the incentive for the contractor needs to be sufficiently substantial to ensure the contractor's collaboration for as long as possible. To limit the contractor's risk, while maintaining a sufficient incentive, any deficit in an alliance fund is not entirely shared 50/50. Instead, a stepwise sharing model is implemented as shown in Figure 3.1.

Imagine a fictional project contracted for €120 million with a very high alliance deficit of €130 million. The budget overrun of the alliance fund is shared between both partners in the alliance, ProRail and the contractor, as shown in Table 3.2. The total cost of the project is now €250 million. For an amount equal to 10 percent of total project costs (€25 million), ProRail and the contractor each contribute 50 percent to cover the deficit. For an amount from 10 percent to 25 percent of €250 million (€37.5 million), ProRail pays 75 percent and the contractor pays 25 percent. From 25 percent to 50 percent the overrun is shared 90/10. Above 50 percent budget overrun, ProRail pays 100 percent of the cost overrun. In the end ProRail pays €101,875 million of the budget overrun and

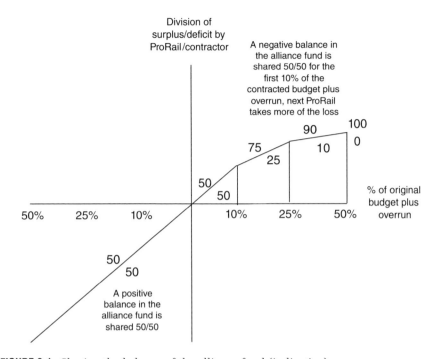

FIGURE 3.1: Sharing the balance of the alliance fund (indicative)

TABLE 3.2: Fictional example of sharing a deficit in the alliance fund

	Sharing	ProRail	Contractor
10 percent of 250 = 25	50/50	12.5	12.5
10 percent–25 percent: 15 percent of 250 = 37.5	75/25	28.125	9.375
25 percent–50 percent: 25 percent of 250 = 62.5	90/10	56.25	6.25
Above 50 percent of 250: 5	100/0	5	0
		101.875	28.125

the contractor pays €28,125 million. This system effectively limits the exposure to risk for the contractor to 11.25 percent of the total building sum (the original budget plus overruns). Such a limit is necessary because contractors are not able to deal with unlimited exposure to risk. Unlimited exposure to risk hampers their ability to attract funds in the capital market. Note that the contractor always stays responsible for any cost overruns within the scope of the construction contract: the deficit sharing only relates to the alliance fund, not to the

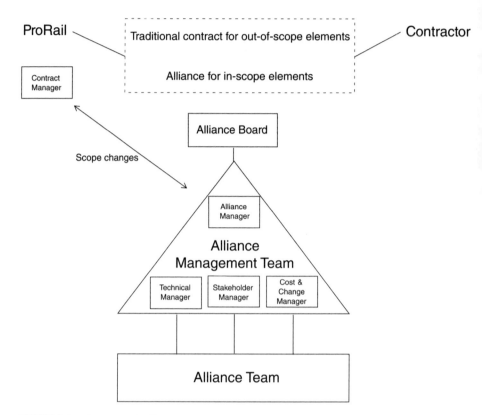

FIGURE 3.2: The ProRail alliance structure

contracting sum. ProRail, on the other hand, remains responsible for any budget overruns caused by scope changes in both contracts.

To manage the alliance, an Alliance Management Team oversees the alliance fund (see Figure 3.2 for an overview of the entire alliance structure). An alliance manager appointed by ProRail leads the team. The other team members may represent either ProRail or the contractor, but the team always consists 50/50 of ProRail and contractor representatives. The alliance manager's team has a number of experts who are knowledgeable about construction (the technical manager), cost management, and managing the stakeholder environment. Each has a team working for him. The Alliance Management Team monitors the progress of the alliance and is authorized, up to a certain limit, to decide on payments out of the alliance fund. The Alliance Management Team makes decisions unanimously.

An additional and financially even more important task of the Alliance Management Team is to identify optimizations, because cost savings flow directly into the alliance fund. The alliance identifies opportunities for optimizations, most of which are found early in its life. In practice some optimizations were substantial. Therefore, the incentive for both ProRail and the contractor to increase the alliance fund appears to be effective. Savings can be substantial because building a railway is highly capital intensive. The budget for the construction of a new railway that connects Schiphol Airport to Amsterdam and its satellite cities is hundreds of millions of euros. The alliance fund counts tens of millions of euros.

Risk management is an important part of the scope. The scope of the alliance includes other elements as well, like the detailed design mentioned previously. Rather than giving the alliance very detailed specifications, ProRail gives the alliance a set of functional requirements. This generates an opportunity to identify optimizations in the reference design. The alliance also has the role of surveyor. It oversees and checks the work of the contractor. Finally, part of the project management is delegated to the alliance.

The Alliance Management Team reports to the Alliance Board, which consists equally of representatives from both partners of the alliance, who each have one vote. The Board appoints the members of the Alliance Management Team, taking into account that the alliance manager has to be a ProRail representative. The Alliance Board has three main tasks during project execution:

- Review the alliance and give the alliance instructions when necessary.

- Decide on all aspects within the scope of the alliance. For anything outside the scope of the alliance, ProRail's standard contracting procedures apply. One individual at ProRail is authorized to deal with a contractor on such issues. This contract manager also is the person who has final say on changes in scope.

- Solve conflicts in the Alliance Management Team. If the Alliance Board cannot reach a majority on the issue at hand, the contract mentions the possibility of arbitrage.

In addition to the previously described structural aspects of the alliance, ProRail recognized that an alliance runs smoother when personal relationships are developed. For that reason various informal and relationship-building processes were implemented. One important mechanism is co-location of the contractor and the alliance staff. Both are housed close together near the building site to facilitate

TABLE 3.3: ProRail guidelines for building trust from the ProRail Alliance Handbook

- Alliance leaders play an important role in developing trust in the alliance. Trust grows through open communication, dealing with problems pragmatically and supporting each other with problem solving.
- Even though there is a formal voting procedure, seeking consensus in decision-making leads to commitment and trust. In this way choices are supported by both partners and serve the interest of the alliance.
- The alliance should operate as one organization. The alliance is at the centre of attention, the partners are not. This is a difficult step to make for the alliance team, but the more the goal of the alliance fits with the interests of the partners, the easier trust is built.
- Sounding out the viewpoints of the partners informally around important decisions creates more trust than preparing a decision without discussing it with the partners.
- Celebrate alliance successes.
- Emphasize that the alliance is a joint enterprise in which everybody has to give and take.
- As a partner, don't do anything unexpected.
- Discuss problems, doubts and difficulties sooner rather than later. Do not hide them.
- Discuss each other's behaviour around giving and taking. Only giving or only taking is not a trust-building tactic.
- Do not try to agree on all the details of the alliance: show that you are prepared to decide about some issues together at a later point in time.

communication. In addition, the Alliance Management Team conducts a team kick-off that includes discussions of each other's personality profiles to ensure that everyone is aware of one another's strengths and weaknesses and of the team's strong points and blind spots.

The ProRail Alliance Handbook lists ideas for informal activities including informal drinks, joint lunches, alliance outings, and celebrating successes. The handbook also lists a number of trust-building rules (see Table 3.3). Attention to the trust side of the alliance is deemed necessary to ease decision making and to increase its resilience in the face of change.

In a handful of alliances, ProRail has applied the alliance structure outlined here with some adaptations based on the nature of the project. So far, its experience suggests that the model is successful and combines flexibility with sound financial management. One thing to take into account is that the governance costs of this type of alliance are high. The first two projects with an alliance based on this model will be ready at the end of 2016. Only then will ProRail and the contractors be sure of the financial results. The coming years will have to show to what extent the model will bring the expected gains and whether the alliance partners continue to collaborate efficiently.

Clearly, the ProRail approach to alliances is primarily control oriented. ProRail managers fulfill key roles such as alliance manager, the scope description is very detailed, and processes to change the scope are elaborate and clearly specified, as is the financial model. Moreover, ProRail recognized that trust was a precondition for success. The code of conduct, co-location with the contractor, and guidelines for trust building emphasize this belief. The control and trust-related elements are examples of the formal and informal elements of the Alliance Design Framework. The strategic imperative of the alliance lies in the value proposition for the partners: lower cost for ProRail, a better margin for the building contractor, and improved risk management. The alliance is aligned with the partners' internal operations via the members of the Alliance Board and the ProRail contract manager. Alliance dynamics are managed via clear decision-making procedures and the financial model that stimulates mutual adjustment of the partners.

When to ally with suppliers

As the examples provided clearly communicate, the variety of relationships between customers and suppliers is infinite. Joint innovation to joint sales – and anything in between – is possible. Yet, some commonalities also exist because certain general conditions, such as the following, need to be met before customer–client collaboration makes sense:

- A sizeable relationship may play a role, but it is neither a necessary nor a sufficient condition to enter into this type of alliance. Size is primarily relevant because the costs of governance tend to be higher for alliances than for traditional contracting. Such costs must be recouped, which is usually easier with larger alliances.

- Similar to the size of the alliance, duration of the relationship is a second feature. If the costs of the initial set-up of the alliance can be earned back over a number of years, an alliance may become financially viable. Moreover, the benefits of investments in an alliance can be recouped more easily in long-term relationships. A Toyota supplier may invest in extra equipment for quality control because it can spread those costs over many years. Such investments lead to new gains in the partnership. However, a supplier to a car manufacturer that continuously changes suppliers may not be willing to make that investment for its customer.

- Knowledge plays an important role in both sides of the relationship. The simple procurement of pens and paper is not knowledge intensive. The pen manufacturer may have world-class capabilities, yet the customer often has nothing to bring to the table to create better pens. In the ProRail, Rolls-Royce, and Toyota examples, both partners have knowledge related to what the alliance is to achieve. Both partners can make a contribution that affects the success of the alliance, providing fertile ground for innovation, knowledge exchange, and creativity. In that case, creating an alliance makes sense. In other cases, classical contracting is a better option.

- Risk and uncertainty are important in an alliance because they make specifying contracts in detail more difficult and require both partners to use their knowledge to solve unexpected problems. They demand mutual adjustment by the partners along the way. The ProRail example shows the degree to which the alliance structure can transform risk into profits.

- New margins must be uncovered to enable a refocus from cost to margin. One of the key insights from the client–supplier alliances previously discussed, is that the focus on the price that a client pays to a supplier is a very narrow, if not naïve, focus. Instead of focusing on price (or revenue from the supplier's perspective; or cost from the customer's perspective), a focus on the margin that both sides realize opens up entirely new avenues for collaboration. In the ProRail example, the contractor's revenue declines but its margin increases tremendously, and ProRail's costs decrease considerably. In project alliances, this margin must be identified early in the relationship. Long-term supplier relationships should experience continuous growth and, therefore, continuous margin improvements (however, this does not mean that margins increase endlessly because competition always forces the partners to give margin away to the final customer).

Notes

1   Different approaches to purchasing are defined in the classic article: Kraljic, P. 1983. Purchasing must become supply management, *Harvard Business Review*, 61, 5, 109–117.
2   Davis, E.W. and R.E. Spekman. 2004. *The Extended Enterprise*, New York, FT/ Prentice Hall.
3   The account of the Toyota network is based on Dyer, J.H. 2000. *Collaborative Advantage*, Oxford, Oxford University Press; Dyer, J.H. and K. Nobeoka. 2000. Creating and managing a high-performance knowledge-sharing network: the Toyota case, *Strategic Management Journal*, 21, 345–367.
4   Lorenzoni, G. and C. Baden-Fuller. 1995. Creating a strategic center to manage a web of partners, *California Management Review*, 37, 3, 146–163.
5   Cusumano, M.A. 1988. Manufacturing innovation: lessons from the Japanese auto industry, *Sloan Management Review*, 30, 1, 29–38.

6   This case is based on De Man, A.P., M. Nevin and N. Roijakkers. 2011. Turning experience into alliance capability: alliance evaluation in Rolls Royce, in: T.K. Das (ed.), *Strategic Alliances in a Globalizing World*, Charlotte, NC, Information Age Publishing, 117–138.

7   Bouncken, R.B. 2011. Innovation by operating practices in project alliances – when size matters, *British Journal of Management*, 22, 586–608.

8   Common Wealth of Australia. 2011. *National Alliance Contracting Guidelines: Guide to Alliance Contracting*, July, Canberra, Department of Infrastructure and Transport.

9   Ibid, p. 42.

10 This case is based on discussions with alliance managers, interviews and the next sources: ProRail. 2011. Handboek Alliantiemanagement, Utrecht, ProRail; ProRail. 2005. *No Guts no Glory*, Utrecht, ProRail; ProRail. 2011. Bouwen aan mobiliteit in het drukste deel van Nederland, *ProRail Magazine*, 8, 3, 17–19.

4

Contractual alliances: The customization of alliance design

The most common alliance form is the contractual alliance. In a contractual alliance, companies do not take cross-shareholdings or form a new joint company. Instead, they enter into a contractual agreement. These agreements may be very complex and detailed or very short and general. The diversity is enormous, which is exactly why contractual alliances are so popular: they give the partners the opportunity to create alliances that fit their very specific needs. Contracts contain anything partners want them to contain, nothing more and nothing less. Contracts are also easier to adapt than shareholding relationships. This flexibility is an added bonus in the fast-paced world of business.

Contractual alliances have not always been the most popular form of collaboration. In the 1970s, approximately half of all alliances were equity alliances. In the high-tech sector today, 90 percent of alliances are contractual.[1] Outside of the high-tech sector and in sectors with less alliance experience, the number of contractual alliances may be a bit lower, at approximately 75 percent,[2] but contractual alliances even in those sectors are clearly the dominant mode of collaboration. In particular, since the 1980s, growth in the number of alliances has primarily been in contractual alliances. During the past decade, equity joint ventures have made a small comeback, particularly as a result of the increase in corporate venturing activities. Large organizations taking an equity stake in small startups to gain access to promising technology are the driving force behind this. However, regardless of its importance, corporate venturing is still dwarfed by the number of contractual alliances.

Next to this quantitative change from equity toward contracts, an important qualitative difference also exists. In the 1960s and 1970s, joint ventures were widely used for internationalization.[3] Companies that wanted to operate in a different country used joint ventures with local partners to market and sell their products in foreign markets. During the 1970s and 1980s, alliances slowly began to focus on production and R&D. This trend took off around 1990 and, with the increase in innovation alliances, the number of contractual alliances grew.

This growth coincided with a change in the way management perceived alliances. In the 1970s, alliances were viewed as activities on the fringe of organizations. This situation changed in the 1980s. Because of their contribution to R&D, alliances became increasingly viewed as a source of competitive advantage. The growing number of alliances and the business they generated also positioned them closer to the core of organizations. An increasing number of organizations entered into alliances that connected to their core competences.

The popularity of contractual alliances is easily explained by the fact that they fit very well with the current business environment. Contractual alliances are easy to create and change; therefore, they fit in a business environment that requires companies to adapt to ever-changing requirements. They also enable organizations to experiment with new knowledge and products at relatively low cost. In addition, of all the alliance types, contractual alliances are the easiest and cheapest to disband, which is compatible with the temporary nature of most 21st century businesses. For many businesses, whether today's partner will be relevant in two years is unpredictable. Contractual alliances make it easier to switch partners, which may, at the same time, make alliances self-defeating. If both partners expect a collaboration to be only for the short term, they will shy away from making long-term investments that might have made their alliance more productive.

Longer-term relationships have a number of advantages in addition to this advantage of larger investments. Longer-term relationships also reduce the transaction costs between companies. Collaborating over time becomes easier, and the costs of writing and enforcing agreements may decline. Long-term relationships also enable deeper knowledge exchange. Partners need time to get to know each other well enough to share knowledge freely, to understand each other, and to discover new opportunities.

One disadvantage to a long-term relationship is that changing partners is more difficult when companies are intertwined. Moreover, learning may be deep in a long-term alliance, but it may not be very broad. By partnering with more companies in the short term, a company gains exposure to different sources of knowledge.[4] However, in general, companies tend to underestimate the positive learning effects of long-term collaboration.[5] Knowledge-sharing and information-sharing open up numerous possibilities for new joint value creation that were not thought of at the start of the alliance. However, the contradictions are clear: longer-term relationships may increase learning but lead to lower flexibility; short-term collaboration may be flexible, but bring lower learning benefits.

The variety of contractual alliances is enormous, and Table 4.1 shows that alliances may serve a variety of purposes. The most important purpose is to reach market-oriented goals. Almost half of all alliances aim to bring new products and services to market. This occurs in channel alliances in IT, which are discussed later in this chapter. Research and development is another important category (18 percent). The combination of distribution and supplier alliances shows that 21 percent of alliances are in the supply chain. This variety underlines the flexibility of contractual alliances and that they are applicable in many situations.

Because of the diversity of contractual alliances, different alliance designs exist in practice. No one best way exists to organize them. Many organizations have a mirror structure or a multiple points of contact model for governing contractual alliances. In a mirror structure, each hierarchical level in the partners has its counterpart in the other partner. The alternative to the multiple points of contact model is the single point of contact or lone ranger model of alliance management, in which one alliance manager or alliance team is responsible for coordinating with the partner's alliance manager or alliance team. In the single point of contact model no other management layers are involved in managing the alliance. This model is used frequently and may be fitting for smaller alliances, but it is not a best practice for important alliances.

TABLE 4.1: Percentage of alliances aiming to achieve a certain goal in 2011[6]

Alliance goal	Percent
Co-marketing, sales, business development	46
Research and development	18
Distribution	11
Co-production	10
Supplier alliances	10
Other	5

TABLE 4.2: Three models for multiple points of contact alliances[7]

Specialization	Joint team	Peer to peer
Partners have different competences and do not intend to learn from each other; it is possible to segment the work (knowledge access)	Partners want to learn from each other (knowledge transfer)	Partners have similar or overlapping competences and do not want to learn (pure coordination)
Alliance teams work in their own company and only collaborate on interfaces between the partners; low level of integration	Alliance teams consist of representatives of all partners and have intensive contact; high level of integration	Alliance teams work in their own company and have intensive contact with the partner's teams; medium level of integration
Alliance teams specialize across companies: partner A's alliance team does X and partner B's alliance team does Y	Alliance team optimized; alliance teams contain specialists from both sides: companies A and B both send people to one alliance team doing X and to one team doing Y	Alliance teams mirror each other; two of everything: partner A's alliance team does X and partner B's alliance team does X; A's team does Y and B's team does Y

The multiple points of contact model can be organized in three ways: specialization, joint teams and peer to peer. Table 4.2 summarizes the main differences between the three models. The specialization model is relevant when companies do not want to learn from each other, but need to combine different competences to create something new. Access to the partner's competence is sufficient to achieve the alliance goal; learning is not required. For that reason it is sufficient to define the interfaces between the two organizations. Teams can focus on their own competence and can work separately. Joint teams are used when knowledge transfer is necessary to make the alliance a success. To achieve knowledge transfer the teams need to consist of representatives from both sides of the alliance and have to work together intensively. Co-location of teams may be necessary. In peer-to-peer alliances the companies do not intend to learn but have to coordinate their activities intensively. Such alliances are mainly used around joint marketing and joint sales, where companies bring a joint offer to the market.

Three cases in this chapter illustrate these main models. The Senseo alliance of Philips and Sara Lee/DE highlights a specialization model in which each partner specializes in its own competence and collaboration mainly takes place on the interfaces between the organizations. The case of Novartis and Orion illustrates how control can be replaced by trust over time in a contractual model when social capital is built. The partners apply a joint team model in which teams with representatives from both sides work on projects. Finally, the HP–Cisco alliance exemplifies one of the most common contractual alliance types: marketing and sales alliances in IT. The case initially shows the lone ranger model. The case also shows a move in the opposite direction from that of Novartis and Orion. By implementing a more elaborate governance structure, the HP–Cisco alliance considerably increased its success. The lone ranger model was replaced by a peer-to-peer model. A common thread is that all models use multiple points of contact.

In practice, combinations of the models are found. In the Senseo alliance the main structure is specialization: Philips and Sara Lee/DE have their own development and production. Collaboration takes place on the interfaces. The alliance also has elements of the joint team model: there is a joint marketing team and joint sales teams visit retailers to sell the product. Similarly, the Novartis–Orion alliance mainly revolves around joint teams, but there is specialization as well. The HP–Cisco alliance predominantly had a peer-to-peer structure, with some joint teams.

Senseo: specialization and complementary competences

The Senseo alliance is a wonderful example of how two companies with complementary competences combined their knowledge to innovate and bring a new product to market. In 2001, Senseo, a new way of making filtered coffee, was introduced into the market. Royal Philips Electronics and Sara Lee/DE (through its DE subsidiary, which in 2012 had been spun off and acquired by another company in 2013) created this new concept. Philips produced an innovative coffeemaker and Sara Lee/DE built on its long coffee blending tradition dating back to 1753 to create coffee pods, which are pre-packaged ground coffee beans in their own filter that can be inserted in the Senseo machine to make one cup of coffee. By 2012, no less than 33 million Senseo machines were sold[8] around the world. The Senseo concept revitalized two markets that appeared to be as mature as they could be: the market for coffeemakers and the market for home-brewed filtered coffee.

The two partners had been in touch for quite some time on an informal basis to exchange ideas about the coffee market in which both were active, albeit with completely different products. Philips was a leading maker of coffee machines, whereas Sara Lee/DE was a leader in coffee. The first serious conversations about a possible collaboration started in 1998. Both partners recognized that their products needed a makeover. Sara Lee/DE was experimenting with coffee blends that led to coffee with a small layer of foam, which later became the hallmark of the first Senseo coffee blends. Philips also developed some ideas about renewing the experience of making coffee in the home.

By combining their thoughts on this topic, they developed a concept aimed at creating more coffee moments during the day. Making only one cup instead of a whole pot of coffee was instrumental. To achieve this goal and to be distinctive from competitors, the key issues were to create the right flavor and the right selection of pods, and to ensure a continuous quality of the coffee. These factors were achieved by fixing the coffee and water quantities used by the machine, which was a different approach from traditional filtered coffee in which the consumer determines both quantities.

The next challenges were to design an attractive machine and to ensure a fast market introduction. A fast introduction was necessary to gain an installed base of Senseo machines in households to pre-empt any competitors and to ensure sales of the pods which bring in high margins. To quickly build an installed base, Philips introduced the Senseo machine into the market at a relatively low price. Philips' low margin on the machine was compensated by the fact that it also shared in some of the revenues that Sara Lee/DE generated from selling coffee pods.

The scope of the contract was limited to the market for "packaged coffee," and the alliance was exclusive for this market. The alliance was renewed automatically in the first years. No separate Senseo company was created because the competencies that the partners contributed were completely different. The production process for the pods was completely separate from that of the machines, indicating that no economies of scale could be created if these production processes were combined into a separate joint venture.

An alliance structure was developed, as depicted in Figure 4.1. A mirror structure was devised in which different levels of the partner organizations were connected to each other. This multiple points of contact model had three hierarchical layers:

- The International Steering Committee;

- National Steering Committees responsible on a country by country basis for Senseo sales; and

- Joint sales teams.

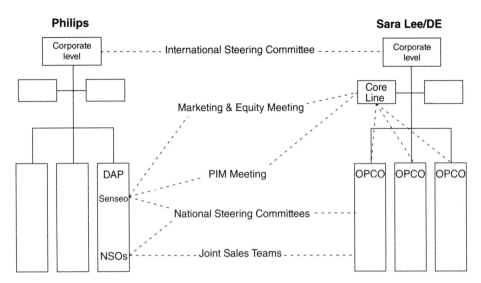

FIGURE 4.1: Governance structure of the Senseo alliance in 2006

In addition to the vertical hierarchical structure, two standing committee meetings exist for discussing marketing and brand development (Marketing and Equity meeting) and product development (the Product Innovation Meeting, commonly referred to as the PIM meeting). The specialization model is clearly visible in the fact that production and development are executed separately by each of the partners, coordinated via the PIM meeting. The joint sales teams are a departure from the specialization model.

The International Steering Committee (ISC) consists of three representatives from the corporate level at each of the partners. The ISC authorizes the business plan and the product roadmap, which describe the planned development of the Senseo machine and the accompanying pods. An annual and an occasional semi-annual review of the National Steering Committees are held to evaluate whether the targets of the national business plans are being met. The ISC meets every two months.

The National Steering Committees consist of representatives from local national Operating Committees (OPCOs) in Sara Lee/DE and representatives from the Philips National Sales Organizations (NSOs) in each country. They develop business plans with a three-year planning horizon for their own country that need to be approved by the ISC. The business plan contains the usual elements such as planned sales and advertising and promotion campaigns. The mirror structure is translated through to the operational level, with local sales teams visiting clients jointly. For example, sales people from both companies visit supermarket chains to promote Senseo.

The Marketing and Equity meeting coordinates the marketing activities and discusses brand development (brand equity, hence its name). This group is worldwide and meets regularly. The costs and desired benefits from marketing activities are set on a case-by-case basis. In mutual discussions, the costs are split among the partners per activity in an attempt to balance them overall.

In the PIM meeting, product managers discuss new coffee blends and new machine models on a continuous basis. Usually, a new version of the machine and a new blend are introduced simultaneously. The PIM meeting also develops the product roadmap for approval by the ISC. In principle, the PIM meeting works globally, but sometimes the products need to be adapted to local demands; for example, the US market requires larger coffee mugs. The interfaces between the machine and the pods are discussed, after which Philips and Sara Lee/DE go their own ways and continue regular discussions and product tests. The partners do not tread on each other's competency areas but respect each other's specialties and, in the end, Sara Lee/DE decides on the coffee blends and Philips on the machines. This process enables each partner to apply its own knowledge in an optimal way, thus avoiding discussions about the why and what of certain product features.

The layered structure of the alliance makes it possible to solve issues that can be resolved at a lower level at the next higher level. This escalation model works well because it stimulates passing problems onto another level without putting too much strain on the lower levels.

A complicating factor in the alliance lies in the internal organization structures of the companies. When Senseo became a big success, Philips opted to create a different business unit for it in its Domestic Appliances division (DAP), with its own profit and loss statement. Thus, most of the decision making is centralized under one manager. At the outset, Philips' main structure is product based, whereas Sara Lee/DE's main structure is country based. In Philips, the Senseo manager can decide on marketing activities. In Sara Lee/DE, the national OPCOs decide on marketing and sales and on whether and when to introduce a new product into their respective markets. Marketing and Equity and product development are centralized in Sara Lee/DE in a department called the Core Line organization. This organization also has the task of stimulating the OPCOs to collaborate with Senseo marketing and product introductions. The business manager who leads the Senseo line of business in Philips also has the role of alliance manager for this partnership. He is the main person to "sell" the alliance within Philips.

Another complicating factor in the alliance is that the planning and control cycles in the organizations are not synchronized. The fiscal year for Philips ends December 31, whereas for Sara Lee/DE it ends June 30. Therefore, the partners also hold a half-year review of the business plans to enable each partner to incorporate the Senseo plans into their budgets for the next book year, which creates some extra work.

Other company differences are related to the production process. Philips needs to plan further in advance to produce new varieties of the machine. Sara Lee/DE needs a shorter time to adapt its processes to new coffee blends. Philips is accustomed to thinking in terms of product roadmaps that describe how the machines can be developed over time, which was not something that Sara Lee/DE did. These differences in ways of working and culture were recognized as a possible source of difficulties. To address them, the companies implemented a number of actions. One of them was holding a session in which cultural differences were analyzed and discussed to increase the partners' mutual understanding. The experience in the alliance showed that these cultural problems could be overcome. The differences in the personal style of the individuals involved were deemed more important. For example, some people are inclined to look at the specifics of the contract, whereas the spirit of the contract is more important for others. Such differences surface in the daily management of the alliance and are managed and addressed by the individuals involved. Mutual adjustment and continuous communication are the key solutions. The mirror image structure contributes to bridging these differences.

During the first four years of the collaboration, no amendments to the contract needed to be made. The lack of amendments does not mean that no negotiations occurred between the partners. In fact, negotiations were continuous but all changes were worked into the business plans, roadmaps, and agreements related to marketing without requiring adaption of the contract. Contractual changes were required when the scope of the alliance changed to include tea in addition to coffee. In 2012, the alliance made further important changes when it took a completely new approach and introduced a Senseo that was not based on pods but on coffee beans. This major innovation for the alliance led to several changes in the collaboration. Philips sold its rights to the jointly owned Senseo trademark to Sara Lee/DE and the parties agreed on a long-term collaboration until 2020.[9]

The Senseo alliance shows a balanced use of control and trust. Control elements such as a governance structure and planning and control cycle are in place, as are agreements on sharing the value. The multiple points of contact model also introduces a hierarchical element in the alliance. Trust elements are also well developed. The focus on value creation and innovation, mutual adjustment, and the attention to bridging company differences are examples of well-developed trust elements.

The complete Alliance Design Framework was filled in. The strategic imperative for the partners was to renew their existing markets and the strategy for the alliance was to introduce a new coffee concept to create more coffee moments during the day. Formal building blocks include the financial model and the governance structure. The attention for cultural differences and the mutual adjustment over the alliance lifespan are important informal elements of the alliance. Internal alignment was achieved via the separate business unit in Philips, the introduction of the core line organization in Sara Lee/DE, and the involvement of top management. Finally, the partners dealt with dynamics through regular reviews, a clear decision-making structure, and the adaptation of the contract to changing markets.

This alliance is a good example of complementarity between partners that brought completely different competences to the table. Struggles over overlapping territories were non-existent. Because complementarity usually implies that the partners work in completely different industries, it may also create a communication problem and a learning problem. The multiple points of contact and the attention to cultural differences alleviated the communication problem. The learning problem that may have resulted from the fact that such different companies may not understand each other[10] did not exist because the partners did not need to transfer knowledge. Access to each other's capability was sufficient,[11] and the partners achieved their goals by defining the interfaces between the Philips and the Sara Lee/DE product.

Novartis–Orion: joint teams building trust

The stability of the Senseo governance structure is remarkable. The balance between control and trust that the partners created fits well with their specific situation. However, this balance may change over time, posing a risk if the partners do not react to changes in a similar manner. Change may also increase trust when the partners are able to overcome the difficulties they face. The latter was true for the alliance between Novartis and Orion. Other than the Senseo alliance, in which control and trust remained balanced in the face of change, Novartis and Orion relied increasingly on a trust-based relationship partly because some of the dynamics of this relationship were predictable. The partners were able to anticipate and predict some of the changes in their alliance structure. Of course, knowing that a structure will need to change is no guarantee that the change will be successful. The Novartis–Orion alliance demonstrates the conditions that need to be met to successfully handle the dynamics.

Parkinson's disease is a serious condition that affects millions of people worldwide. Although the disease has no cure, progress has been made in the search for drugs that reduce the severity of the disease. Pharmaceutical companies make great effort to bring these drugs to the market. Novartis and Orion do so through a partnership in which Novartis markets and sells Orion's anti-Parkinson drugs Comtan and Stalevo (both based on a drug called entacapone) in various regions of the world. Their alliance has not been without challenges. First, drug regulations around the world are extremely strict and evolve over time, sometimes unpredictably. Therefore, ensuring compliance in all parts of the value chain for bringing pharmaceutical products to the market requires close collaboration. Second, their alliance consists of a smaller (mid-sized pharma) company and a big pharma organization. Orion is the smaller partner and, at one point, as much as 30 percent of its revenue depended on its anti-Parkinson's drugs. Novartis is one of the world's largest pharmaceutical companies and has various other sources of revenue (although Orion's anti-Parkinson's drugs have sold very well). Therefore, the companies' sizes and interests diverge. Finally, the alliance tracks the products' lifecycle. It started in the development phase, moved into full-blown sales mode, and is now matured given that the two products are losing patent protection in some markets. Although managing such dynamics places a significant strain on any alliance relationship, Novartis and Orion made it work.

By successfully managing these challenges, Novartis and Orion have kept their alliance alive and kicking since 1996. A well-thought out alliance design was one of the key success factors, but it only worked because the companies were willing to mutually adjust and compromise. The contract between the parties was good to rely on to initiate the collaboration, but some of its parameters needed to be adjusted throughout the lifecycle of the alliance. Initially, many control elements were present in the alliance; however, over time the partners placed greater emphasis on trust and understanding each other's operations. As the alliance matured, formal interaction between the partners through a committee structure was replaced by greater emphasis on informal communication and decision making. This dynamic was not only the result of moving through different phases of the alliance lifecycle, but also resulted from conscious attention to building trust and personal relationships. That the people working in the alliance formed a stable group over time greatly supported this result.

Starting up

In 1996, Orion was working on a drug that later became Comtan. Because Orion had a limited market and sales reach, it sought a partner to market its product in countries in which it lacked adequate coverage. The Swiss-based pharmaceutical company Sandoz sought a neurology product to supplement its product portfolio in this area and licensed the product from Orion. In 1997, Sandoz merged with CibaGeigy to become Novartis. A year later, Comtan was approved for sale in the European Union. Under the terms of the first contract, Novartis also obtained the right of first negotiation to a follow-on combination product, Stalevo, and the two companies concluded a deal around that drug in 2000. Whereas Orion developed the product for US and European approvals, Novartis was engaged as the global marketing partner that could help Orion obtain the approvals needed from authorities throughout the rest of the world, such as Japan. National governments have different demands that must be met before approving drugs. Typically, each individual country demands different tests on patients for drugs, called clinical trials. One of the purposes of the alliance is to ensure consistency between the various clinical trials and to foster learning across different trials. In 2003, the US and European Union approvals for Stalevo were secured and the drug was launched. Orion exclusively marketed the product in its own region, primarily Northern Europe, Central Europe, and parts of Eastern Europe, whereas Novartis exclusively marketed the drug in other regions. The deal consisted of three elements:

• License: Orion licenses the product and brand to Novartis;

• Supply: Orion manufactures the drugs and supplies them to Novartis; and

• Distribution: Novartis distributes the drugs outside Orion's regions.

Elements of the deal

The supply relationship is a noteworthy element in the scope of the agreement. Orion produces Comtan and Stalevo and delivers them to Novartis. In some other alliances of a similar nature, the big pharma company takes over production, which normally leads to a loss of control for the smaller company because the bigger company can develop new IP (intellectual property) around the product by modifying it. In this case, Orion kept control over production and, hence, over most of the IP developed in the relationship. For that reason, the need to work in close collaboration with Novartis and to gain its appropriate support on manufacturing and regulatory issues in its territory was even more acute than in a pure licensing relationship: because it kept the production, Orion retained a strong position but also required access to Novartis' regulatory knowledge.

Novartis compensates Orion by paying for the cost of goods sold and a royalty component on sales in its regions. The companies agreed on a cost sharing arrangement for new development initiatives and new marketing initiatives. This cost sharing is based on the relative benefit that either party receives from the initiative: if a partner has x percent of the market potential/revenues, it will pay x percent of the costs. However, if an initiative will not benefit one of the partners, then the other party may still go ahead with it but will also have to carry all of the investments on its own. An example of the latter occurred when Orion developed a smaller Stalevo tablet. Orion saw this product as an important addition to its offering. However, because Novartis estimated that the additional benefit was limited in its own markets, it chose not to participate in this new tablet's development. As a side note, this fact did not undermine the alliance because the focus on consensus building was a fundamental operating principle: no consensus, no deal. Other costs of managing the alliance, such as travel and personnel costs, are borne by the company that incurs them. Overall, the alliance is not a 50/50 business, but it is in balance and focuses on providing a fair return to both partners. In 2011, Orion's net combined sales of entacapone products (Comtan, Comtess, which is Orion's own brand of Comtan, and Stalevo) was €266.7 million.

In the beginning of the alliance, the partners adhered to a strict annual clock for the planning and control cycle that involved various formal committees. After 16 years, this process has become more informal and occurs more on an as needed basis. Regular business reviews are still held. One important mechanism to ensure control at the strategic level is the partnership survey that the companies use to stay on track. The survey measures various aspects of the alliance and is a useful feedback tool to identify whether the partners are still satisfied with the alliance and to highlight its weaker and stronger areas. The tool provides guidance for where management attention is required.

Once the product was launched, the parties realized that to be successful, tighter collaboration was necessary. One of the reasons was because in the different countries in the European Union, the drug was approved under the same centralized approval process and would benefit from consistent marketing messages, even globally. In addition, the drug was in a different stage of development across the world. In one country, the drug may already have been approved, whereas in another region, clinical studies were still taking place to meet the requirements of the local authorities that needed to approve the drug. Knowledge sharing also made the alliance more effective. Feedback from the market needed to be shared to ensure that, among other reasons, any safety-related matters were dealt with consistently. Intensive collaboration helps optimize the management of this process through better exchange of knowledge and information across geographies.

Alliance structure

To ensure efficient collaboration, an alliance management structure was implemented. Early in the 2000s, Novartis started to implement best practices for alliance management. Its increased use of alliances demanded that the company invest in building strong capability in this area. Orion, recognizing the same need, followed and matched the alliance management structure that Novartis developed, which greatly facilitated the companies' ability to collaborate. Figure 4.2 shows the formal alliance structure at that time, which was not speci-

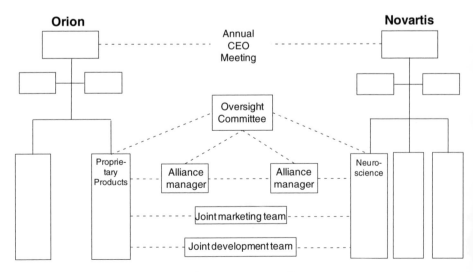

FIGURE 4.2: Governance structure of Novartis–Orion alliance

fied in the contract but was implemented in practice after the inclusion of Stalevo into the alliance. The structure has been stable since, although it has become much less formal.

The governance structure consists of the following elements: the oversight committee, alliance managers, joint development teams, and joint marketing teams. The annual CEO meetings depicted in Figure 4.2 are not formally part of the governance structure but are courtesy meetings held even if no direct reason exists to meet. The relationship building that occurs through these meetings is important because, should a major event occur in the alliance, the CEOs are able to find rapport much quicker and more adeptly when they know each other. Therefore, the meetings are relevant to the overall governance picture.

The oversight committee, consisting of the Orion head of proprietary products business and the head of Novartis' neuroscience franchise, met frequently in the early years of the alliance. Sixteen years down the road, it is no longer a standing committee but has become an ad hoc committee. Today, almost any issue can be dealt with at a lower level. Should the need arise to involve senior management, the alliance managers know on whose door to knock.

The alliance has two operational teams. Team members work in their own organization but meet regularly by telephone or face to face and communicate on an ongoing basis. The joint development team consists of neurologists on both sides of the alliance and, by and large, each discipline has a counterpart in the other organization. The marketing team ensures consistency in labels and branding. Novartis adds its own look and feel to the product. Regulatory changes occur frequently, and the marketing team needs to ensure consistency in its marketing messages that must be, at all times, in compliance with the regulations. Over time, the alliance emphasized either marketing or development, among others, depending on where the product was in the product lifecycle and on the time and resources dedicated to the alliance. For example, a greater emphasis was placed on marketing as products got to later stages of the development phase.

The role of the alliance managers has the following three dimensions:

* Overseeing the health of the alliance. Alliance managers know about everything that happens in the alliance and must pick up the signals if actions need to be taken to advance the alliance. They must also monitor the informal elements of the alliance, such as communication, trust, and the soft skills required from participants in the alliance. Managers check whether

the various functions are able to collaborate productively with their counterparts in the other organization.

- Advise internal stakeholders on the general aspects of the alliance. In each of the two organizations, different people are involved in the alliance and they usually only see a small part of it. The broader perspective of the alliance managers may help them decide on the right course of action when faced with an alliance-related decision.

- Manage the contract. All changes in the contract go through the alliance managers. They are also responsible for renegotiations. Note that alliance managers carry out renegotiations, not a different team. Organizing renegotiations in this manner ensures that a renewed deal fits with the existing alliance, that all relevant knowledge of the alliance is incorporated in the renegotiation, and that the end result will be executed because the deal is renegotiated by the same individuals who are responsible for its implementation.

An escalation mechanism is in place between the different levels. The rule is that issues are escalated first to alliance managers and next to senior management. The contract mentions an international arbitration procedure but that has never been used. Escalation of issues is important to avoid an issue becoming a burden at the project level. Projects need to continue and disturbance of the relationship at a project level would damage the core of the alliance. This line of communication is strictly adhered to and is seen as a success factor of the alliance. Alliance managers are always involved in the process of defining the agenda of higher level management meetings to ensure consistency in communication and thus build trust.

In addition to this structure, each partner still has its own control and decision-making procedures. Therefore, investments or major changes in the alliance must go through internal company processes. The parties' patience may have been tested at times, but frustration was avoided through good communication on where in the decision-making process the companies were. Over time, companies came to understand each other's processes and, hence, impatience all but disappeared.

Relationship building: consensus, respect, and social gatherings

The formal aspects of the alliance may form its backbone, but its long-term success depends largely on the attention paid to informal aspects. A logic that alliance management applied is to give both sides equal voice in the alliance and to strive for consensus. Despite the size difference of the partners, this approach seems to work well. Both partners appreciate each other's expertise, whether in development (Orion) or in marketing (Novartis). The complementarity in expertise implied that few, if any, conflicts regarding overlapping areas of the alliance exist. One danger to an alliance between a small and a large partner is that the smaller partner may not feel taken seriously. The clear roles and responsibilities and the consensus principle ensure that such a situation is avoided.

In addition, Novartis gives Orion quite some attention, as is underscored by the annual CEO meeting. In the same vein, on all levels in the alliance, people know each other quite well and social events are organized. The good relationships are supported by relatively low employee turnover. Most of the staff working on this alliance have been involved in it for a long time. The benefits of such tenure in terms of open communication and working toward a common goal are clear. As one of the alliance managers observed, "If someone walked into a team meeting once, they would not be able to tell who was an Orion staff member and who was from Novartis. They were all focused on maximizing the joint business, not on realizing their own company's agenda." The individual experts in the alliance are free to liaise with one another as they see fit, as long as all pertinent parts of the organizations are informed of what is being discussed. This relationship aspect also shows up in small ways. Orion's Christmas card and small Christmas gift is highly appreciated by Novartis as a gesture of friendship. The little things count in developing a close working relationship.

Coping with change

As previously mentioned, many issues may affect an alliance. Certainly, over a 16-year period, many issues have arisen. Perhaps equally important, as having the right design and structure in place at the outset of the alliance is having a process and the willingness to adapt to changing circumstances. The contract is not formally reviewed regularly, but it has been through a multitude of renewals and changes. Some examples of amendments are as follows:

- Originally, the two companies agreed to co-market the products in France, Germany, and the United Kingdom. Later, this arrangement turned out to be suboptimal and the partners agreed that Orion would market the drug in the UK and Germany, whereas Novartis would focus on France. The companies pay cross-royalties on sales generated in these areas.

- Financials also needed to be reviewed periodically even though the general balance originally negotiated largely remains.

- Few industries are as hit by patent expiration as the drug industry: once a drug patent expires, imitators (called "generics" in the industry lingo) quickly come to the market and offer the drug at lower prices. In some countries, generics have arrived and, consequently, the sales forces have been scaled back, which has required changes in contractual terms.

The dynamics of the business are also reflected in the alliance's governance. The initial governance structure as depicted in Figure 4.2 was important to kick-start the alliance. Over time, the alliance has become much less formal and extensive formal planning and control was abandoned. The oversight committee is no longer a standing committee. Two reasons exist for this change. The first reason is that, at an operational level, the working relationships in the joint development team and the joint marketing team are such that, in combination with the alliance managers, the vast majority of issues are resolved there. The excellent relationships and open communication ensure fast problem solving. In this regard, the maturity of the alliance does not necessitate extensive governance procedures. The second reason for this change is that the alliance has advanced far enough in the product lifecycle to merit a shift in focus from development to marketing work. The lifespan of the alliance is related to the patents on the drugs. As patents expire in more countries, the alliance will become smaller. For example, in the USA, Stalevo is now off patent and generics have become available in the market. Consequently, activities in the USA are now at a much lower level than before.

Any of the events previously mentioned could have been a source of conflict and sometimes they were. However, the resilience of the alliance in dealing with the dynamics is an important part of its long-running success. The following conditions enabled the partners to make a successful transition to a new alliance structure:

- The knowledge that the alliance, similar to any other pharma alliance, follows a known lifecycle, and everybody knew that change would come and in what direction it would occur;

- The build-up of trust on all levels, strengthened by the limited churn of people working in the alliance;

- Mutual adjustment. The many contract changes could not have been achieved without such a spirit. Obviously, ups and downs occur, but more important than that is that the companies were prepared to give and take to overcome the problems. Naturally, this situation was helped along by the fact that the business was successful. Without a successful business, the alliance could have been short-lived. However, in this case, the spirit of collaboration that developed over the years clearly strengthened the alliance, is important to its longevity, and made it more efficient;

- Maintaining some basic hygiene, even when that did not seem necessary; for example, the CEO meetings continued regardless of whether important points needed to be discussed; and

- Alliance managers had responsibility for designing and implementing changes, which represents an application of the subsidiarity principle that states that actions should be taken at the lowest level whenever possible. In addition, by keeping the design and implementation of changes in one hand, the transition can be smooth.

In terms of trust and control, the alliance defined clear control elements that remain important. However, they are complemented and partly substituted by trust elements that help the alliance move forward. The overall structure builds on joint teams, but some specialization takes place as well. Other than in the Senseo alliance, the competences overlap. Both partners have capabilities in development and marketing, but they are not equally strong in those areas. In terms of the Alliance Design Framework, the value proposition for both partners lies in generating sales. The alliance is necessary to ensure the necessary knowledge exchange takes place. The formal elements include among others the contract, financial model, and the governance model. Social gatherings, an emphasis on consensus, and the emergence of trusting personal relationships constitute the informal elements of the alliance. The alliance managers have the lead in maintaining internal alignment, which they achieve by working with internal stakeholders. They also play a leading role in managing the dynamics as they are responsible for contractual changes. The spirit of mutual adjustment further facilitates the management of change.

IT partnering and the HP–Cisco alliance: from lone ranger to peer to peer[12]

For market-oriented alliances in IT to have light alliance designs is very common. These alliances often operate through the lone ranger model in which the alliance manager is largely on his own, sometimes with a team behind him, but without multiple points of contact on different hierarchical levels. Most IT companies go to market using a "sell-to," "sell-through," or "sell-with" model. Sell-to means selling software or hardware to a company. For example, Cisco sells its products to IBM for IBMs own internal use. Sell-through means selling products through the sales channel of another company. For example, IBM resells Cisco products to IBM clients. These channels may also go both ways, as Cisco may incorporate IBM products in its own products and sell those to Cisco customers. These are pure channel alliances; Cisco uses IBM as a reseller and vice versa. In the sell-with model, companies team up to go to market and visit clients jointly to sell their solutions together. In many of these partnerships, all three elements are mixed: a partner may be a client, a reseller, or an equal in going to the market. This complexity makes it difficult to get an accurate picture of business done with a partner and, as each of these three roles requires a different approach, conflicts of interest may exist. For example, should a certain client be approached through the sell-through or the sell-with approach?

Figure 4.3 shows the use of various go-to-market approaches in the IT industry. Companies may use various routes to market simultaneously. A 74 percent majority of the companies use a form of sell-with relationship in which joint

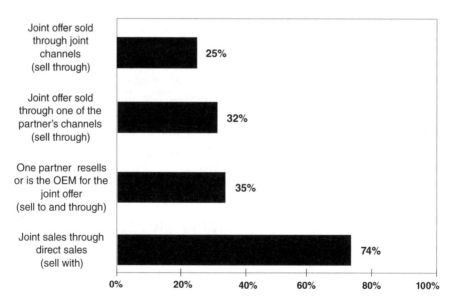

FIGURE 4.3: Percentages of companies using a particular go-to-market approach in IT in 2013[13]

sales teams go to market. A quarter of the companies have a joint offer that is also sold through joint channels and 32 percent sell a joint offer through one of the partner's channels. Reseller relationships or relationships in which one partner is the original equipment manufacturer (OEM) that integrates a partner's technology in a new offer are used by 35 percent of companies.

The performance of these alliances is predominantly measured using revenue-related metrics.[14] The vast majority of these alliances at least measure incremental revenue (93 percent) generated through the alliance. New customer wins (87 percent) and the integration of solutions (52 percent) are the next most popular metrics. However, revenue is notoriously difficult to relate to alliances. Many sales may be generated with a partner without the influence of the alliance and, the other way around, salespeople may not always recognize that a sale benefited from an alliance being in place.

In the lone ranger model of alliance management, an alliance manager has the task to stimulate the sales force to sell the partner's products. Because the sales force usually does not get an extra incentive for alliance-related sales, the alliance manager's task is difficult. The strength of the solutions offered by the partner is his main weapon for convincing sales managers to collaborate with the alliance partner. Involvement of higher levels of management to support the alliance is often absent or limited, meaning that the alliance manager and his team are on their own. The alliance manager needs to have highly developed influencing skills, as he has no formal power to force people to work with the alliance. Channel alliances can be successful though. However, when a stronger alliance design is put in place, the results may improve significantly, which clearly occurred in the case of HP and Cisco.

One of the interesting features of the IT industry is that many IT companies focus on a narrow product range. By necessity, this type of focus requires them to integrate their products with those of other companies to offer their clients a complete solution. At the same time, the product range of the larger IT companies broadened sufficiently over time to make them each other's competitor. Therefore, dealing with co-opetition,[15] or cooperation with a competitor, is part of the daily activities of alliance managers in the industry. The collaboration of Cisco and HP, which was successful from 1997 to 2010, was a great example of IT alliances: highly successful until the market and the partners' strategies changed and competition overrode collaboration.

In the Cisco–HP alliance, as in many other IT alliances, alliance managers played the central role. Most IT alliances have limited formal governance structures in place beyond the responsibilities given to the alliance managers. In the first half of its existence, the Cisco–HP alliance was no exception to that rule. However, in the second half of its lifecycle, a stronger governance model was introduced, giving more backing to the alliance managers who – still – continued to carry the main responsibility for the alliance. The new model had a tremendous effect on the business.

In 1997, HP and Cisco entered into an alliance comprising four different areas: IP telephony, service and network management, mobility/wireless, and data center networking solutions. In these areas the companies had complementary technologies and services. Their aim was to integrate them and in that way serve their clients better.

The original alliance mission was co-marketing of enterprise networking solutions to HP and Cisco's joint customers. Figure 4.4 depicts the structure of the alliance in late 2002. Each side nominated an alliance manager responsible for the relationship whose tasks included: (1) developing a strategy for the alliance and getting it accepted in the organization, (2) motivating business unit and sales people to execute the strategy, and (3) developing plans for new products and technologies. To achieve these tasks, they set up virtual strategic alliance teams in their respective organizations that consisted of all of the functions that needed to interact with the alliance partner. An important part of the function of the alliance manager was to ensure alignment of his own organization with the alliance. Executive commitment to bring business units in line with the collaboration was indispensable for this alignment because not all units collaborated automatically. At the most operational level, collaboration existed between individual HP and Cisco employees, which involved joint sales visits or attending joint training sessions. No dedicated sales force for the alliance existed; instead, the sales people in each organization sold the alliance's offerings together with their counterparts from the other organization.

One element that brought the two companies together was a jointly created business plan that was translated into joint metrics. The metrics measured sales and market share in the target markets. During business planning, cultural differences came to the fore. HP was used to conducting significant planning before introducing a product into the market. Cisco's approach was the other way around: they tried out products in the belief that detailed, upfront business planning was difficult in its fast-paced business.

The internal operations of the two organizations had an important effect on alliance performance. Cisco had a global centralized alliance function that was

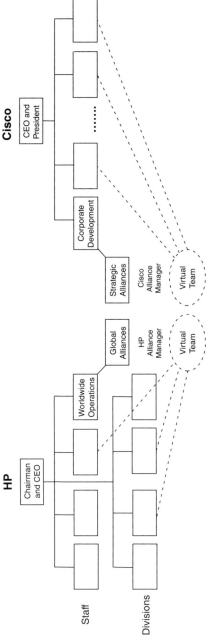

FIGURE 4.4: Structure of the HP–Cisco alliance (summary, late 2002)

part of the Corporate Development unit. One unit in the alliance group represented the alliance to the Cisco sales force. In HP, the alliance manager initially reported into the HP marketing organization and later reported into the sales group. In the first half of 2002 the alliance management role was split from the sales role and investment in alliance management increased. The Cisco alliance was managed from the Global Alliances unit. From then on, HP alliance management was able to focus more on alliance strategy and executive alignment instead of on daily sales activities.

Obtaining organizational alignment in each of the organizations remained a daunting task. The success of the alliance depended critically on the collaboration of everybody involved. The targets for sales managers played a crucial role in this success. Initially, the HP sales people who sold Cisco equipment received a commission and counted the sales toward their targets. Therefore, they benefited from selling Cisco products regardless of whether HP benefited. This system was changed in 2001 into one in which the sales people received a bonus when they achieved a certain goal. The result was a decline in sales of Cisco gear via HP. At Cisco, the sales people were compensated partly on HP's resell of Cisco products. Therefore, the change in HP affected them adversely.

The meeting structure supporting the governance structure was straightforward. The two virtual teams had a biweekly call to discuss issues related to the sales channel. Some felt that more structure was necessary. For example, no strong escalation mechanism existed if conflicts arose. Conflicts arose because the alliance was not exclusive. Exclusivity was not an option for the alliance because clients sometimes demanded a particular product or service from a particular supplier. Therefore, Cisco sold services from HP competitors and HP sold products from Cisco competitors. The latter also included some of HP's own products that competed with Cisco's. Consequently, disagreements occurred and, in the absence of an escalation procedure, put pressure on the alliance.

Characteristic of this alliance design was the central role of the alliance managers. Their ability to influence their organizations made the difference between alliance success and failure. With little escalation possibilities, their formal position in the organizations provided them with limited support. A more formal structure would have made them less of a "lone ranger" in their organizations.

That conclusion was supported in 2002. During that year, the companies reviewed the alliance and believed it could be expanded to include optical technologies (integrating Cisco's products with HP's management services in this area) and storage (ensuring interoperability between Cisco's network products and HP's storage solutions). To ensure further success, Cisco's alliance team recognized the need to get closer to the Cisco sales organization, whereas HP needed to develop a more strategic view of the alliance, in addition to its sales orientation. Moreover, a new governance structure for the alliance was proposed that resolved the difficulties previously mentioned. Although this structure changed over the years, the core of the structure remained relatively stable in the following manner:

- A governing committee was established comprised of five to six people at the executive level that met four times a year. At this executive level, regular reviews of the business plan took place. The people on the committee formed a cross-functional team, with its members having backgrounds in products, sales, or alliance management. The alliance managers and their teams prepared the meetings, briefings, and reports for this committee, which normally came to a mutual agreement on the issues before them.

- If no consensus emerged, an escalation procedure was agreed on. Issues were escalated depending on the topic, to those persons for whom the issue was most relevant, to ensure that issues were escalated to managers who had the knowledge to deal with them and the mandate to implement the decisions made.

- On a regional basis, groups were set up in which peers from both sides met at every level. They reviewed performance and discussed the business pipeline for their respective regions.

- CEO meetings were now integrated in the alliance structure and were held at least once a year. Over time, these meetings became more irregular and started taking place on an as needed basis.

- Rules of engagement were agreed on regarding how to engage with customers and how to deal with co-opetition.

The alliance managers remained the focal point of the alliance, and with more formal backing behind them, they had an easier time doing their job. Still, their most powerful tool was not the formal structure but their (and their teams') capacity to convince sales people and the business of the value of the joint services offered with the alliance partner. Sales teams' incentives were not changed and these teams were rewarded for their sales regardless of whether the sale was made through the alliance. In this way, the alliance competed for the attention of the sales teams with all other routes to market that they had at their disposal. Only the strength of the joint offer persuaded sales to invest their time in an alliance service. One thing that made a difference in the new governance structure was that the investment in alliance management was increased. With more people to promote joint services in the internal organization, the effectiveness of alliance management improved. The changes in the alliance management structure of the HP–Cisco alliance bore fruit. Five years after the introduction of the new structure, business had grown by 200 percent.

However, the issue of co-opetition did not go away but increased over time. At first, the overlap in the product portfolios of the companies grew organically. Cisco increasingly moved into offering complete systems in traditional HP territory by investing in the server and storage market. It did so by partnering with, among others, storage company EMC and software company VMware. HP took a big step in 2009 when it acquired 3Com, a direct competitor to Cisco. These changes meant that, in the balance between cooperation and competition, the competition side dominated. Consequently, Cisco and HP did not renew the alliance contract in 2010. The companies continue to work together where clients expect it.

In contrast to the Novartis–Orion case, the HP–Cisco case shows that an increase of formal governance can also make an alliance more successful. The introduction of more control elements improved the alliance. The overall structure is a peer-to-peer model with teams operating in each of the partners separately, but with regular meetings. In addition, some joint sales teams existed. The final structure of the alliance followed the Alliance Design Framework closely. The strategy was to co-market to joint customers. The structure became more formal with more rules put in place. Informal communication in the teams increased. One of the most interesting features in relation to the Alliance Design Framework revolves around internal alignment. The changes in the incentive model for the sales forces clearly affected the alliance. After the last restructuring the effectiveness improved. The investments in alliance management enabled the alliance managers to better "sell" their alliance internally and thus increase alignment. Finally the management of dynamics improved once a new decision-making structure and an escalation procedure was put in place.

Although the alliance manager remains at the core of the alliance, support from a governance structure sends a clear signal to the rest of this organization that the alliance and, therefore, the alliance manager require their attention. This situation helps reduce the problem of aligning the internal organization with the alliance, which was a challenge during the early phase of the alliance. The case also shows that even when trust is not at its highest level because the companies are competitors, having a successful alliance that runs longer than a decade is still possible.

When to use contractual alliances

The three cases show the diversity of contractual alliances. They can be applied in very different settings and may develop in different directions over time. The Senseo structure was relatively stable and balanced control and trust. The Novartis–Orion alliance developed from control to more trust and the HP–Cisco alliance strengthened control. All three alliances were successful.

A number of conditions make the contractual model particularly relevant. First, the model is useful in situations in which partners have complementary, rather than similar, competences and do not have the goal of learning from each other. Instead, they seek access to their partner's competences to combine them with their own.[16] Sara Lee/DE does not have the ambition to produce coffee-making machines and Philips does not aim to develop competences as a coffee blender. They need each other's competences to create a coffee concept. More far reaching integration in a joint venture or a merger is not necessary to achieve this goal. No economies of scale are to be realized by using these organizational forms. They would even be counterproductive because experience shows that the track record of combining diverse competences under one roof is not very positive. Alliances enable companies to combine their knowledge in innovative products across company or sector boundaries. In the IT industry, this ability is particularly valuable because few IT companies deliver complete solutions to their customers on their own. They tend to specialize in certain technologies that next need to be combined with those of one or more partners. As the HP–Cisco example shows, in a fast-moving industry, companies with once complementary competences may develop over time in such a way that their competences start to overlap. This phenomenon often results in the end of an alliance because the partners are no longer complementary.

Second, contractual alliances have limited scope. The collaboration relates to a limited area rather than an entire business or a value chain. In both the Novartis–Orion and the Philips–Sara Lee/DE alliances, only one or two products are part of the scope of the alliance. Over time, different product varieties may develop, but the core of both alliances is clearly limited to two drugs and one coffee maker, respectively. Such focus represents the strength of contractual alliances, which enable organizations to focus on very specific areas.

The definition of the interfaces between the companies in these areas becomes a key success factor.

Third, contractual alliances are useful when speed is required. Building a competency from scratch requires a long-term view and a substantial investment. Combining existing competencies leads to faster results in the market. As speed becomes an essential competitive requirement, the more frequently contractual alliances will be used. Speed can also be maintained in an alliance because combining the thinking power of two organizations may enhance the alliance's ability to develop innovations, to make improvements, and to react quicker to changing demands.

The combination of complementarity and limited scope does not mean that contractual alliances are by necessity small. Each of the examples discussed in this chapter generated substantial business for the partners and at interesting margins. The alliance design was instrumental in achieving this result. The cases show how varied alliance designs may be. Trust and control elements can be observed in all of them, but the precise structures differ substantially – representing another strength of contractual alliances: structures can be custom made for the specific task at hand. No one best way of organizing alliances exists.

Notes

1   Duysters, G.M. and A.P. de Man. 2003. Transitory alliances: an instrument for surviving turbulent industries?, *R&D Management*, 33, 1, 49–58.
2   Pekàr, P. and M. Margulis. 2003. Equity alliances take centre stage, *Business Strategy Review*, 14, 2, 50–62.
3   This paragraph and the next are based on Dussauge, P. and B. Garette. 1999. *Cooperative Strategy*, New York, John Wiley & Sons.
4   Duysters, G.M. and A.P. de Man. 2003. Transitory alliances: an instrument for surviving turbulent industries?, *R&D Management*, 33, 1, 49–58.
5   Dyer, J.H. 2000. *Collaborative Advantage*, Oxford, Oxford University Press.
6   Duysters, G., A.P. de Man, D. Luvison and A. Krijnen. 2012. *The State of Alliance Management: Past, Present, Future*, Canton, MA, The Association of Strategic Alliance Professionals.
7   This table is inspired by Everett, C. and J. Hollings. 2010. *Changing the tires while driving*, presentation at the ASAP Summit, Anaheim CA, 2 February.
8   *De Financiële Telegraaf.* 2012. Philips verkoopt merkrecht Senseo, 26 January.
9   *De Financiële Telegraaf.* 2012. Ibid.
10 Lane, P.J. and M. Lubatkin. 1998. Relative absorptive capacity and interorganizational learning, *Strategic Management Journal*, 19, 461–477.
11 Grant, R.M. and C. Baden-Fuller. 2004. A knowledge accessing theory of strategic alliances, *Journal of Management Studies*, 41, 1, 61–83.

12 The description of the HP–Cisco alliance till 2002 draws on interviews with HP and Cisco representatives and Casciaro, T. and C. Darwall. 2003. *The HP-Cisco Alliance,* Harvard Business School case study 9-403-120, Boston, Harvard Business School Publishing. HP and Cisco representatives also provided the information about the period after 2002. For more on alliance management in Cisco see the book by Cisco's VP of Strategic Alliances: Steinhilber, S. 2008. *Strategic Alliances: Three ways to make them work,* Boston, Harvard Business Press.

13 Thanks to Norma Watenpaugh for providing these figures. Further details can be found in: Watenpaugh, N. 2013. *Market Makers: 2013 best practices in go-to-market alliances,* Gillroy, CA., Phoenix Consulting Group.

14 Watenpaugh. 2013. Ibid.

15 Brandenburger, A.M. and B.J. Nalebuff. 1997. *Co-opetition,* New York, Doubleday.

16 Grant, R.M. and C. Baden-Fuller. 2004. A knowledge accessing theory of strategic alliances, *Journal of Management Studies,* 41, 1, 61–83.

CHAPTER 5

The virtual joint venture model: Air France/KLM, Delta Airlines, and Alitalia

Contractual, bilateral alliances may be shaped in many ways. One of the more far-reaching models is the virtual joint venture. In a virtual joint venture, companies combine parts of their businesses and operate them as if a separate company – but do not create an independent legal entity. Essentially, companies collaborate and pool their profits, which are shared based on an agreed-on allocation mechanism. The virtual joint venture is the accountable entity and its goal is to optimize profits. The remainder of the partners' businesses remains independent. Compared with a "real" joint venture, which has a separate legal entity, this type of alliance is called a "virtual" joint venture.

Despite its complexity, the popularity of this model is slowly growing. An increasing number of alliances seek to achieve a 50/50 profit-sharing arrangement (or 1/3, 1/3, 1/3 when three companies are involved, for example). To do so requires a number of conditions to be fulfilled. First, a virtual joint venture model is easiest to achieve when the partners' contributions are of a similar size. Most alliances do not fulfill this condition, making the creation of a virtual joint venture model more difficult. In this case, a solution may be to divide profits according to the contributions made by each partner. Even though this solution may make financial sense, the feeling of what is fair and just is quite different compared with a 50/50 arrangement. Such an argument may not be rational, but if partners do not believe that a profit-sharing arrangement is fair, the alliance's development may be hampered. Emotion often overrules reason.

A second condition is that organizations need to have a high level of accounting maturity. The virtual joint venture demands that partners be financially transparent toward each other because they have to provide insight into all of the costs and revenues within the scope of the alliance. Open book accounting, in which the alliance partners allow each other to study their financials in detail, is a requirement. Such an approach only works[1] when all parties have a clear benefit, have the will to implement the approach, have accurate – and preferably – similar accounting standards, and have sufficient staff to do the work. The latter point is not insignificant: managing a virtual joint venture is more time consuming than when simpler financial models are used.

Third, companies need to have a strategic and cultural maturity. In a virtual joint venture, companies become interdependent in the core of their business, which the staff may see as a loss of autonomy and independence. In the KLM–Northwest case, discussed in detail below, the two companies slowly grew toward the model over time, thus diminishing these feelings. Other companies that do not have this history behind them may have to implement the model on a step-by-step basis.

Given these restrictions, pure virtual joint venture models are not common, but partners in many alliances strive to come close to the pure model. Cost and benefit sharing in supply chain relationships is one example. A limit on the use of this model is competition law. In particular, when direct competitors pool their profits, cartels may emerge that are counter to antitrust regulations. Antitrust issues are relevant for all alliances, but companies that aim for a virtual joint venture should pay particular attention to the antitrust implications of their collaboration.

Once established, the benefits of a virtual joint venture are manifold. By running an alliance as a separate business, companies find that they can increase their flexibility. Because of the profit sharing that takes place, partners focus on increasing the overall profit of the alliance instead of bickering about who gets what share of the pie. Therefore, adapting the alliance to changing circumstances is much easier. The ultimate example of this concept is the alliance between KLM and Northwest Airlines that survived major changes in the airline industry and was the forerunner of the current alliance between Air France/

KLM, Alitalia, and Delta Airlines. The history of this alliance provides a fascinating view into the dynamics and management of one of the world's most complex and successful alliances.

Ready for take-off: the KLM–NWA alliance

One of the longest running and most successful alliances in the airline industry, that between Air France/KLM, Delta, and Alitalia, is rooted in an alliance between KLM and Northwest Airlines (NWA) dating from 1989. The alliance survived major turbulence and two major mergers in the airline industry. What characteristics enabled this alliance to survive in this challenging business environment?

1989–2004: the invention of the virtual joint venture

The virtual joint venture model was pioneered by the American carrier Northwest Airlines (NWA; acquired by and merged into Delta Airlines), and KLM, a Dutch airline and currently part of the Air France–KLM group. The model has been surprisingly stable and has withstood major downturns in the airline industry, such as the decline in demand after the terrorist attacks on the New York World Trade Center on September 11, 2001. Even after two mergers involving the original partners, the basic notion behind the virtual joint venture model remains intact and is taken as the point of departure for what currently is an alliance between three parties: Air France/KLM, Delta (including Northwest), and Alitalia (partly owned by Air France/KLM). Although other alliances exist in the airline business that have more partners, none of them has achieved the intensity of cooperation of these companies. Table 5.1 presents some key figures of the alliance.

Airlines have entered into increasing numbers of alliances since the early 1990s. Although other alliances exist, the best known are the three large ones: oneworld, SkyTeam, and Star Alliance. Alliances are important in the airline business for the following reasons:

- Deregulation. Airlines used to be a heavily regulated business with strong government involvement. Over the years, government intervention has decreased. An increasing number of countries are entering into Open Skies

TABLE 5.1: Key 2010 figures of the Air France/KLM, Delta, Alitalia alliance[2]

The virtual joint venture:

- Represents 26 percent of the airline industry's total trans-Atlantic capacity
- Operates 250 flights daily across the Atlantic
- Offers service to 500 destinations in Europe and North America
- Covers routes between Canada, United States, Mexico, and Europe, and those connecting Amsterdam and India, and North America and Tahiti
- Is structured around seven hubs – Amsterdam, Atlanta, Detroit, Minneapolis, New York-JFK, Rome-Fiumicino, and Paris-CDG
- Generates approximately US$10 billion in annual revenues
- Is a long-term business arrangement effective until at least March 31, 2022
- Employs more than 100,000 employees at Air France–KLM; more than 70,000 employees at Delta; and more than 14,000 employees at Alitalia

Agreements that allow each carrier based in those countries to fly to any city in the other countries.

- Competition. New entrants such as low-cost airlines and the new airlines from the Gulf States are entering the industry and pressuring existing carriers.

- Overcapacity. In combination with the previous two trends, overcapacity has led to lower rates for many carriers.

- Expansion drive. The desire to grow and offer more destinations to passengers causes companies to search for partners.

- Restrictions to the growth of airlines. For example, the rights to fly to a particular destination are usually limited. To offer passengers flights to that destination, an alliance partner can help.

- Restrictions on foreign ownership. Many countries forbid foreign carriers to own national airlines. Alliances are used as an alternative when cross-national mergers and acquisition are not allowed.

Combined, these forces have eroded the financial results of airlines, causing airlines to seek to increase revenues and lower costs through alliances. Most alliances start by focusing on increasing revenues. By combining route networks and ensuring easier transfers, airlines can offer more destinations and better service to their passengers, typically through code sharing, which allows passengers from more than one airline to be transported in one plane.

For example, consider the initial alliance between KLM and NWA. The alliance enables KLM to offer more American destinations to its passengers, whereas NWA sells tickets to all of KLM's destinations in Europe. The operational model of the alliance revolves around a hub and spoke system. NWA flies its passengers to Amsterdam from across the USA to a few airports – the hubs – such as Detroit. There, passengers transfer to either a KLM or an NWA plane and are flown across the Atlantic to Amsterdam. This is code sharing: the plane flies under both a KLM and an NWA code and carries passengers from both airlines. From Amsterdam, passengers are transported to other European cities through the KLM network. In short, the companies deliver passengers to each other's networks. By aligning arrival and departure times of connecting flights, passengers receive better service. More destinations, better service, and a higher occupancy rate on cross-Atlantic planes results in increasing revenues and lower costs.

The first step toward the alliance was taken in 1989, but a number of years passed before it adopted the virtual joint venture model. Figure 5.1 shows the timeline of the KLM–NWA alliance.

In 1989, KLM was one of a group of investors in NWA that purchased the company and took it off the stock market. As part of this leveraged buy-out, KLM obtained 19 percent of the shares and a seat on the board. KLM sought a possible partner in the USA for some time and jumped at the opportunity to participate in the leveraged buy-out. At the outset, the notion behind the collaboration was to strengthen the KLM freight business. Collaboration on the

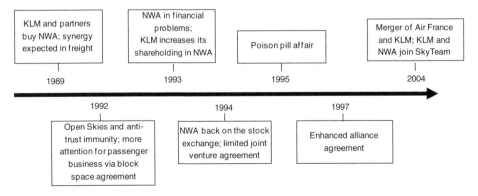

FIGURE 5.1: Timeline of the KLM–NWA alliance (1989–2004)

passenger side was not high on the agenda. Subsequently, the passenger business turned out to be the real goldmine for the alliance.

In 1992, the American and Dutch governments concluded an Open Skies Treaty that enabled KLM to fly to more destinations in the USA. Similarly, NWA increased its frequency of flying to Amsterdam, enabling the companies to generate higher profits from their collaboration. Soon after the Treaty was signed, the American government gave the two parties antitrust immunity, meaning that nothing could stop the two partners from intensifying their collaboration. The commercial and operational collaboration initially focused on the Detroit–Amsterdam route. The benefits of collaborating in the area of freight were disappointing because the route networks for freight were not complementary. Therefore, the alliance shifted its attention toward passenger transport. KLM did not yet operate its own flights to Detroit. The first step in passenger transport was a "block space agreement" in which KLM bought blocks of seats in NWA's planes, which were sold to KLM clients. When this strategy turned out to be successful, KLM also started flights to Detroit.

In 1993, NWA was on the brink of bankruptcy after the market collapsed in the wake of the Gulf War. At the last moment, management was able to turn the situation around when its staff agreed to a pay cut. KLM supported NWA and invested new capital in the carrier. Consequently, KLM received stock options that could increase its shareholding in NWA to 25 percent, the maximum allowed under American law, which stipulates that non-American carriers are not allowed to control American carriers.

In 1994, the story continued with the return of NWA to the stock exchange. KLM and NWA upgraded their alliance with an agreement known as the limited joint venture agreement, which remained in place for three years. The governance structure of this limited joint venture developed rapidly (see Figure 5.2) until an Enhanced Alliance Agreement replaced it in 1997. As part of the limited joint venture agreement, an Alliance Committee was created that consisted of senior executives of both carriers. Two working groups were added soon after: the Network Group and the Passenger Group. The Network Group decided on which types of airplanes flew on which routes and how often with the goal of optimizing their use. Substantial cost savings could be realized when, for example, a smaller aircraft replaces a large Boeing 747 on routes that do not fill the Boeing to capacity. Because of the alliance, the Network Group made use of the fleets of both partners, significantly increasing the opportunities to optimize the use of aircraft. The Passenger Group was dedicated to marketing and sales. Later, these two working groups merged into a Joint Venture Operating Committee, which became the main governing body of the alliance.

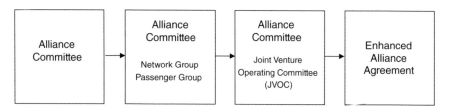

FIGURE 5.2: Changes in the structure of the KLM–NWA alliance

The scope of the alliance was clearly defined as comprising all transport between the USA and Europe. Some collaboration existed in other areas, notably in Asia where the partners collaborated on marketing and the sharing of business class lounges. In addition, the frequent flier programs were connected and passengers could earn credits on all KLM and NWA flights. However, execution of joint flights (code sharing) only took place on the North Atlantic route between the USA and Amsterdam. The alliance was successful and profitable.

In 1995, the situation changed dramatically. The relationship between the parties was seriously threatened when the NWA board introduced a defensive tactic against a hostile takeover in the form of a poison pill, which would considerably raise the cost of a takeover. The NWA board voted 11 to three in favor of a poison pill that would limit KLM's ability to exercise the stock options it received in return for helping Northwest Airlines avoid bankruptcy in 1993. The stock options could bring KLM a 25 percent stake, but the NWA board effectively established the limit at 19 percent. KLM considered the poison pill as an attack on its position as shareholder and initiated a court case to contest it. The animosity between the two boards increased and, consequently, the Alliance Committee stopped meeting. Intriguingly, this situation did not end the meetings of the Joint Venture Operating Committee. At the operational level, the alliance's activities not only continued but also intensified and became increasingly successful.

Naturally, this situation could not continue for long. Despite the substantial commercial success in the short run, in the long run the situation at the board level was untenable. In 1996, an opportunity arose to revive the board-level contacts when KLM's CEO retired. Studying the partnership again, KLM's conclusion was that it did not want to jeopardize the alliance, but did not yet drop the lawsuit against NWA. KLM's true interest was not so much to own a stake in NWA but to ensure a long-term collaboration. KLM believed that only a long-term collaboration would deliver benefits and ensure KLM's success in the

longer run. Without the 25 percent stake, NWA would be able to change partners. However, with KLM's shareholding, tensions between the two companies
would continue. A solution required KLM's long-term interest to be secured
while selling its shares in NWA. The solution came in 1997 when the two
companies entered into a long-term contractual alliance agreement: the
Enhanced Alliance Agreement.

The Enhanced Alliance Agreement

The Enhanced Alliance Agreement took the alliance to another level. The main
points of this agreement, which introduced the virtual joint venture model, are
as follows:

- Extension of the scope of the alliance. The entire North Atlantic route was
  included in the alliance, also comprising Mexico and Canada. In addition,
  India would be involved in the alliance.

- Commitment to grow to a 50/50 capacity share in a few years.

- Joint marketing and product development. KLM closed its own sales offices
  in the USA, Canada, and Mexico. NWA did the same in Europe, the Middle
  East, and Africa. In these areas, the carriers would sell each other's tickets,
  a major sign of commitment: in those days, sales were done through sales
  offices instead of the Internet. Closing down those offices was an almost
  irreversible step because ending the alliance implied that both partners
  would lose a considerable part of their sales network and staff.

- Sale, in phases, of KLM's shares in NWA to the NWA Corporation.

- Both companies made one non-executive board position available for each
  other. Thus, even without equity stakes, the partners would be represented
  on the highest level in each other's organizations.

- An annual settlement of the alliance profits on a 50/50 basis. This provision
  entails that the alliance would operate as if a separate company in which
  each party has a 50 percent stake, without actually creating a separate legal
  entity for that company.

- An exit fee was agreed to be paid by the partner wanting to leave the
  alliance.

- A 10-year contract that is automatically renewed each year after the first 10
  years pass. After the first decade, each partner can terminate the alliance

but with a three-year term of notice. Effectively, the alliance would run for at least 13 years, which met KLM's need for a long-term relationship. It also increased the possibility to invest in the alliance, as investments could be earned back over a longer period. To achieve the alliance goal substantial investments were necessary in IT, sales and marketing organizations and aligning the route network.

Given the earlier animosity between the two companies, seeing them enter into such a far-reaching deal was surprising. The Enhanced Alliance Agreement substantially extended the alliance. However, in reality, the agreement in many ways formalized what had already happened in practice. Despite the disturbed relations at the board level, on an operational level the collaboration was extended, refined, and improved and went far beyond the contract of the limited joint venture agreement.

The Enhanced Alliance Agreement also required a new governance and management structure. The Joint Venture Operating Committee was not able to manage the increase in activities that emanated from the new agreement. A new governance structure was implemented, as shown in Figure 5.3. The core idea was to create a multiple points of contact structure, through which people on different hierarchical levels have their counterparts in the partner organization.

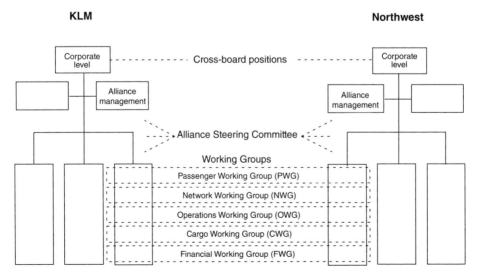

FIGURE 5.3: Governance of the KLM–Northwest alliance 1997–2004

The cross-board positions are the first element of the governance structure. They emphasize the relevance and importance of the alliance relationship for both companies and give them considerable insight into each other's organizations. Of course, the board positions are broader than only the alliance; they relate to the entirety of the organizations. In practice, the board positions meant that the KLM CEO became a non-executive director of Northwest, whereas the Northwest CEO became a member of KLM's Supervisory Board. This change reflected the difference in corporate governance structures in the USA and the Netherlands, with the USA having one-tier boards and the Netherlands having two-tier boards.

Despite the size of the alliance, it does not have many hierarchical layers. The most important governance body is the Alliance Steering Committee, in which executive vice presidents and senior vice presidents are represented who are responsible in their own departments for some of the functional areas relevant to the alliance. These departments include sales, network (which planes fly on which routes), and finance. The Alliance Steering Committee decides on alliance policy and is authorized to make many important decisions. If the Alliance Steering Committee is not able to make a decision, the CEOs may get involved. Important decisions are also sent to the CEOs for approval. The Alliance Steering Committee meets four times a year, and these meetings were not to be cancelled under any circumstances. The executive vice presidents responsible for commercial affairs at KLM and NWA are the co-chairmen of the committee. Each committee meeting also has an informal agenda, such as visiting a sports match or similar, which helps create good personal relationships that support collaboration throughout the alliance. The informal gatherings are also relevant because management positions in both companies change regularly and they help ensure that new members of the committee are rapidly integrated into the committee.

Decision making is based on consensus, which is supported by the 50/50 profit split. The companies agreed to balance the number of flights that each would operate to avoid imbalances. Although NWA was bigger than KLM, in the alliance the contributions of the two partners were balanced to ensure joint decision making and to help gain further organizational support for the alliance. Because of the 50/50 profit split, both parties are automatically interested in optimizing the alliance instead of engaging in opportunistic behavior. The interest of the alliance is the same as the interests of KLM and NWA.

The next level of collaboration is comprised of five working groups. The network and passenger groups are the most important and their functions are similar to the network and passenger groups in the limited joint venture agreement. An operations working group focuses on all ground handling processes, including luggage and catering. The cargo working group focuses on the freight business. Finally, the financial working group is responsible for financial settlements. Communication between the two airlines in these working groups is very frequent and usually takes place daily. New developments in the market, as well as in the alliance, require continuous coordination and the development and implementation of new policies. The working groups are not standalone entities: members of the working groups are part of the line management of KLM and NWA. They have to implement the policies they develop themselves in the working groups. Therefore, the lines of communication between the organizations and the alliance could not be shorter. Because the interest of the alliance is the same as that of the partners, the incentives for the companies' staff are automatically aligned with both the alliance and company performance.

The final element of the governance structure is the role of the alliance management departments. They review progress, mediate in conflicts, and prepare the meetings of the Alliance Steering Committee. Around 2004, when both companies became members of the SkyTeam alliance, the alliance management departments also became responsible for aligning the alliance with SkyTeam. In short, the alliance management departments have a supporting role: the actual management is done in the business. The NWA and KLM departments meet every three to four weeks.

The governance structure laid down in the Enhanced Alliance Agreement proved enormously resilient. The alliance has grown substantially and it experiences many and sometimes extreme changes in the business environment. However, the structure as shown in Figure 5.3 has remained unchanged until a round of mergers occurred in 2004.

Much of this resilience lies in the financial structure, as the financial incentives are perfectly in line with the interests of the two partners. All costs and revenues that the partners make on the North Atlantic route are made transparent. In the Enhanced Alliance Agreement, the partners negotiated over the costs and revenues to be attributed to the alliance. For example, costs include fuel, depreciation, and staff and, for each of these, the contract provides a clear definition. The contract includes an incentive for the companies to sell each other's tickets beyond the North Atlantic route: when KLM sells an NWA ticket for a flight from Detroit to Las Vegas, KLM also earns on that sale. This strategy provides a great incentive for sales people to sell "color blind"; for them, whether they sell their partner's ticket or a ticket of their own company does not matter as both count toward their sales target. This system can only work with open book accounting: both companies have the right to check the books of the other company. In the end, all revenues are added, all costs are subtracted, and what is left is shared 50/50. Such sharing usually requires a settlement in which the company that generated more profits from the alliance than the 50 percent pays the difference to the other one.

The benefits of this financial model became clear after the 9/11 attacks on the New York World Trade Center, which led to an immediate and unparalleled drop in air travel. KLM and NWA were able to adapt their business to the changed conditions within a couple of weeks, whereas other alliances took months. In the other alliances, the partners did not have a 50/50 model; hence, negotiations about which airline would reduce capacity on which route took a long time. For KLM and NWA, whether KLM or NWA cut back on flights did not matter because the profits were pooled and any cutback affected both airlines in the same way.

A relevant note to add in this regard is that both specialists and generalists are involved in the alliance. A mix of specialists and generalists is especially important in a dynamic environment because it ensures that specific knowledge is available to deal with many different types of changes, while at the same time the generalists can help to place specific issues in the broader context of the alliance. The latter is important to prevent specific issues from dominating the alliance, whereas the former ensures that all relevant aspects of an alliance are covered. People also play multiple roles in the KLM–NWA alliance, enabling them to connect different issues and spot potential clashes before they occur. For example, a member of the alliance management department may also be on one of the working groups. Such linking-pin functions ensure a better flow of information and force people to consider issues from different perspectives, ensuring that the alliance is not ruled by narrow interests. In a dynamic environment, weighing the pros and cons of handling issues and coming to an effective decision quickly are important. Multiple roles ensure that such processes occur.

However, success is not only the result of the governance model and the financial incentives. The motivation of the personnel and the improved relationship between the two companies opened up further opportunities for learning and innovation. Knowledge transfer has had a positive effect on both organizations. For example, e-business lessons learned were exchanged, increasing the effectiveness of e-business implementation. Over time, the companies have also come to understand their differences. For example, in the United States good service means something different than in the Netherlands. Although these differences may not be bridged entirely, they are now understood and do not lead to conflict or irritation inside the companies.

One remaining question is why the virtual joint venture structure was developed for this alliance. Why was not a formal joint venture set up with its own legal entity? Three answers to this question exist:

- Isolating part of the business into a separate legal entity is not possible. For example, a formal joint venture would have needed its own aircraft to fly the North Atlantic route. However, optimal use of aircraft requires them to fly on the route that is most logical and profitable. They may fly from Washington to Amsterdam and next to Tokyo. If part of the capacity was separated in a legal joint venture, such optimization would not be possible.

- Detailed research into the joint venture option showed the partners that, in fact, this option was more complex than the virtual joint venture. For a variety of legal reasons, the relationship of a joint venture with the mother companies would be difficult to organize.

- At the start of the Enhanced Alliance Agreement, the companies doubted that internal organizational support and commitment for creating a legal joint venture would exist. Such support would have created a separation between the two parents and the joint venture, enabling the joint venture to be seen as a separate entity. Creating incentives for KLM and NWA staff to collaborate with the joint venture would have been next to impossible. The elegance of the virtual joint venture is that it is integrated into the normal day-to-day business and makes aligning the incentives for the staff with those of the alliance easy.

By the end of 2003 and in early 2004, KLM merged with Air France, and both KLM and NWA joined the broader SkyTeam alliance, of which Air France was already a member. At the time of KLM's merger with Air France in 2004, the alliance had revenues of almost $3 billion and has always been profitable.

Control, trust, and the stability of the virtual joint venture

Before moving to the next part of the story, which deals with the effect of this merger, Table 5.2 summarizes the reasons why the virtual joint venture was

TABLE 5.2: Sources of stability in the KLM–NWA virtual joint venture[3]

- Seamless alignment of incentives between the alliance, the partners, and the staff through the 50/50 profit-sharing arrangement
- A clear vertical division of labor in the governance structure, with each level having clearly defined responsibilities
- A mix of specialists and generalists
- People in the alliance fulfill multiple functions
- Extensive use of informal communication channels

such a stable structure. In the early days of the alliance between KLM and Northwest, the governance structure was frequently changed. The sources of turbulence were not only external (regulations, changes in technology, and demand) but also internal (financial problems, board-level politics). In contrast, during the 1997–2004 period, the dynamics in the alliance and the business environment were absorbed, not via structural changes but within the existing governance structure. The virtual joint venture was able to cope with a high level of turbulence.

Structural aspects of the alliance are one part of the explanation. The 50/50 profit sharing and the alignment of incentives that is connected to the alliance clearly form the basis of its stability. Cross-board positions and the governance structure with its various groups and committees are other control elements. However, control is not sufficient for the alliance to be successful. Involving the right mix of people and an extensive use of informal communication are also necessary, ultimately leading to a balance between control and trust in the alliance. Trust, which was at a low point during the poison pill affair, could be rebuilt because people changed – opening up an opportunity to start with a clean slate – and because the new joint venture structure ensured perfect goal alignment. The chance that one of the partners would resort to actions that would damage the other partner was minimized because the 50/50 profit-sharing arrangement ensured that both partners shared any damage that ensued. The virtual joint venture makes the partner's behavior predictable. In this way, the alliance's new control elements supported the rebuilding of trust. The resulting mix of control and trust is necessary to manage an alliance of this level of complexity.

2004–2012: continuing to fly high – the effect of mergers

Although major mergers often spell the end of an alliance, this did not occur after the 2004 merger between Air France and KLM. Instead, the merger opened

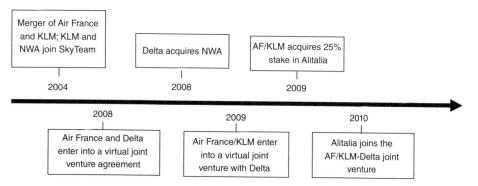

FIGURE 5.4: From KLM–NWA to AF/KLM–Delta–Alitalia 2004–2010

up new possibilities for the alliance. Air France had an alliance in place with Delta Airlines in the USA since 1999. In theory, this alliance created opportunities to coordinate across the three airlines, Air France/KLM, Delta, and Northwest. However, the American antitrust authorities did not grant antitrust immunity for intensifying the collaboration between the three companies: in December 2005, NWA did not receive permission to join the Air France–Delta alliance. Hence, the situation was that Air France and KLM merged, but each of these companies still collaborated with their own alliance partner; in other words, a separate Air France–Delta alliance and a separate KLM–NWA alliance existed. In 2007, the Association of Strategic Alliance Professionals presented the latter alliance with an Award for Alliance Excellence in recognition of its innovative alliance model.

In 2008, the situation changed rapidly (see Figure 5.4). Air France and Delta extended their previous alliance to a virtual joint venture agreement modeled on the KLM–NWA virtual joint venture. Later that same year, Delta acquired NWA. By that time, antitrust authorities loosened the rules for collaboration. Further enabled by the takeover of NWA, Air France/KLM and Delta were now allowed and able to intensify their collaboration. This situation led to a new virtual joint venture agreement between Air France/KLM and Delta. Finally, in 2010, Alitalia joined these two parties following the acquisition of a 25 percent stake by Air France/KLM in the Italian carrier in 2009.

Therefore, the current situation is a virtual joint venture between three airlines. The joint venture is modeled on the original KLM–NWA alliance but with some differences (see Figure 5.5). First, the combination Air France/KLM and Alitalia

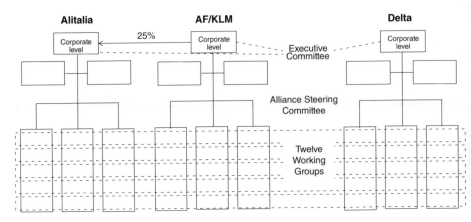

FIGURE 5.5: The Air France/KLM, Delta, Alitalia virtual joint venture as of 2010

are partners in the alliance. Even though Air France and KLM merged, they each still retain quite some autonomy. With the addition of Alitalia, the European part of the alliance consists of three organizations. In the USA, Northwest was completely absorbed by Delta and, hence, only one American airline was party to the deal. For this reason, the Europeans hold their own meetings, in which they agree on profit allocation and capacity among them before moving into talks with Delta.

A second change from the original structure is that CEO roles were transformed. After Delta acquired NWA, the cross-board positions ceased to exist. These positions turned out to be not as useful as originally thought because the boards dealt with much non-alliance business. In the new system, the Air France/KLM and Delta boards meet annually. In the new structure, the CEOs are members of an Executive Committee that is actively involved in governing the alliance (in the KLM–NWA alliance, the CEOs only acted as an escalation mechanism). The CEO committee meets frequently and is comprised of four CEOs: two from the Air France–KLM Group (one Air France CEO, one KLM CEO), the Alitalia CEO, and the Delta CEO. Decision making is still based on consensus. The Executive Committee defines the strategy for the virtual joint venture with regard to:

- Changes in the alliance agreement. Given the complexity of a four-party deal, predicting whether all of the agreements entered into during contract signing were adequate is difficult. The Executive Committee was created to handle the necessary changes in, for example, governance, financial settlement, and capacity planning.

- Collaboration with other partners, which may relate to collaboration in the SkyTeam alliance and other relevant partners.

- Implementation of changes in the governance structure, such as nominating the right persons for the Alliance Steering Committee.

A third change to the structure is the growth in the number of working groups. Currently, 12 working groups are responsible for implementing and managing the agreement in the sectors of network, revenue management, sales, product, frequent flyer, advertising/brand, cargo, operations, IT, communications, e-commerce, and finance.

A regular meeting structure is in place that also enables people to meet informally. They are structured in "joint venture weeks," which are weeks in which all groups meet, albeit one group may meet on Monday and another on Tuesday. The benefit of combining these meetings in one week is to ease communication among the various meetings. The need to meet informally has diminished with the increased experience in operating the alliance. Still, the organizations meet face to face instead of using videoconferencing.

The Alliance Steering Committee is still in place and consists of approximately a dozen individuals. On the European side, the individuals represent a mix from different functions (marketing, controller, operations) and nationalities (Dutch, French, Italian) to ensure that each of the airlines is represented. Some ASC members also have a role in a working group, whereas others do not. Working groups with no ASC representative report separately to the Alliance Steering Committee.

The contract is now a 12-year contract. After that a three-year term of notice exists. If no notice is given, the alliance is automatically renewed. The contract provides more opportunities for partners to go their own way. For example, when one partner wants to continue flying on a loss-making route, doing so is possible but that airline has to pay for it. Moreover, some changes in the cost structure have been incorporated in the new contract. For example, a ceiling has been defined for some costs to ensure that not all of those costs are an expense for the alliance. Finally, in the KLM–NWA alliance, the two airlines closed their sales offices in each other's territory. Such closures have not yet been realized in the new constellation and Air France and Delta still maintain their own sales offices in Europe and the USA, respectively.

Governance as a source of success

The most striking elements of this case are the longevity of the alliance, the depth of integration achieved in the virtual joint venture, and the major changes that have occurred without disrupting the alliance. Obviously, pressure from the business environment and the initial operational success play an important role in keeping these companies together. However, the reaction to this pressure has been particularly inventive. The main strategic imperative lies in the possibility to generate revenue by profit pooling.

In the Enhanced Alliance Agreement, control elements seem to dominate. The seamless incentive structure and clear cost and revenue-sharing guidelines are instrumental in creating and maintaining alignment. However, this structure also created trust between the partners because it made their behavior predictable. Other control elements, such as the committee and working group structure, ensure smooth decision making and communication, particularly because many people fulfill multiple roles: members of the Alliance Steering Committee participate in working groups, line managers are in working groups, and representatives of the alliance departments participate in different decision-making bodies. Such elements constitute the formal elements of the Alliance Design Framework and ensure internal alignment.

As in the first phase of the alliance's development, the formal structure is only part of the story in the post-merger phase. The partners also invest in the informal elements of the Alliance Design Framework. Attention to building personal relationships is strong and consensus decision making ensures that each partner has sufficient breathing space. With the last transformation to the Air France/KLM, Delta, and Alitalia alliance, the partners also realized that a good contract was an important but not sufficient condition for success. That a contract would cover all possible futures was unlikely, because of the complexity of the alliance and the dynamic business environment. Realizing the open-ended nature of the contract, a stronger involvement of the CEO level was ensured. The CEOs could fill the gaps in the contract and have the authority to adapt the alliance to changing conditions, thus ensuring adequate management of alliance dynamics. Heavy emphasis on control is counter-intuitively mixed with a high level of trust, providing for the flexibility that makes this alliance the benchmark in its industry.

This alliance also meets the three requirements of a solid alliance design. First, it ensures value creation through a smart financial model. Second, it ensures protection of the partner's interest through the control procedures and the decision-making structure implemented. Third, it enables the alliance to cope with change through direct CEO involvement.

When to opt for the virtual joint venture?

As the case makes clear, the virtual joint venture is by no means an easy solution to the challenges of collaboration. The case shows a number of circumstances that need to be met for the virtual joint venture to be a serious option, beyond those already mentioned. These circumstances are:

- Substantial benefits need to be present, whether in generating revenue or in cost savings. In this case, the revenue increase generated by connecting the networks was immediately visible.

- Long-term collaboration is necessary to ensure that the investments made to achieve the economies of scale and scope can be recouped. Investments in the route network and IT systems were substantial.

- A complete business is involved. The alliance comprises all activities, whether sales, marketing, route network, or flight operations.

- A clear scope can be defined. The North Atlantic route was chosen as the scope.

- The contribution of the partners is balanced. Without a balance in the size of the contributions on both sides of the Atlantic, the 50/50 profit share would not be possible.

- The cost of the transfer of resources to a separate legal entity is prohibitive. It does not make sense to transfer aircraft to a separate company because doing so would reduce the possibilities for optimizing their use.

- Companies are willing and able to achieve a high level of integration and openness. The strategic and cultural requirements to make this work are high.

Notes

1   Kajüter, P. and H.I. Kulmala. 2005. Open-book accounting in networks: potential achievements and reasons for failures, *Management Accounting Research*, 16, 179–204.
2   http://nieuws.klm.com/alitalia-joins-air-france-klm-group-delta-air-lines-in-industry-a-s-leading-trans-atlantic-joint-venture-en/; http://news.delta.com
3   De Man, A.P., N. Roijakkers and H. de Graauw. 2010. Managing dynamics through robust alliance governance structures: the case of KLM and Northwest Airlines, *European Management Journal*, 28, 171–181.

CHAPTER **6**

Equity alliances and joint ventures

Equity alliances, which are alliances in which some form of shareholding exists, are used with some regularity. The vast majority of alliances are non-equity alliances, but the number of equity alliances is not to be ignored. Three forms of equity alliances exist: joint ventures, minority stakes, and cross-shareholdings. Figure 6.1 shows that for 60 percent of companies, equity alliances comprise less than 20 percent of the alliances in their portfolio. Only 2 percent of the companies have an alliance portfolio comprised almost entirely of equity alliances. In the latter cases, public–private partnerships and fiscal reasons seem to be the reason behind the choice for joint ventures. Overall, fewer than 20 percent of alliances involve some form of equity. However, differences in sector and in alliance type exist. For example, for R&D alliances, the number of joint ventures has decreased over time to less than 10 percent, but differences between industries are substantial.[1] That equity stakes constitute a minority of all alliances does not imply that they are less important. In fact, the use of equity signals a long-term commitment. Although a minority, their importance is quite high.

Joint ventures come into existence when two or more companies jointly set up a separate legal entity. This new organization may be one in which they both participate as shareholders, but not all joint ventures are equity based. Other legal forms that do not necessarily require shareholdings, such as cooperatives, are also used to structure joint ventures. Minority stakes occur when one organization

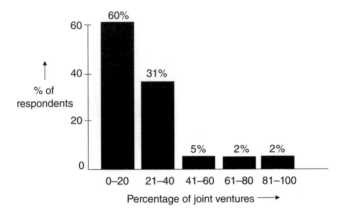

FIGURE 6.1: Percentage of equity alliances in company alliance portfolios in 2011[2]

takes a minority share in the equity of another organization. In the KLM–NWA alliance, KLM owned 19 percent of the shares of NWA. Cross-equity stakes occur when organizations are each other's shareholders. Reliable recent figures on the number of cross-equity stakes are not available, but they appear to be quite rare. Cross-equity stakes seem to occur most often in so-called quasi-integration alliances in which the partners want to approach the effect of a merger. The best-known example is the Renault–Nissan deal. Renault owns 43.4 percent of the shares in Nissan, whereas Nissan owns 15 percent of the Renault shares. Each owns 50 percent of the shares in a joint venture that, among others, manages the purchasing for the two companies.[3] The integration between the two companies has gone so far – even sharing the same CEO – that for all intents and purposes the entity is no longer an alliance but a merger.

Minority stakes and cross-equity alliances are usually part of a much broader deal between organizations. The equity stake is embedded into a broader con-tractual agreement. Their governance tends to be similar to contractual alli-ances, with the addition of a corporate governance element: minority stakes and cross-shareholdings tend to come with board seats. Joint ventures have a different dynamic. The creation of a separate legal entity with its own management introduces an additional player over and above the partners in the joint venture.

Reasons for equity alliances

Different reasons exist for why companies enter into equity alliances. The first and most logical reason is the financing needs of one of the companies involved.

New joint ventures require their own capital; therefore, partners have to invest. Other examples include the financing of ventures.[4] Corporate venturing increases innovativeness by investing in startup companies. Because startups are strapped for capital, a larger company can invest in them, thereby guaranteeing access to the startup's innovative ideas and creating an equity alliance.

Financing needs may also be why companies invest in their suppliers. ASML is the world's leading producer of lithography machines, which are indispensable in the production of computer chips. The development of each new generation of machines requires increasing R&D expenses, to the extent that the investments became too risky for ASML to make. Therefore, the company approached Intel, Samsung, and TSMC, its most important clients. The three companies took a stake in ASML, ensuring innovation in lithography machines for themselves and giving ASML a market for its products. With Intel (15 percent), TSMC (5 percent), and Samsung (3 percent) taking almost a quarter of ASML's shares, the company generated an investment of €3.9 billion. The three investors also committed to invest an additional €1.4 billion in R&D.

A second use of equity is to deal with information asymmetry when working toward a merger, acquisition, or transfer of part of a business from one firm to another.[5] Information asymmetry exists when the seller of a company has more information about its business than the buyer. This situation is true for every sale, but the problem is particularly acute when buying and selling businesses. The "buyer beware" mantra is particularly applicable here because many of a company's characteristics are difficult to assess from the outside. A due diligence process hardly provides one with a good view into the capabilities, quality of staff, and level of knowledge of a takeover partner. These elements only become clear sometime after a deal is closed. By slowly building up their equity holdings over time, companies may get to know each other better and, hence, gain a better perspective on the quality of each other's organization.

Philips Electronics has regularly used joint ventures to exit a business. It sold its white goods division to Whirlpool through a joint venture, enabling Whirlpool to gain a clear view of the business. If the price of the remaining shares in a joint venture is made dependent on the joint venture's performance, acquirers reduce the risk of paying too much. Similarly, Philips set up joint ventures with LG Electronics to exit their display business. In 2012, Philips and TPV implemented a joint venture around Philips' television business. TPV obtained 70 percent of the shares for "a deferred purchase price." The price that TPV will pay is 70 percent of an amount equal to four times the joint venture's average annual earnings before interest and taxes. Philips has an option to sell the remaining 30 percent shareholding in the joint venture for a consideration calculated as 30 percent of the same formula.[6] In this way, both companies deal with information asymmetry and with unexpected market developments.

Another similar mechanism regarding takeovers of businesses occurs when a company sells a part of its business to another company and simultaneously takes a stake in the acquiring company. When Siemens sold its IT division to the French IT firm Atos, it acquired a minority stake in Atos, ensuring Atos that Siemens would remain a client for some time. The deal also gave Siemens some control over Atos, which as a result of the deal became an important supplier to Siemens.

As a step toward a full merger or an acquisition, an equity stake may also make sense from a monitoring perspective. Equity stakes may come with a seat on the board of the company to be acquired, enabling an acquiring company to monitor developments in the target company. In doing so, the acquirer obtains privileged access to knowledge and information and the ability to raise arguments in board discussions that may help guide the discussion in its desired direction.

The third reason for taking a stake in a partner company is value capture, particularly capturing the "private benefits" of an alliance. Any alliance has common benefits, which are benefits for both parties, and private benefits, which are benefits realized by only one of the partners in the alliance.[7] For example, if a small company partners with a large, established company with high brand value, that smaller company's market value may increase more than the size of the collaboration would warrant because the small company also increases its reputation and reduces its risk. Part of the brand of the established company rubs off in a positive way on the small company, and this benefit only accrues to the small company. The larger company may want to capture part of that value. One way to do so is to take an equity stake in the smaller company. Other private benefits may reside in knowledge spillover, increased innovation, or a better image in general.

Sometimes, the private benefits are substantial. The collaboration between General Motors and Toyota in their NUMMI joint venture enabled Toyota to learn not so much about American manufacturing technology but, more importantly, about the American market and ways to enter it. An important part of the value that Toyota generated from the NUMMI joint venture was not generated internally but externally by applying the market lessons learned in other parts of Toyota. If General Motors would have wanted to capture part of that value, it could have taken a stake in Toyota to profit from the increased company value. Judging the magnitude of private benefits and whether they are substantial enough to warrant an equity investment is difficult. However, the option exists and it can be a valuable part of the alliance's financial model.

Equity stakes have two effects on value appropriation: increases or decreases in the share price and dividend payments. For both elements, partners may make further agreements. They may agree to compensate each other for falling share prices and minimum and maximum dividend payments may be agreed on. In this way, companies can balance their financial interests in the face of market uncertainty.

A fourth reason to enter into an equity deal is to pre-empt competitors or to make a credible threat against them.[8] Taking a stake in a focal company may enable a shareholding company to signal to its competitors that the company is its territory. The stake may be accompanied by a blocking vote that prohibits any other company from taking over the focal company or that limits the focal company from licensing its technology to competitors of its shareholder. All such actions block a rival from access to technology, clients, or other resources that it might desire. A related argument is to make a credible threat against a competitor. The minority stakes that the Mexican telco América Móvil took in the Dutch telco KPN and the Austrian telco Telekom Austria in 2012 were explained by some in the popular press as a credible threat against Spanish Telefonica's growth in the Latin America market. By entering Telefonica's backyard, América Móvil warned Telefonica not to be too ambitious in Latin America because it could retaliate in Europe. However, the real drivers behind the minority stakes have not yet been disclosed.

A final reason to enter into equity deals, and specifically cross-shareholdings, is "to seal the deal," in other words, to ensure goal alignment between partners. When two partners take a stake in each other's business, they become co-dependent and the risk of opportunistic behavior by company A toward its partner company B is reduced. After all, such behavior would also damage company A because it would reduce the value of its shares in company B. In management-speak, such cross-shareholdings are labeled a "credible commitment." The less forgiving language of economics professors refers to it as creating "mutual hostages."[9] The latter is probably nearer to the truth. Of all of the reasons to enter into equity alliances, creating a credible commitment is the weakest. The business plan behind the alliance should be strong enough to stand on its own and to commit the partners to the alliance without artificial tricks such as cross-shareholdings. Additionally, if the fear of opportunistic behavior exists, then taking each other hostage is unlikely to turn that fear into trust.

Joint ventures

Joint ventures can be used for any conceivable goal. However, in practice, they are used more frequently to reap economies of scale, to share the risks associated with big projects, and to gain access to foreign markets than for R&D and innovation. For the latter, more flexible contractual alliances are usually better options. As partners integrate their activities into a single new company under a single management team, joint ventures are very suitable for creating economies of scale.

That a new company is created does not imply that joint ventures are run as independent organizations. Whereas shareholdings for companies listed on the stock market tend to be spread over numerous organizations and individuals, in joint ventures a limited number of partners hold the company's shares. Therefore, these partners have considerable say in a joint venture's operations.

Table 6.1 lists more differences between a joint venture and an "independent" company. First, shareholders in independent companies are rarely more than investors and tend not to have intensive operational ties with that company. In contrast, shareholders are often a client or a supplier of a joint venture they own. Such a client–supplier relationship may be tied directly to the core process. In many cases, a partner also delivers supporting activities such as administration or HR services. Next, non-executive board members or members of a supervisory board tend to be employed by the shareholders, for example they may be business unit managers in one of the parent companies. In independent companies shareholders do not have such a relationship with board members. The upshot of this situation is that board members are more heavily involved in managing conflicts between shareholders and monitoring transactions that a joint venture makes with its parent companies. Transactions between a joint venture and a parent may be a source of profit or loss to the parent companies. To prevent one of the partners from siphoning profits from the joint venture by charging a high price for a service it delivers or by paying a low price for a service it receives, such transactions are scrutinized at the joint venture board level. Therefore, whereas board members of independent companies primarily focus on strategic decisions, risk management, and CEO succession, they are more operationally involved in joint ventures.

TABLE 6.1: Differences in joint venture governance compared to independent companies[10]

"Independent" company	Joint venture
• Shareholder is investor in the company	• Shareholder is investor and a client or supplier to the joint venture
• Non-executive or supervisory board members are not employed by shareholders	• Non-executive or supervisory board members are employed by shareholders
• Board members oversee strategic decisions	• Board members also manage conflicts between shareholders and monitor transactions with parents
• Management team is neutral and represents interests of all shareholders	• Management team is not neutral and is (or was) employed by one of the shareholders
• Broad scope	• Limited scope

A further difference lies in the fact that the management team of joint ventures is not neutral. In most instances, the people on the management team either are or have been employed by one of the partners. If they are involved full time in the joint venture, at a later date they will likely return to be employed by one of the partners. Therefore, they will represent the interests of one of the partners instead of equally representing the interests of all shareholders. Finally, a joint venture is usually limited to a narrow scope of products or services that it is allowed to provide. Moving outside that scope is likely to lead to competition with one of the parents. Therefore, joint venture managers face constraints on their freedom to maneuver.

These differences raise additional governance problems in a joint venture. The risk of conflict between the partners is considerable. To avoid such conflicts, a number of precautions can be taken.[11] One such precaution is to appoint an outside (non-executive) director or member of the supervisory board. Such a person can play a neutral role in the joint venture and may bridge differences of interest between the parent companies. Second, the heavy operational involvement of board members makes appointing persons with a general business background insufficient. Instead, people with specific knowledge relevant to the joint venture should be appointed, which may mean that, for example, a business unit manager is also a non-executive director or management team member in a joint venture related to his business. To align the management team and board members with the goals of the joint venture, they should be reviewed and rewarded at least partly based on joint venture performance. To deal with less than transparent transactions between joint ventures and their parents, the parents should agree upfront on auditing mechanisms. Independent parties may play a role in such agreements.

Finally, the management of the joint venture runs the risk of being overruled by the partners. If that happens, the success of the joint venture will be undermined. Therefore, joint venture managers should be empowered to make important decisions such as hiring and firing of key staff and signing off on capital expenditures. In reality, the CEO of a joint venture will always have a smaller mandate than the CEO of an independent company. However, the mandate should empower the CEO to run the business without continuous interference from the shareholders.

Many of the elements listed in the right-hand side of Table 6.1 become evident in the case of the Obvion joint venture. By striking a balance between dependence and independence by using a variety of mechanisms, Obvion was able to grow a sizeable business while serving its shareholders. This situation illustrates how carefully designed checks and balances help to achieve a desired effect.

The Obvion joint venture

In 2001, Rabobank – at that time the only privately held triple A-rated bank in the world and the largest provider of mortgages in the Netherlands – faced a strategic challenge. Increasingly, mortgages were sold through financial intermediaries instead of bank branches. At the same time, ABP, one of the world's largest pension funds, also faced a mortgage-related question. As an instrument of diversification of its fixed income investments, between 1980 and 2001 ABP had built up a portfolio of mortgages sold exclusively through intermediaries worth €5 billion. In 2001, that ABP should be active in this retail business by itself was no longer self-evident. The origination and servicing of a mortgage portfolio was not its core business. After all, ABP was not a bank; it was active in mortgages as an investor that invested its participants' pension savings with the objective of providing them with good pensions after their retirement. A deal between the two companies was self-evident: by collaborating with ABP, Rabobank could build a position in the intermediary channel and protect its leadership. By collaborating with Rabobank, ABP could remain an active investor in Dutch residential mortgages with limited risk without having to run an extensive operation and without the complexity of operating in a retail market. In terms of the Alliance Development Framework, the strategic imperatives were clear.

Because the two partners intended to create a completely new business of selling mortgages through intermediaries, they selected a joint venture structure for their alliance. Given that the move was most strategic for Rabobank, it became the majority shareholder with 70 percent of the shares, thus obtaining strategic control. ABP owned the remaining 30 percent. However, economically, the division was 50/50. Control-wise, ABP was a minority partner; however, economically, it shared equally in the value created. For example, the companies agreed that dividends were shared 50/50 (in reality, dividends were not paid because Obvion retained all of its earnings to meet the ever-stricter regulations that demanded higher levels of equity in financial institutions).

ABP's existing portfolio of mortgages was managed but not owned by Obvion. The servicing of this portfolio gave Obvion a head-start in the market and relieved ABP from a substantial, non-core activity. Ownership of the mortgages was not transferred to the joint venture because doing so would have required Rabobank to compensate ABP financially, which would require a very substantial capital investment. Together with the management of the portfolio, the entire staff of ABP Hypotheken (ABP Mortgages) moved from ABP to Obvion.

Figure 6.2 depicts the structure of the Obvion joint venture. The joint venture is governed by a shareholder agreement, a shareholder meeting, and a supervisory

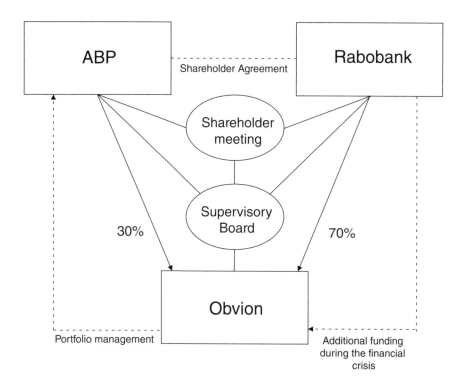

FIGURE 6.2: Obvion joint venture structure

board. The shareholder agreement stipulated a number of elements that described the relationship between the two parties. It was not consulted over the lifetime of the joint venture. The governance bodies in place and the excellent relationships between the members of the supervisory board were more than sufficient to deal with the issues that emerged. Resorting to the contractual provisions was not needed.

The shareholder meeting consisted of senior members from both organizations. For example, Rabobank's chief financial officer represented the bank in the shareholder meetings. The shareholder meeting appointed Obvion's CEO, who always had his roots in Rabobank. Another responsibility of the shareholder meeting was to decide on sales of shares to a third party should the occasion arise.

The supervisory board consisted of four people: two for each partner. At least one of the two has to be a board member of the partner he represents. One of the Rabobank supervisory board members acted as chairman of the supervisory board of the joint venture and had the decisive vote in case of a split vote. The board's membership did not overlap with the membership of the shareholder meeting, allowing the supervisory board to focus on the joint venture's interest without getting into a conflict of interest. The shareholder role was separated from the supervisory role. One of the most important tasks of the supervisory board was to approve the annual business plan. Decision making was guided by consensus, which was always reached because, among other reasons, the members of the supervisory board had a very good rapport.

The Obvion CEO is responsible for writing the business plan. Part of the business plan is the funding plan that outlines where and how Obvion will attract funds to finance its mortgage portfolio. This funding plan also needed to be approved by the chief financial officer of Rabobank.

Obvion is free to determine its product pricing and the precise mortgage products that it wants to offer, and to handle its own marketing and communication. The scope of the joint venture is strictly limited to mortgages in the Netherlands: it is not allowed to offer other banking products because doing so would be too competitive to Rabobank's offerings. With its mortgage offering, it already competes with Rabobank's products, raising the occasional eyebrow from Rabobank staff who fear cannibalization. The presence of a Rabobank board member on the supervisory board was instrumental in protecting Obvion's status as an independent company.

Obvion attracts 80 percent of its funding itself using secured funding instruments such as securitization. Rabobank attracts funds for its activities through senior unsecured funding and does not use secured funding instruments. Because Obvion is not allowed to attract savings by offering savings accounts (which would compete with Rabobank) or issuing senior unsecured bonds, its main method for obtaining external funding is securitization in which bonds backed by a portfolio of mortgages are sold to investors. These transactions are carried out in the European capital markets and the bonds are sold to a diversified global investor base primarily comprised of European investors.

Whereas Obvion faces some constraints imposed by its parent companies, it also benefits from them. Even though it could not use the Rabobank and ABP brand, as a new company it benefited from the fact that it had two such strong partners behind it. The brand names of the partners rubbed off on the Obvion brand name, which was true in both the consumer market and the securitization market. Regarding the latter, Rabobank guaranteed the financial swaps behind the securitizations (at an arm's length fee). As an important and trusted player in the financial markets, Rabobank's backing was a valuable asset to Obvion.

However, the practice of securitization made it difficult for Obvion to attract funding when the financial crisis hit the markets in 2007. Investor appetite for securities vanished overnight, and throughout 2008 and 2009 the securitization market was weak and even closed during prolonged periods. Without a supplementary source of funding, Obvion could not have continued operating in the mortgage market. Therefore, Rabobank stepped in to ensure that Obvion was still able to lend money to homeowners. In contrast, ABP did not support Obvion, leading to an imbalance in the relationship.

Other imbalances started to emerge as well. As a pension fund, ABP was more interested in liquid investments instead of the difficult-to-dispose-of stake in the joint venture. It looked at Obvion more from an investor's viewpoint, whereas Rabobank saw the business as an integral and strategic cornerstone of its position in the Dutch mortgage market. To ABP, profitability and growing the value of the company were its prime interest; to Rabobank, the joint position of Rabobank and Obvion in the mortgage market was the most important issue.

Taken together, all of these elements led to the conclusion that a full takeover of Obvion by Rabobank was the best solution. Because the relationship between the two parent companies remained friendly over the years, ABP and Rabobank agreed on an amicable divorce in 2012. ABP sold its shares to Rabobank, its representatives on the supervisory board resigned, and Obvion became a 100 percent daughter of the bank. Thus ended a successful collaboration that saw, despite difficult years in the capital market, Obvion's mortgage portfolio grow to €30 billion. Moreover, based on sound funding and risk management, Obvion provided responsible and high quality mortgages to more than 180,000 customers. It employed 350 full-time equivalent staff at the time of the full takeover. The ties with ABP were not completely severed: the remainder of the ABP portfolio that Obvion managed since its inception is still in Obvion's care. The joint venture helped both partners meet their objective. Rabobank gained a considerable foothold in the intermediary channel, whereas ABP obtained a good return on investments. When market circumstances changed, ABP could make a graceful exit from this form of investment in Dutch residential mortgages.

Most of the elements listed in Table 6.1 apply in this case:

• The shareholder is a client of or supplier to the joint venture. Obvion manages ABP's mortgage portfolio, and Rabobank backs the swaps behind the securitizations.

• Board members are employed by the shareholders. Board members from both partners sit on the supervisory board.

• The joint venture management team has a background in one of the partners: Obvion's CEO always hails from Rabobank.

• The joint venture has a limited scope: Obvion is a monoliner and sells only mortgages. It is not allowed to sell other products to customers and its external funding predominantly comes from securitization.

All of these elements suggest that Obvion was highly dependent on the parent companies. And it was. However, note that some measures were taken to ensure Obvion's independence. For example, the separation between membership of the shareholder meeting and membership of the supervisory board ensured that shareholder interests would not dominate the entire joint venture. A behavioral element is that the member of the Rabobank supervisory board acting as chairman of the Obvion supervisory board protected Obvion's independence. Without these measures, Rabobank might have put too many limits on Obvion and, consequently, Obvion's growth might have been constrained. The balance between being dependent on the parents and operating independently as a company is a fine one. In terms of the Alliance Development Framework, this relates to the element of internal alignment that needs to be managed.

A balance was also struck between trust and control. Typical control elements included the 70/30 shareholding that gave Rabobank control at the shareholder meeting. That Rabobank nominated the CEO was another important control mechanism, as was the fact that the Rabobank chief financial officer needed to approve the funding plan. Interestingly, the presence of a shareholder agreement, a shareholder meeting, a supervisory board and the accompanying rules and regulations create the impression of very strict control procedures in terms of governance. However, this case shows that such strict governance was only true to some extent (obviously, ABP, Rabobank, and Obvion being financial institutions, the operational and financial control was also in practice very strict). The contract was never looked at (until the very end) and the good relationships between the members of the supervisory board stimulated consensus decision making. More than control, trust formed the basis of this successful joint venture, but both the formal and the informal element of the Alliance Development Framework received attention in this joint venture.

Ownership structures

The most visible part of an equity joint venture is the shareholding arrangement. Companies may be very particular in wanting 50/50, 49/51, 51/49, or any other division. All of these discussions are irrelevant if the goal of the alliance is not kept in mind (bar any fiscal consequences of the shareholding arrangement that local authorities may have devised). Table 6.2 lists the pros and cons of perfect equality and a majority/minority structure, assuming that the division of shares is representative of what happens in the rest of the joint venture. However, this assumption is a significant one to make because joint venture partners may agree on an almost infinite set of divergences from the shareholding structure. In the Obvion case, the shareholding was 70/30, but economically the split was 50/50. Or, one partner may have a majority, but the partners may still agree that all decision making will be based on complete agreement between the shareholders. Alternatively, the minority shareholder may be entitled to higher dividends. Therefore, shareholdings are not necessarily indicative of the balance of power in a joint venture. In fact, in most cases, contractual provisions guarantee rights to a minority shareholder that go over and above the size of its holdings in the joint venture.

Equal ownership, equal decision making, and equal financial stakes in a joint venture simplify governance in many ways. At first sight, the approach is very balanced and enables the partners to control each other. In situations of less trust, such as when competitors want to keep an eye on each other, a 50/50

TABLE 6.2: Joint venture ownership structures and their implications

	Applicable when:	Advantages	Disadvantages
50/50 ownership	Less than perfect goal alignment; partners make contributions of equal value; low trust	Equal share of risk, revenues and costs is highly transparent; possibility to control partner	Decision making can get stuck and speed may be lost
Majority/ minority structure	High goal alignment; high trust; one partner makes larger contribution	For the majority shareholder: more control; ability to steer alliance in its direction; financial consolidation For the minority shareholder: less investment in the joint venture and the goal can still be achieved; less risk	For the majority shareholder: higher investment, higher responsibility; partner may free-ride; less knowledge transfer from partner to joint venture For the minority shareholder: partner may act opportunistically; no consolidation

joint venture makes sense. Likewise, when strategic goals may diverge, a 50/50 agreement makes more sense because it prevents one partner from steering the joint venture in a direction that fits less with the other partner's aims. Naturally, a 50/50 joint venture is also applicable when the partners make contributions of equal value to the alliance.

Research showed that partners in a 50/50 joint venture book similar results from operations.[12] When the shares are not equally split between the partners, whether both partners achieve the same results depends heavily on the goal alignment between the partners. When both partners have the same goal for the joint venture and trust each other, a minority partner's position is quite good. In that case, the majority partner will guide the joint venture in a direction that is also beneficial to the minority partner. Joint ventures in the oil industry to exploit oil fields often have a majority/minority structure. The aim of both partners is the same: to operate the oil field as efficiently as possible. To do so, having one partner run the operations is most efficient (and safer) than having to discuss and compromise continuously regarding a variety of issues. Only when the goals are not congruous and partners distrust each other is the minority partner in a disadvantageous position.

The drawback of a 50/50 shareholding is that decision making can come to a halt. The advantage lies in the equal commitments that the partners have made.

If both contribute equally, both have an incentive to continue to contribute to the alliance in the same way. When the shareholding is not equal, the majority partner is likely to invest more in the management of the joint venture, thereby further increasing its control and possibly to the detriment of the minority shareholder. The majority shareholder has ample opportunity to behave opportunistically and steer the joint venture in its direction. The downside of a majority position is in the greater responsibility and the possibility of free-riding by the minority partner. A joint venture may benefit from the knowledge that a minority partner brings; however, because most of the benefits of that knowledge will flow to the majority partner, the minority shareholder may not be amenable to sharing all of its knowledge.

A majority shareholder that is in control of the joint venture may also consolidate the joint venture on its balance sheet and income statement (note that such consolidation does not always occur: accounting standards on consolidation are complex and vary across countries). Such consolidation can be attractive because it optically increases the firm's revenues and profits.

The focus on who owns the majority in an alliance overlooks other important mechanisms. The partner's intention can be quite different than expected. For example, the NUMMI joint venture shows that the real benefits for Toyota were only partly connected to its shareholding in the venture. Therefore, companies focused on obtaining a majority share may be aiming for the wrong thing. They may be prepared to give up many assets for a 1 percent majority, which may gain them operational control but may lose them strategic control.

Moreover, equity stakes and associated dividend rights are not the only financial elements of joint venture deals. Shareholders are often clients of or suppliers to the joint venture, which opens up another opportunity for financial gain. By setting transfer prices high or low, partners can appropriate some of the joint venture's profits. If a partner supplies a joint venture with certain goods or services, he will charge a price for that. That price will incorporate a certain margin that accrues to the partner. For that reason, contracts between joint venture partners often contain provisions for transfer pricing.

The shareholder agreement describes these provisions, along with the rules that regulate the relationship between the shareholders in the joint venture. The shareholder agreement contains details for the dividend policy, voting rights, transfer pricing, and the like. More than the division of shares, the rules agreed to in the shareholder agreement govern the joint venture. The case of Americhem and EuroPower clearly underlines that the real financial implications of a joint venture may diverge from the shares the partners hold.

Americhem and EuroPower

What does an entity do when it generates so much electricity that it cannot use all of it? The entity creates a joint venture with an energy company that can sell the surplus electricity. Such a situation was a driver behind the joint venture between Americhem and EuroPower (the names Americhem, Euro-Power, and Amepco are pseudonyms). Americhem, an American chemical company, and EuroPower, a European energy company, started their joint venture in 1997 on an Americhem site in Europe. Americhem was interested in combined heat and power (CHP), a technique to simultaneously generate electricity and steam, both necessary for its chemical plant. Steam is an essential part of Americhem's production process and it needs to be generated onsite. CHP seemed an economically attractive technology because the demand for both steam and power was believed to be growing. Americhem already operated one CHP turbine that transformed gas to heat and electricity, and a second one would satisfy the expected increase in demand.

There was one catch: with a second CHP turbine, Americhem would generate more electricity than it needed and, at that time, the company was not allowed to legally deliver excess electricity to the national grid. These were the days before the liberalization of the European energy market. Therefore, Americhem set up a joint venture with EuroPower, which was an energy company and, thus, could sell electricity. Americhem contributed its existing CHP turbine to the joint venture and the partners jointly invested in a new second gas turbine. Americhem was the majority partner, owning two-thirds of the joint venture, and EuroPower had the remaining one-third ownership. The joint venture was christened Amepco (Americhem EuroPower Company). A shareholder agreement between the two partners contained a number of provisions on decision making and conflict resolution, among other areas.

As part of the collaboration, Amepco entered into a 10-year agreement to deliver its excess power to EuroPower and a 15-year contract to deliver steam and power to Americhem. If neither of the parties ended the alliance after these terms passed, the agreement automatically renewed for another year. A supervisory board consisting of two senior managers was created that had to approve the business plan proposed to them by the daily management of Amepco. The day-to-day management team consisted of two Americhem staff members and

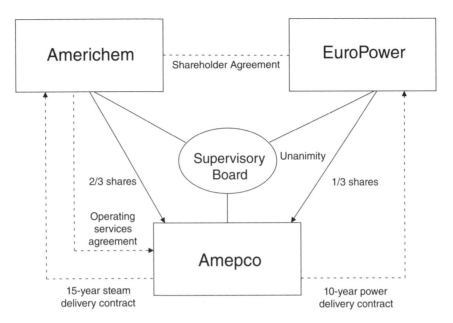

FIGURE 6.3: Structure of the Amepco joint venture

one EuroPower representative. The supervisory board was to meet at least twice a year; in practice, it met on average three times. The Americhem staff carried out daily operation of the turbines through an operating services agreement that ensured the supply of services and products from Americhem to Amepco needed to operate the CHP turbines. Figure 6.3 shows the legal structure of the joint venture and the related agreements.

Amepco's main risk was related to the equipment's uptime. When the turbines ran continuously, Amepco made a profit that the partners shared. The original business case estimated that a good return on investment over the entire lifetime was feasible. Any downside risk or upside potential associated with fluctuating power prices was borne by EuroPower. Because Americhem paid for the gas needed to operate the turbines, it carried the price risk on gas. This arrangement ensured that Amepco would generate relatively stable profits, provided that the turbines ran on a continuous basis.

The joint venture experienced difficulties during the first few years. The new turbine that Amepco built was the first of an upgraded model, and several installation errors were made during its construction. During the first four years of its operation, the turbine operated only half the time because of unplanned outages. After the teething problems were solved, the turbine's performance improved. The joint venture entered into a stable and profitable phase and served both partners well.

After 10 years, the contract relating to the delivery of power to EuroPower ended. By then, the world was quite a different place compared with a decade earlier when the contract was signed. The energy market was liberalized, which changed its pricing structure and increased the risk of price instability for electricity. Therefore, EuroPower, which was selling the excess power generated by the turbines, was exposed to additional risk. In the renegotiations after 10 years, the partners agreed that Amepco would now carry the risks and profits associated with price swings in the electricity market, thus changing the incentives: for Amepco and EuroPower, the best option was to operate Amepco at full capacity when power prices were high and at low capacity when prices were low.

At approximately the same time, Americhem sold some of its businesses located on the plant site. The new owner moved the businesses elsewhere and closed the plants on the site, substantially decreasing the need for steam. Moreover, during the 2009 economic crisis, Americhem's plant did not operate at full capacity, further decreasing demand for steam. Therefore, Americhem preferred to temporarily shut down one of the turbines. It had no use for the steam that Amepco generated but still had to pay for the gas used. EuroPower preferred that both of the turbines remained operative when power prices were good. The changing market circumstances caused dis-alignment in the financial incentives of Amepco, Americhem, and EuroPower: profits for Amepco and EuroPower meant higher costs for Americhem. The internal alignment as demanded by the Alliance Design Framework was lost.

The decision-making process led to a stalemate, primarily because the joint venture agreements were not flexible enough to manage this unforeseen reality. Although Americhem owned two-thirds of the joint venture, the shareholder agreement between the two partners stipulated that decision making required unanimity. The Amepco management team was not able to reach a mutually acceptable solution and escalated the problem to the joint venture's supervisory board, which consisted of one senior manager from EuroPower and one from Americhem. Because both of these managers operated at some distance from the joint venture, they informed themselves by asking their representatives on the Amepco management team about the conflict. Hence, they were informed by the same people who were unable to reach consensus. Consequently, the stalemate was not resolved.

Communication between the partners deteriorated, also influenced by the fact that the membership of the supervisory board changed on both sides. When new individuals get involved, they always need time to develop mutual trust and understanding. The shareholder agreement stated that arbitrage was the next and final step for conflict resolution. In 2009, EuroPower filed a case with the local arbitration institute. The "benefit" of the arbitration process was that it forced both parties to do some further fact finding to clarify the issues to the arbitration panel. After two hearings, the arbiters were reluctant to impose a decision: they demanded that Americhem and EuroPower should have one more attempt to solve the issue based on the new facts and the insights gained into each other's positions. If that attempt was unsuccessful, then they might issue a ruling. By the end of 2010, Americhem and EuroPower reached a settlement.

This settlement was the starting point for both partners to re-examine the potential of the Amepco partnership after the 15-year alliance period which would end in 2012. Experts from both sides gathered to review the joint venture. Further future synergies were jointly explored and a number of them were identified. Among the proposals for improvement were more flexible contracts for electricity offtake by EuroPower, a revised operating agreement with Americhem, and the delivery of new services from EuroPower to the joint venture. However, strategically, the fit between the partners was limited. EuroPower made a strategic decision to withdraw as an equity partner from the partnership. New business areas (for example, in operations and maintenance) might form the basis of a possible new cooperation between the parties after 2013.

Reflecting on the events that led to the conflict of interest, the management team identified some lessons learned. First, the original design of the alliance was not flexible enough to adapt to ever-changing circumstances. The design may have made perfect sense in 1997, but a 15-year contract without automatic reviews did not fit in a rapidly changing environment. When two basic assumptions behind the joint venture changed, the joint venture was not redesigned. The liberalization that took place undermined the assumption of relative price stability. The drop in steam demand attributable to economic circumstances and restructuring in Americhem undermined the assumption of growing demand for steam and power. These two changes should have triggered an earlier rethink and redesign of the alliance. A more flexible contract that would have provided for managing such changes would have made this easier to realize.

A second point was that any not so obvious opportunities for collaboration were unexploited because of the initial design of the joint venture. Americhem operated the joint venture and one manager from EuroPower collaborated with Americhem on a daily basis. EuroPower has expert knowledge in a variety of areas, such as in operating and maintaining gas turbines. This expertise was not optimally exploited by both parties in the past. Influenced by the conflict of interest on the operational principles, neither party explored these opportunities in sufficient depth. A change in the division of labor between the partners could have created new synergy-generating opportunities.

Third, the managers concluded that once the tensions occurred, the partners did not spend enough joint time and effort on finding a mutually acceptable solution. No serious attempts were made to "see issues through the other partner's eyes." In the past, the absence of a strong collaborative relationship led to a formal yet inefficient approach to problem solving.

The Amepco joint venture shows that joint ventures can have complex designs. From a distance, the relationship may seem simple: two parties owning shares in a joint enterprise. The entire financial picture is more complex given the multiple client and supplier relationships between the joint venture and the partners. Moreover, in an ever-changing market, incentives may easily become misaligned, which underlines the importance of managing alliance dynamics: even joint ventures that have been successful for a decade may have to be thoroughly redesigned when circumstances change. In terms of the Alliance Development Framework, the analysis made by the management team highlighted that the informal elements and the management of dynamics were not sufficiently developed to cope with changing strategic imperatives. The logical explanation for this lies in the fact that at the outset the two companies operated in relatively stable markets.

The joint venture between Americhem and EuroPower primarily relies on control elements. This control focus was successful for a decade because it fitted well with the demands of the business to operate CHP turbines as efficiently as possible. An emphasis on control does not guarantee that a joint venture can deal with changes in the market. Doing so requires mechanisms to review the alliance on a regular basis. Changing markets and changing incentives need to be monitored to ensure that the financial results of the partners remain fair and balanced for all involved.

As the previous discussion shows, the relationship between a joint venture and its parents is not a passive shareholding relationship. Various ties exist between the parent companies and the joint venture, and balancing the parent–joint venture relationship is a delicate act. A best practice is to ensure that a joint venture either works with the governance processes of one of the partners or has a well-developed separate governance process.[13] When defining the responsibilities of the joint venture manager, companies may also distinguish between elements that are completely at his discretion and elements that require input from the parent companies. Joint venture managers may also attend the strategy sessions of the parent business units that are closest to them to ensure alignment with the partners as demanded by the Alliance Development Framework.

An important role in maintaining alignment between the parents and the joint venture lies with the supervisory board or non-executive board members. The joint venture manager is appointed by the shareholders, the joint venture's supervisory board, or one of the shareholders. Supervisory or non-executive board membership of joint ventures has different characteristics than that of "regular" companies because the ownership structure of joint ventures is different from that of a listed company. Members of a joint venture's board are often put in place not as neutral supervisors but to control and monitor the joint venture from one of the partner's perspective. Doing so may entail that the non-executive or supervisory board members meddle with the operational affairs of the joint venture too much for the joint venture's good. A number of guidelines are relevant to the composition of the board:[14]

- Add a neutral third person not related to the parents. This person will be more objective and look after the joint venture's interest instead of being a watchdog on behalf of one of the parents. He or she will also be in a better position to ask the painful questions and to help partners reconcile their differences.

- For larger joint ventures, board members representing various functions may be appointed. Do not skimp on board size for a sizeable joint venture. For example, having an audit committee may make sense.

- Ensure that sufficient seniority exists on the board to instigate change or to decide to dissolve the joint venture.

- Ensure that the board members have knowledge of the joint venture's business. Nominating somebody to the board simply because a director from one of the partners needs to be on the board is not a best practice.

- When a client–supplier relationship also exists between a partner and the joint venture, separating the client–supplier relationship from the membership of the board is best. To avoid conflicts of interest, the board member representing that partner should not be responsible for the client–supplier relationship with the joint venture.

TABLE 6.3: Exit clauses around shares in joint ventures[15]

- *Right of first refusal.* If partner A wants to sell its shares in a joint venture to a third party, it first has to offer them to partner B against the same conditions the third party offered to partner A. If B decides not to buy the shares, they may be offered to the third party.
- A *right of first offer* exists when partner A wants to sell its shares, but no third party has been approached yet. In that case, partner B may make a first offer on A's shares. If A deems that offer too low, A may offer the shares to a third party.
- *Texas shoot-out:* The partners in a joint venture each make a sealed bid for the shares of the joint venture. The highest bidder wins.
- *Russian roulette:* Partner A has the right to make an offer for the shares owned by partner B; however, as soon as A has made the offer, B has the right to buy A's shares for the price offered by A. This mechanism forces A to offer a good price in its initial offer.
- *Drag along:* If partner A owns the majority of the shares in a joint venture and wants to sell the shares to a third party, the minority shareholder B is obligated to offer its shares to the third party against the same conditions.
- *Tag along:* The right of a minority shareholder B to require a third party that wants to buy the shares of partner A – which owns the majority of a joint venture's shares – to extend the same offer price per share to B.
- *Lock-up:* The obligation of a shareholder not to sell his shares during a certain period.

As in other alliance types, the exit of joint ventures should be thought through in advance. One extra complication exists when exiting joint ventures: What to do with the shares? Partners face a variety of possible challenges. For example, if one partner wants to sell its shares to a third party, is that allowed? What if both partners want to acquire 100 percent of the joint venture? Joint venture agreements may stipulate clauses that address such situations. When a joint venture is sold to one of the partners or a third party, a valuation issue arises. Of course, an independent party may determine the share price. However, other mechanisms also exist. Table 6.3 lists types of agreements that partners may enter into to address the thorny issue of selling and valuing shares.

When to use joint ventures?

Joint ventures are primarily used to create economies of scale, to build market power, or to create new businesses (as in Obvion). Because setting up a joint venture requires more durable legal structures, they tend to have a long time horizon. Shares in a joint venture are difficult to sell; therefore, companies need to be sure that the joint venture will be around for a long time. In addition, integrating a business under one management needs to make sense. If no benefits are to be had from that, a joint venture is not the solution. In the cases of Obvion and Americhem–EuroPower, such integration was logical. Obvion needed to build a new business and the assets in the Americhem and Euro-Power joint venture also benefit from being in one company. One drawback of joint ventures is that setting them up takes time. Contractual agreements are faster to create; hence, joint ventures are less suitable to quickly react to new opportunities in the market.

Companies with little alliance experience sometimes prefer joint ventures because they believe that joint ventures are easier to manage. At first sight, a separate company looks clearer than a contractual alliance. In addition, equity ownership gives companies the sense that they own something tangible. In this chapter, a closer look revealed that joint ventures have many intricacies similar to those of contractual alliances, as well as some special ones. For that reason, ease of management is not a strong argument for choosing the joint venture option.

Notes

1   Hagedoorn, J. 2002. Inter-firm R&D partnerships: an overview of major trends and patterns since 1960, *Research Policy*, 31, 477–492.
2   These numbers are based on the Fourth State of Alliance Management Study database.
3   These numbers are based on Renault Nissan. 2013. *Alliance facts & figures 2012–2013*, http://blog.alliance-renault-nissan.com/sites/default/files/Alliance_facts_and _figures_2012_2013.pdfdownloaded, 24 January 2013.
4   Dushnitsky, G. and M.J. Lenox. 2005. When do incumbents learn from entrepreneurial ventures? Corporate venture capital and investing firm innovation rates, *Research Policy*, 34, 615–639; Dushnitsky, G. and M.J. Lenox. 2006. When does corporate venture capital investment create firm value?, *Journal of Business Venturing*, 21, 753–772.
5   Balakrishnan, S. and M.P. Koza. 1993. Information asymmetry, adverse selection and joint-ventures: theory and evidence, *Journal of Economic Behavior & Organization*, 20, 1, 99–117.
6   Philips press release, 1 November 2011, *Philips and TPV sign agreement on Television joint venture.*
7   Dyer, J.H., H. Singh and P. Kale. 2008. Splitting the pie: rent distribution in alliances and networks, *Managerial and Decision Economics*, Vol. 29, 137–148; Khanna, T.R., R. Gulati and N. Nohria. 1998. The dynamics of learning alliances: competition, cooperation and relative scope, *Strategic Management Journal*, 19, 193–210.
8   Folta, T.B. and K.D. Miller. 2002. Real options in equity partnerships, *Strategic Management Journal*, 23, 77–88.
9   Williamson, O.E. 1983. Credible commitments: using hostages to support exchange, *American Economic Review*, 73, 4, 519–540.
10 This table and the related discussion are among others based on Bamford, J. and D. Ernst. 2005a. Governing joint ventures, *The McKinsey Quarterly*, Special edition: Value and Performance, 63–69 and De Man, A.P. 2006. *Alliantiebesturing*, Assen, Van Gorcum.

11 This paragraph is based on Bamford and Ernst. 2005a. Ibid.

12 Yan, A. and B. Gray. 1994. Bargaining power, management control, and performance in United States–China joint ventures: a comparative case study, *Academy of Management Journal*, 37, 6, 1478–1517.

13 Bamford, J. and D. Ernst. 2005b. Getting a grip on alliances, *Corporate Dealmaker*, winter, 29–32.

14 This is based among others on Bamford, J. and D. Ernst. 2005b. For more on the link between corporate governance and joint ventures see: Reuer, J.J., E. Klijn, F.A.J. van den Bosch and H.W. Volberda. 2011. Bringing corporate governance to international joint ventures, *Global Strategy Journal*, 1, 54–66.

15 Based on: Ariño, A., J.J. Reuer and A. Valverde. 2005. The perfect "pre-nup" to strategic alliances: a guide to contracts, *Critical Eye*, June–August, 52–57 and Freshfields Bruckhaus Deringer. 2003. *Joint ventures: a survival guide*, February.

CHAPTER 7

Multi-partner alliances: The more the merrier?

In addition to alliances between two partners, alliances involving larger numbers – or sometimes even vast numbers – of partners exist. This chapter analyses the structures of such multi-partner alliances. In high tech sectors, the average number of multi-partner alliances has been stable over the years. Approximately 15 percent of all alliances in this sector have more than two partners.[1] Multi-partner alliances are common, particularly in IT-related sectors. The need to combine technologies and to work on standardization and interoperability of products drives IT firms to collaborate in larger constellations. In other sectors, such as biopharma, the number of multi-partner alliances is much smaller because technologies in those sectors traditionally operate on a standalone basis. However, given the advent of the use of IT in biopharma and with increased pressure to share R&D expenses, the number of multi-partner alliances in biopharma seems to be increasing.

Apart from the technological drive of firms to enter into multi-partner alliances, other reasons exist for frequent multi-partnering. Competition is one such reason. Companies can combine their strengths to compete with a large competitor. To compete with Microsoft's initiatives around identity management on the Internet, its competitors joined forces in the Liberty Alliance to develop a competing offer. Similarly, when Vodafone became a powerful player in the European telecom market, Deutsche Telekom, Telecom Italia, TeliaSonera, and Orange joined forces to form the Freemove alliance as a countervailing power.

Other reasons to set up multi-partner alliances, such as reaping economies of scale, sharing risk, or exchanging knowledge, are not unique to these structures. Bilateral alliances may be formed for these same reasons. However, multi-partner alliances open up more opportunities to achieve these goals: as more partners join, the benefits that can be realized increase. Obviously, a limit exists to the number of partners that can join an alliance, and multi-partner alliances come with a number of challenges that increase in importance when the number of partners increases.[2]

First, relationship building becomes more complex. Each partner must build a relationship with all other partners in the alliance. As more partners join an alliance, the relationships tend to remain shallow and significant trust may fail to develop. Such a situation diminishes the benefits of the alliance because exchange of knowledge and information is less likely when relationships are superficial. Therefore, alliances with many partners usually focus on less far-reaching goals that do not reach deeply into alliance members' organizations. Only over time might such an alliance deepen and intensify its relationships and goals.

Second, each partner has its own strategy and goals. The chance that all strategies fit together decreases as more partners join. As a result, multi-partner alliances find it difficult to define projects that benefit all members. Therefore, the scope of multi-partner alliances tends to be narrower than the scope of bilateral alliances. For the same reason, the projects that a multi-partner alliance executes will have longer-term strategic effects instead of an immediate impact on competition in the sector.

The third challenge is to discover partners' opportunistic behavior. Monitoring the contributions of all partners and determining whether they are actually committed to the alliance or whether only lip service is paid is difficult. Free-riding and profiting from the work of others without contributing oneself is easier to cover up and more likely to go undetected in multi-partner alliances. One solution to this problem is to increase control procedures, which in turn makes the alliance less flexible and increases governance costs.

Decision making is a fourth challenge. Consensus is often difficult to reach and democratic decision making may hold back the entire alliance. In practice, many multi-partner alliances have a dominant partner (or partner group) that guides the decision making in a certain direction. This partner must understand its specific role and exercise restraint in using its power by taking into account the interest of others. The METRO case discussed in this chapter illustrates such an alliance structure.

Finally, the composition of multi-partner alliances is rarely stable. Over time, existing partners leave and new partners join. The inflow and outflow of members require continuous management attention. New relationships need to be built and old ties are severed. Multi-partner alliances are time consuming and require more management hours than bilateral alliances, thus limiting the number of alliance members.

Because of the aforementioned reasons, only well-designed multi-partner alliances are viable. The following four different models for multi-partner alliances have emerged in practice:[3]

- A general assembly or democracy model in which all partners vote on decisions. In the purely democratic model, the one-man one-vote rule is applied. Other models may specify different voting rights, such as in relation to partner size.

- The lead partner model, in which one dominant company acts as the first among equals in the alliance and has a more significant decision-making role. A variant of this model is a lead partner group comprised of a smaller inner circle of partners that guides a larger alliance.

- The alliance support office, which is a central office created by the partners to support the alliance's administrative processes. Alternatively, the alliance support office may have an active decision-making role.

- Joint ventures in which the partners participate as shareholders and the joint venture manager has its own decision-making responsibility.

The general assembly: the Prominent cooperative

Early in the 1990s, Dutch tomato growers were confronted with a major loss of market share. The growers had a leading position in Western Europe but sacrificed tomato flavor by increasing the quantity of production. German consumers who for years formed the most important markets for Dutch tomatoes stopped buying them from one day to the next. They qualified Dutch tomatoes as "water bombs," or flavorless vegetables that tasted like water. In response, tomato growers started thinking about new ways to improve and differentiate their products. Because these growers were small family businesses, they estimated that the risks connected to innovation would be too significant for their individual companies. Therefore, they sought likeminded entrepreneurs to create cooperatives involving multiple partners.

One such cooperative is Prominent tomatoes in the Netherlands, which started in 1994 with six vine tomato growers that owned 20 hectares of greenhouses, in which tomatoes are grown in the Netherlands. In 2013, the cooperative had 23 members that owned 206 hectares of vine tomatoes in greenhouses. Prominent's mission is to produce vine tomatoes in a sustainable way in harmony with the environment and society. The cooperative is an instrument that helps its members operate their business profitably. Hence, the primary strategic imperative is not to build Prominent as a business but to strengthen the partners' businesses by collaborating.

Figure 7.1 depicts the structure of Prominent as of 2006, when it had 22 vine tomato growers as members. The cooperative has a board whose members are elected from the membership. The cooperative owns a holding that, in turn, is the mother company of a number of daughters. One daughter is a packaging company in which specialized machines package tomatoes for different markets.

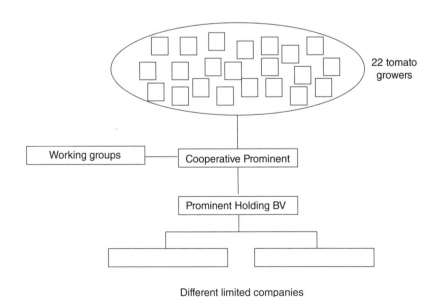

FIGURE 7.1: Structure of the Prominent cooperative

Another daughter company is a greenhouse in which the partners experiment with new technologies for growing tomatoes, such as new forms of lighting that influence the growth of plants or energy-saving technologies. For the partners to experiment with these technologies on their own is much too expensive. Jointly, they can afford making investments into innovative efforts, and the lessons learned from these innovations are available to them. Next, the individual growers decide whether they want to implement the lessons learned in their own greenhouse.

Members are obliged to participate in management of the cooperative. They do so by serving on the board, being a member of a working group, or being involved in running the daughter companies. Working groups focus on themes such as marketing or purchasing. The advantage of this approach is that it fosters specialization, wherein some growers are good at purchasing and others have a great feel for marketing. Growers choose the job they are most competent at, gather even more knowledge and expertise in that area through experience, and increase the benefits for all members. Individual members are obliged to follow the decisions made by the working groups; in other words, if the purchasing working group decides that a certain supplier is the best, all members need to purchase from that specific supplier. Another obligation is that they have to follow a number of rules for growing their vine tomatoes to ensure quality and realize the mission. Essentially, the cooperative handles all non-core – in other words, all non-growing-related – activities of the members. The alliance is also open ended. Many of the ideas that it implemented were not thought of at its start 20 years ago.

The board consists of a handful of members and meets on a weekly basis. The board is accountable to the general meeting of members that takes place each month. Important investments, such as the creation of a new daughter company, are subject to agreement by the members. When a proposal is put to a vote, the partners do not quite follow the one-man one-vote rule. Instead, the number of votes that a grower has is directly related to the number of hectares he owns, up to a maximum of five hectares. The working groups report to the board on their activities.

The partners also learn from one another in the core of their business: improving the growing of tomatoes. They visit one another's greenhouses to learn the latest tricks of the trade. An obligatory excursion to one of the partners' greenhouses is held each week. A quality test of the tomatoes produced by the growers occurs on a biweekly basis, making transparent the quality scores of each grower.

Over time, the collaboration intensified. For example, not all membership obligations were instituted in the beginning. Moreover, the daughter companies were created over time and managers were hired to run the daughter companies. Because not all members agreed with all of these decisions, some left and new ones were asked to join. The number of members is maintained at between 20 and 25. New members have to meet specific criteria. They must be located in the same region, must grow a particular species of vine tomatoes, must have a similar philosophy about the direction of their company, and must be willing to be involved in the cooperative. The requirement to be located in the same region as the other growers has a long historical background. That particular region is the world's leading horticultural region. It is relatively small and culturally homogeneous, and most Prominent partners know one another informally because they are neighbors, relatives, or members of the same sports clubs. Such relationships foster trust among the members. Because the cooperative conducts important aspects of the growers' business, a high level of trust is necessary. The informal relationships among the partners ensure that this trust exists.

Based on the size of their businesses, the members give loans to the cooperative for a five-year period (or until they leave the cooperative, whichever is earlier). Any profits remain in the cooperative. A maximum of 10 percent of the profits from the daughter companies is available to hired managers of those companies as an incentive. The individual members receive profits from being a member through improvements in their knowledge, lower purchasing prices, and better sales prices.

Prominent shows a mix of trust and control elements. A number of obligations are tied to being a member. Simultaneously, partner selection, regular joint meetings, and visits to the greenhouses ensure that relationship building occurs. Trust is recognized as an important mechanism in the alliance. The conscious policy to allow only regional tomato growers to join the cooperative is an example. Over time, a slight trend has emerged to increase control. As investments in the daughter companies grow and the concept of the cooperative develops, the parties are feeling the need to strengthen the formal rules.

The high reliance on the informal elements of the Alliance Design Framework enabled the alliance to adapt to changing circumstances. The ability to manage dynamics is also fostered by the fact that internal alignment is not a challenge. The companies are small family businesses and the owners participate in the alliance themselves. As a consequence decision making is fast. A final condition that helps to manage dynamics is that exit is easy. Partners that might otherwise hold back change can leave the alliance easily.

Prominent is not the only cooperative to have emerged from the crisis in the early 1990s. Other growers set up similar initiatives, also around other crops, flowers, and potted plants. The "water bomb" disappeared as a result of these efforts. In 2005, the Dutch growers regained their position as the most important suppliers of tomatoes to the German market.

In the general assembly model, the ultimate power lies with the general meeting of the members of the alliance. Voting is a normal procedure and is used often as a mechanism to decide on issues. This model is relevant when the investments and risks of the partners are relatively similar. When they are not similar, the lead partner model may be more relevant.

The lead partner:[4] METRO's Future Store Initiative

How do you keep more than 50 partners focused on and aligned with innovation? The German METRO Group, the third largest retail chain in the world, answered that question by designing a trust-based network. After a strategy review, METRO decided that the way to differentiate its supermarket chains from competitors was to apply more technology in their stores. Because METRO is not a technology company, it asked one of its main suppliers, Intel, how to innovate. In 2001, they jointly came up with the idea to create the Future Store Initiative. This Initiative aimed to build the supermarket of the future in a real-life setting. To fill the supermarket with the latest technology, more than 50 partners were invited to contribute their ideas and technologies.

A crucial issue was the development of an RFID (radio-frequency identification) standard for supermarkets, which did not yet exist at the initiation of the Future Store Initiative in 2002. RFID chips are tags that send out a radio signal that can be used for a variety of purposes. For example, tags can be attached to a crate of Coca-Cola when it leaves the factory for delivery at a supermarket. Once the crate arrives, the radio signal can be picked up and the presence of the crate is automatically registered in the IT systems of the supermarket. This process saves handling costs and provides opportunities for optimization. For technology companies, the Future Store Initiative was an appealing idea. By developing an RFID standard, a new market could open up, enabling the Initiative to sell its technologies to the supermarket sector. In addition, the Future

Store Initiative is a real-life store; therefore, the partners showcased their technologies not in an experimental setting as they usually did, but in a supermarket where people shopped, enabling the benefits of the new technology to be shown in practice. Finally, many technology companies already focused on retailing or were evaluating that market. Joining the Future Store Initiative could help them to realize their strategy for the retail market. The strategic imperatives of the partners combined well with the value proposition of the Future Store Initiative.

RFID was not the only technology to be implemented. Partners were invited to contribute their ideas on anything that could enhance the shopping experience. Over time, the partners proposed technologies such as:

- Personal shopping assistants: the ability for a customer to email his/her shopping list to a shopping cart for display on a small screen.

- Intelligent scales: scales that automatically recognize the fruits and vegetables placed on them.

- Self-checkout: different systems for self-checkout were attempted in the store.

- Electronic advertising displays: rather than having the in-store paper advertising that displays what is being offered, electronic displays save on handling costs because manually changing all of the paper ads is not needed.

- Information terminals: an example is a wine terminal that enables shoppers to search for the wine that best matches their taste. Next, a spotlight in the ceiling shines on the shelf where the chosen bottle is located.

In December 2002, METRO selected an existing supermarket, removed everything inside, and invited the partners in the Initiative to implement their ideas. Broadly, the Initiative has six types of partners: RFID partners, trade technology partners (specializing in retail technologies), brands (producing consumer goods), IT technology and service partners, software companies, and other service providers. To accommodate the fact that some partners contributed to many projects in the Store, whereas others worked on only one project, three levels of partnership were defined: platinum, gold, and silver. At the launch of the Future Store, the Initiative had three platinum partners: Intel, SAP, and IBM.

METRO invited partners that it knew well to participate. It had relationships with some of the partners that went back decades. Moreover, many of the partners knew one another as well, leading to a web of personal relationships. When certain competencies were missing, METRO relied on the partners to bring in their best relationships, leading friends of friends to join the network. Most partners were suppliers to METRO, even though the Future Store Initiative was strictly separated from the purchasing relationship with the suppliers. METRO did not even make commitments to buy technologies from the suppliers who participated in the Future Store Initiative in the event that it decided to roll out that technology in other stores. Still, METRO was an important customer and the companies certainly did not want to disappoint it. METRO also invited partners for clearly specified roles. The major competitors in the software industry, Microsoft, Oracle, and SAP, were involved. To ensure that they did not compete directly, each was given a specific role to play that did not overlap with the role of its competitors. For example, Oracle was asked for the databases and SAP was asked for its ERP software.

The partners were asked to make a financial contribution to the project. Each partner invested some cash into a fund that was primarily used for marketing the outcomes of the Initiative. In addition to that contribution, the partners were free to decide on how much staff and resources they would make available to the project. The minimum requirement was at least one person as a point of contact. No obligation existed to contribute more. Each partner carried its own expenses. "Revenues" included learning, reputation building, and – hopefully in the future – the opening up of a new market.

Approximately 50 partners participated at the start of the Initiative. In 2013, this number had grown to more than 75. In addition to the software partners already mentioned, additional partners include well-known consumer goods producers such as Coca-Cola, Danone, and Henkel; RFID experts such as Checkpoint; retail technology vendors such as Mettler Toledo; technology providers such as Cisco, Fujitsu, IBM, and Siemens; and other service providers such as Accenture, DHL, and Visa. Some outflow of partners occurred, but overall participation grew.

Because the Future Store Initiative was meant to be a long-running project, a structure for the alliance needed to be implemented. Figure 7.2 shows the formal structure that was devised early in the project. An executive committee was created with representatives from the platinum partners. It held regular meetings and decided on marketing and communication, and on the exit and entry of partners. Within the executive committee, METRO played the leading role and had the final authority on all decisions. All partners are invited to two to three marketing committee meetings a year, at which time progress is reviewed and evaluated. Four project teams focus on the four areas

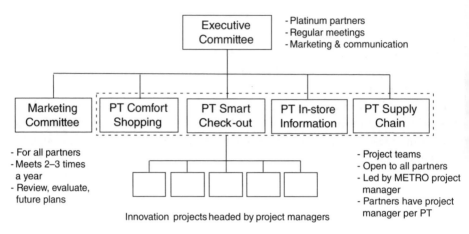

FIGURE 7.2: The structure of the Future Store Initiative in 2005

of innovation identified by the Future Store Initiative: comfort shopping, smart checkout, in-store information, and supply chain. A METRO project manager heads each project team. Next, project teams coordinate the individual innovation projects, each of which has a manager.

Legally, only a short memorandum of understanding was signed that primarily contained intentions, accompanied by a non-disclosure agreement. These documents highlight the vision behind the alliance and the required resource commitments, as previously described. No exclusivity exists within the Initiative: competitors may enter the network and existing partners may enter into similar relationships with competitors of METRO. Partner's proprietary and confidential intellectual property that is contributed to the Future Store Initiative remains as such. However, all lessons learned in the Initiative are open and may be used by the partners in any way they see fit. No end date is set for the alliance. The concept was to continue to innovate and not to make the Initiative a one-time project. In short, the Future Store Initiative was based on few formal agreements.

Why does an alliance with such limited agreements work? Partners contribute because they see the opportunity to increase the pie and break open a new market. That vision was appealing. In addition, the partners do not want to disappoint an important client. Finally, even though the resource commitments they have to make are substantial, from an innovation perspective the partners can innovate at a much lower cost than on their own. Because the partners make their own investments and have no guarantee that they will get any business out of it, no exclusivity could be demanded and IP rules have to be flexible. If METRO asked for exclusivity, the partners might have opted not to join the project. Moreover, METRO does not profit from exclusivity. Especially with regard to RFID, METRO aimed to set a standard and the more that companies use the standard, the higher the chance that the standard is widely accepted. In addition, more important than owning all innovations at one point in time is to continue to innovate. The Future Store Initiative enabled METRO to do just that.

The early phase of the project was particularly noteworthy. After the first discussions took place with Intel in 2001, in 2002 a location was selected for the Future Store in an existing supermarket. In September 2002, that store was stripped and an aggressive deadline of April 2003 was set for its reopening. To add to the pressure, German supermodel Claudia Schiffer was hired to open the store, which guaranteed major media attention. Therefore, the April deadline had to be met and all of the technology needed to work flawlessly. If not, the partners would suffer major damage to their reputation.

People working for the Initiative were required to be present on site. A fun target, good existing relationships, high time pressure, colocation on a single location, and the risk of reputation damage in front of the world press combined to create strong social capital among the participants. A Future Store community came into being. A website listing the competences of all of the individuals involved in the Future Store Initiative also enabled the right people to get connected and resulted in a culture of collaboration.

For the rest, the project was not overly structured. No detailed planning occurred upfront but deadlines were set on the go. METRO paid close attention to execution and getting the details right. In this way, the necessary structure was combined with room for self-organization, and the combination proved fruitful. METRO did not have to exercise its power much and intervened only on rare occasions. For example, it decided that IBM should be the system integrator of the project once it became clear that having a system integrator was necessary.

In 2013, the Initiative was still operational. Some technologies are being rolled out and further research is occurring, as is continuous experimentation. To keep the network vital, METRO continued to set new challenges, such as creating an RFID center to showcase technologies. The introduction of new partners into the alliance is also a way to keep the alliance fresh, to gain access to new ideas, and to signal that existing partners could not rest on their laurels. Finally, the network is kept fresh by co-opetition. The presence of competitors in the alliance stimulates companies to continue to contribute their best efforts even when they have no legal obligation to do so.

The benefits of participating in the Future Store Initiative lie in learning about technology implementation, understanding the business consequences of technology use, and gaining access to a network of specialists. The marketing impact of the Future Store was also valuable and the store opening achieved worldwide media coverage. For many partners, that alone compensated for the investments they made. METRO gained access to many new technologies that enhanced the shopping experience. The effect of the technologies on consumers is measured and many shoppers rate their satisfaction with the technologies as high.

As the structure shows, METRO is not just a first among equals but has a final say on most issues. However, METRO realizes that it cannot dictate the alliance. For the alliance to be successful, each partner must be able to realize its benefits as well. Although the formal structure gives METRO the lead, in practice METRO manages the alliance much more on a consensus basis and ensures that everyone is heard, all interests are taken into account, and communication lines are open. Such tactics help maintain the commitment of the partners.

The governance of the Future Store Initiative is almost completely based on trust, and mechanisms were built in to ensure that trust-based governance was effective, including an appealing vision that ensured intrinsic motivation of the partners to contribute, a focus on value creation, the choice of partners they trusted, and a limited number of rules. Yet, some control elements also existed. METRO is a big client for most of the partners, which acts like a stick for the partners alongside the carrot of opening up a new market. The worldwide publicity that was ensured by, among others, hiring a world-famous model to open the store also meant the risk of reputation damage if the technologies failed in front of the eyes of the assembled world press. Moreover, note how different mechanisms reinforced one another: the fun vision, the colocation, the time pressure, and risk of reputation damage together created the high performance culture of the alliance. Note that all of these relate to the informal elements of the Alliance Design Framework and that the formal structure is limited.

Given the number of partners of the Future Store Initiative, the burden of coordination may become great. In the Future Store Initiative, the burden is lessened by relying on self-organization. Because separate projects are defined that operate quite independently from one another, coordinating much across projects to ensure consistency is not needed. Still, the investments that METRO Group has to make in governing the alliance are substantial. When the burden of coordination becomes too high, an alliance support office may be useful to ensure consistency in coordination across partners and alliance projects.

The alliance support office: SkyTeam

Alliance support offices make sense when the number of partners in an alliance grows. Two varieties of support offices exist. One is an alliance support office that is completely operational and that supports the implementation of the decisions that partners agreed to. The institution is primarily occupied with carrying out the decisions made by the partners. In the second variety, the alliance support office plays an active role in decision making and may even take the lead in the alliance. The office has the power to enforce implementation of alliance policies in individual alliance partners. In both varieties, the alliance support office may also act as a broker among partners, attempting to reconcile differences and act as a go-between.

The first type of alliance support office is used by the large airline alliances of SkyTeam, Star Alliance, and oneworld (see Table 7.1 for details about these alliances). The alliance structure was chosen over mergers for a variety of reasons. For example, in most cases, the level of integration required to achieve the benefits of collaboration does not require more far-reaching integration through mergers or acquisitions. In addition, mergers between airlines in different countries face various legal obstacles. Sometimes these obstacles are

TABLE 7.1: Three airline alliances compared (2012)[5]

	Star Alliance	SkyTeam	oneworld
Founding year	1997	2000	1999
Number of members	27, including Lufthansa, Singapore Airlines, United Airlines	17, including Air France/KLM, Delta, Alitalia	12, including American Airlines, British Airways, Japan Airlines
Passengers per year (in millions)	679	531	324
Destination countries	193	178	149

anti-trust related, sometimes governments limit the acquisition of national carriers by foreign companies, and sometimes treaties between countries regarding the use of airspace make such mergers legally complex. The three main alliances circumvent these problems.

Airline alliances were primarily initiated to combine networks through code sharing and to combine frequent flyer programs, allowing passengers to "earn and burn" their frequent flier miles across the alliance partners. This tactic enables an airline to offer more destinations to its passengers. To achieve this goal, airlines primarily seek to collaborate with complementary airlines that fly different destinations rather than with direct competitors that fly the same routes. This complementarity results in a lower level of integration in these alliances than in the Air France/KLM, Delta, Alitalia alliance. However, more recently with alliances having their route networks in place, they have started to focus on realizing more customer benefits, which requires closer collaboration around service levels, transfer processes, and the like.

This development also has implications for the governance of the alliances. For a long time, SkyTeam had no centralized office; however, coordination needed to increase given the increase in membership and greater focus on customer benefits. Now, the central SkyTeam office has approximately 30 employees that work with the members in different working groups to align the partners. Working groups focus on promotion, product and service, and operational processes. Pricing and optimal use of capacity are outside the scope of the alliance because they have immediate anti-trust implications.

Figure 7.3 presents the structure of the SkyTeam alliance. The strategic decisions in SkyTeam are made by the Governing Board, which consists of the CEOs of the member airlines. They decide on the activities that require priority and have the final say on new members joining the alliance. The SkyTeam's centralized office has a managing director who, together with his management team, is responsible for implementing the strategic plan as decided on by the Governing Board. Next to this operational task, the managing director also develops proposals to put to the Governing Board.

The main functions of the centralized office are:

- Preparing the decision making, in other words, developing proposals with the members about projects to be put to the Governing Board;
- Facilitating implementation of the decisions made; and

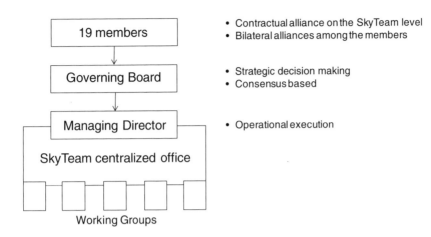

FIGURE 7.3: SkyTeam governance structure in 2013

- Executing some operational tasks, such as acting as a spokesperson for the alliance and taking care of advertising.

To the greatest degree possible, decision making by the Governing Board is done by consensus. Because of the differences in strategy and maturity of the partners, achieving consensus on all issues is not always possible. Therefore, if consensus cannot be reached, a smaller group of partners may still decide to implement a certain decision. In that case, the others are not obliged to follow. Hence, integration occurs at different speeds to allow for company differences. This is a mechanism to deal with dynamics in the alliance.

New members are obligated to enter into bilateral alliances with the other partners. These alliances provide the backbone for implementing the SkyTeam policies. SkyTeam has many basic requirements regarding IT, service levels, code sharing, use of airport lounges, safety, and frequent flyer programs. Working groups ensure consistent implementation of these requirements across the members. They consist of members of the centralized office and representatives from the member airlines and play an important part in ensuring internal alignment of the partner organizations with the alliance. To implement all of the requirements usually takes approximately 1.5 years. Because of these investments, exit from the alliance can be expensive, especially because members also have to pay an exit fee.

The other two airline alliances have a similar structure. The oneworld alliance has a management company and a Governing Board consisting of the CEOs of each of the member airlines. The chairmanship of the Governing Board rotates annually. The Star Alliance structure is somewhat different.[6] Its Chief Executive Board guides the strategic decision making, and the alliance has one layer more than the other two alliances. The Alliance Management Board, consisting of the alliance managers of the member airlines, acts as the Supervisory Board to the Star Alliance GmbH, the centralized office of the Star Alliance. This office coordinates, monitors compliance to standards, stimulates the exchange of best practices among the members, and develops alliance products and services. Sounding boards and advisory groups fulfill similar functions as the SkyTeam alliance working groups. The Star Alliance has approximately 75 standards in different areas that are enforced across all members to facilitate collaboration.

In terms of control and trust, the previous description of the role of alliance support offices in the three airline alliances shows that their focus is clearly on control. They emphasize the formal elements of the Alliance Development Framework over the informal ones. However, this control is not strategic but primarily operational. To the extent that these offices take on more of the decision making and are able to enforce alliance policies, their role becomes more strategic. The alliance offices in the airline business have a pure coordination role, which makes them different from joint ventures that also have an operational task to produce something or deliver a commercial service.

The multi-partner joint venture: the Holst Centre

The Holst Centre, a research center in which companies and universities share common infrastructure for the development of flexible electronics and sensors, uses the joint venture model. Partners include Agfa, ASML, Bayer, DuPont, Philips, Solvay, Sony, Fujitsu, and many more. The reason behind this joint venture is scale economies. By sharing the physical infrastructure as well as some basic research projects, the partners are able to lower their cost of innovation compared with a situation in which they would do everything in house. In this case, self-coordination is not a feasible option. To optimally profit from the economies of scale, centralization is required.

Multi-partner joint ventures do not differ much from bilateral joint ventures, as discussed in Chapter 6 and not repeated here. Naturally, they face the more challenging task of keeping many partners satisfied that may have conflicting goals. The Holst Centre solves this challenge by carefully balancing the partners' common and private benefits by conducting research that benefits all partners and setting up projects that may benefit only one or a subset of part-

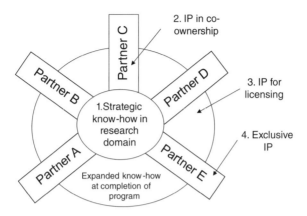

FIGURE 7.4: IP structure Holst Centre[7]

ners. This balance becomes clear in Holst's IP (intellectual property) policies, which reflect a continuum from jointly owned to individually owned IP.

The Holst Centre distinguishes different types of IP, each with its own ownership policy. Figure 7.4 shows the different flavors. First and not shown in the figure is background IP that partners contribute: this IP is owned by the contributing partner. Second, a joint research program delivers IP that represents strategic knowledge in the research domain. Partners pay an entrance fee to participate in the Holst Centre, which gives them a non-exclusive license on this IP. All partners receive exploitation rights, but they do not own the IP. The next step is when partners participate in specific research programs carried out jointly by the Holst Centre and one or more partners. The Holst Centre and the partner(s) that collaborated on it co-own this IP, which is licensed to the other partners. IP for licensing refers to IP that may be created by Holst itself or may be generated by the partners but is of little interest to them. This IP is not co-owned and can be licensed by Holst to third parties.

Finally, exclusive IP is generated in a research program exclusive for one partner. The Holst Centre limits this type of research to special circumstances. It only occurs when other partners agree and one of the following three situations occurs: 1. a partner must bring in own IP to create the new IP and it cannot create this new IP itself; 2. a small- or medium-sized company is involved and part of the IP created by the collaboration can be brought into the strategic know-how in the research domain; 3. a spin-off is created from IP that is not used by the partners, and the spin-off then receives ownership of or an exclusive license to the IP.

Assigning various property rights to partners is an important part of the deal structuring of alliances. Because it helps set the incentives that the partners have to collaborate, such assignments affect governance. The more aligned the property rights are with the alliance's and the partner's strategic imperatives, the easier governing the alliance becomes, making it clearly a control procedure. In fact, the Holst Centre relies more on control than on trust. The lesson from the Holst Centre in relation to multi-partner alliances is that to accommodate different interests, a continuum of projects can be created, each with different levels of participation from partners. This creates flexibility and enables the alliance to cope with dynamics. In addition this flexibility makes it easier for a larger number of partners to align with the alliance, because they can choose which participation level is most appropriate to them.

When to use different multi-partner alliance models

"The more the merrier" is not a saying that applies to alliances. The management of multi-partner alliances is challenging. The cases discussed in this chapter show a number of general features of multi-partner alliances:

- Consensus seeking. Some form of democracy or consensus is at work, even when the alliance has a lead partner or strong central joint venture management. In the end, the lead partner also depends on the commitment of others to achieve his goal. Enlightened self-interest ensures that the lead partner applies unilateral decision making with caution.

- Common core. Minimum standards for partners to join are set, and partners are free to move beyond those standards. Prominent has rules and procedures for growing tomatoes that everyone must meet, but the partners are not obligated to implement the latest lessons learned in the experimental greenhouses.

- Accommodation of differences. Different speeds and levels of contribution accommodate differences among the partners. In the Future Store Initiative, some partners contribute significantly and become platinum partners; others contribute less and become silver partners. In SkyTeam, all members must meet minimum conditions, but some get there faster than others. The Holst Centre defined different levels of participation.

- Limited scope. In terms of development over time, most multi-partner alliances start with a limited number of projects. Over time, the relationships may broaden or deepen.

TABLE 7.2: Different multi-partner structures compared

	General assembly	Lead partner	Alliance support office	Joint venture
Decision making	Alliance partners vote	Consensus-oriented lead partner	Alliance partners vote	Joint venture managers, coordinating with their board
Task coordination	Low	Low	High	High
Self-coordination	High	High	Medium	Low
Division of risk	Equal	Unequal	Equal	Equal
Accountable entity	Partners	Partners	Partners with some targets for the support office	Alliance

- Operational focus. Operationally, alliances have either tight control (METRO, SkyTeam) or high trust (Prominent) to prevent the partners from engaging in opportunistic behavior.

- Exit and entry. The collaboration is not sensitive to changes in the composition of its membership. If one member leaves, the alliance should not collapse. Of course, the exception is when the partner leaving is the lead partner.

The cases reveal a number of differences between the forms of multi-partner alliances (see Table 7.2). The core difference lies in the decision-making model used. The dynamics of decision making are quite different and range from voting to consensus to lead partner decision making. The cases reveal a number of underlying patterns that explain why the decision-making mechanisms differ.

The general assembly model is applied when the required task coordination is low, which is the case when alliance projects do not need to be coordinated and partners do not have to follow all of the rules of the alliance. In the Prominent case, the separate projects executed could primarily function on a standalone basis and the partners only had to follow the basic growing requirements. Compared with SkyTeam, in which all partners need to implement all rules consistently, the demands on coordination are lower in Prominent. In the Holst Centre, the coordination of joint research and the physical infrastructure is a significant task that requires the joint venture structure.

The ability of partners to coordinate among themselves also determines the choice of form. The better the partners know each other, the higher the social capital and the larger the number of people having direct access to one another's organizations, the more self-coordination is facilitated. If the level of self-coordination is medium or low, an alliance support office or joint venture is necessary.

The choice for a lead partner is primarily related to the presence of one party that commits more resources to the alliance and, therefore, faces greater risk. Such a partner that is trusted by other partners may reasonably become the lead. A final issue in determining the choice of form is the optimal level of accountability. A joint venture is a sensible option when the use of a jointly owned asset needs to be optimized. In that case, the joint venture is not only a vehicle that legally owns the asset, but is also accountable for putting it to good use. In the general assembly model and the lead partner model, no separate accountable entity exists. In the alliance support office model, most of the accountability lies with the individual partners. The alliance support office only has to account for efficiently delivering its services, and targets may be defined to measure the office's efficiency.

Notes

1 De Rochemont, M. 2010. *Opening up for innovation: the antecedents of multi partner alliance performance*, PhD thesis, Eindhoven, Eindhoven University of Technology.
2 Dyer, J.H. and K. Nobeoka. 2000. Creating and managing a high-performance knowledge-sharing network: the Toyota case, *Strategic Management Journal*, 21, 345–367; Garcia-Canal, E., A. Valdés-Llaneza and A. Ariño. 2003. Effectiveness of dyadic and multi-party joint ventures, *Organization Studies*, 24, 5, 743–770; Gomes-Casseres, B. and J. Bamford. 2001. The corporation is dead . . . Long live the constellation!, in: A.P. de Man, G.M. Duysters and A. Vasudevan (eds.), *The Allianced Enterprise*, Singapore, Imperial College Press, 31–40.
3 This list combines insights from: Gomes-Casseres, B. and J. Bamford. 2001. The corporation is dead . . . Long live the constellation!, in: A.P. de Man, G.M. Duysters and A. Vasudevan (eds.), *The Allianced Enterprise*, Singapore, Imperial College Press, 31–40; Provan, K.G. and P. Kenis. 2007. Modes of network governance: structure, management, and effectiveness, *Journal of Public Administration Research and Theory*, 18, 229–252; Parkhe, A. 2001. A culture of cooperation? Not yet, in: A.P. de Man, G.M. Duysters and A. Vasudevan (eds.), *The Allianced Enterprise*, Singapore, Imperial College Press, 119–122.
4 Graczewski, T. and A.P. de Man. 2006. *Partnering for the Future: The Case of the METRO Group Future Store Initiative*, white paper Eindhoven, Eindhoven University of Technology.
5 Retrieved from www.staralliance.com, www.SkyTeam.com, www.oneworld.com, in June 2012.

6   Findeisen, H. 2009. *Taking Flight: How Star Alliance is helping airline alliances navigate today's challenging business environment*, Presentation at the Association of Strategic Alliance Professionals Summit, Fort Lauderdale, USA, February 9–12; Lavietes, J. 2011. Star Alliance continues to Soar, *Strategic Alliance Magazine*, Q4, 30–33.
7   Source: www.holstcentre.com.

CHAPTER **8**

Managing the dynamics: Mutual adjustment and continuous negotiation

Because alliances are unstable, their design must change over time. Those changes may be small, minor, and incremental, or major restructurings. Sometimes the changes are planned, and, at other times, unexpected changes force partners to redesign their alliance. This chapter discusses the sources of change, how to deal with incremental change, how to identify the need for radical change, and the ways to build change mechanisms into the alliance at the outset. In doing so, it fills in the element of managing the dynamics in the Alliance Design Framework.

Research provides some insights into the frequency of change. A study into changes in the governance of alliances found that, among the 145 alliances analyzed, 44 percent underwent changes in the governance structure.[1] These modifications included changes in the contract, changes in the governance board, and the introduction of new formal monitoring systems in alliances. Therefore, although only these three elements were measured, a substantial number of alliances experienced adaptations post-formation. This study only focused on changes in the formal alliance structure that may occur after renegotiation of the alliance.[2] Other research indicates that the informal structure may change as well. When trust is built between partners, the use of formal governance mechanisms tends to decline.[3] A rarer occurrence is an alliance that turns into a merger or an acquisition. In general, few alliances lead to mergers

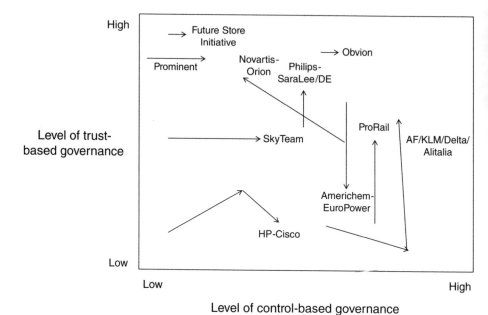

FIGURE 8.1: Development of alliance designs

or acquisitions, with the possible exception of joint ventures that are often acquired by one of the partners. Such an acquisition event is rare, particularly in technology alliances. Technology alliances lead to mergers or acquisitions in only 2.6 percent of the cases.[4]

Figure 8.1 shows how the cases discussed in the previous chapters developed over time regarding their balance between control and trust. Many changes in the alliances occurred:

- In ProRail alliances, the main developments relate to scope changes. These changes occur regularly, particularly during the early phases of ProRail's alliances.

- The Senseo alliance of Philips and Sara Lee/DE expanded once the market grew. The scope of the alliance grew from just packaged coffee to other beverages, such as packaged tea. The most recent addition is its innovative series of coffeemakers based on coffee beans. In addition, this alliance turned mutual adaptation into an art. The partners dealt with many changes without having to review the formal structure for a long time.

- The Novartis–Orion alliance followed a lifecycle based on the processes specific to the pharmaceutical industry. It started with an emphasis on development, adding marketing and winding down the activities once the drugs got off patent. In addition, the structure became more informal once trust was established.

- Initially, HP and Cisco relied almost completely on their alliance managers and held two weekly calls to review the pipeline. They then built a full-fledged and effective governance structure including CEO-level involvement until both companies changed their strategies to such an extent that they ended up in each other's territory.

- The Air France/KLM–Delta–Alitalia alliance already went through various iterations when it was the KLM–Northwest alliance. After its start, it added a network and a passenger group, and then a joint venture operating committee. Finally, the alliance changed to an Enhanced Alliance Agreement after trust reached a low point with the companies suing each other. Trust was rebuilt and a series of mergers and takeovers required the partners to adapt the alliance.

- Americhem and EuroPower faced changes in the business environment and in the strategy at Americhem. They restructured the financial deal around the alliance, but in the end had to dissolve it.

- Obvion was a stable alliance until the financial crisis changed the situation and Rabobank acquired it.

- SkyTeam created a separate office to oversee and execute the increasingly complex arrangements between its members. Entry of new members over time led to repeated changes in the alliance.

- Prominent created a number of limited companies to experiment with innovation. Some partners left when they found that the alliance rules became too strict. The alliance continues to broaden its scope.

- The Future Store Initiative was a stable structure that seemed designed to handle dynamics. The most relevant changes included defining separate swim lanes for the IT partner to avoid conflicts arising between them, and the entry and exit of partners.

Sources of dynamics

As the cases show, different sources of dynamics exist in alliances. The first type of source is internal. Companies may change their strategies, organizational structures, alliance managers, CEOs, and operating procedures. Each of these may affect the status quo of the alliance in a positive or negative manner. Sometimes, changing faces may bring renewed vitality to an alliance; alternatively, the new faces may not be able to establish a healthy working relationship with one another. Any change needs to be carefully monitored and the partner making the change should consider its effect on the alliance. Americhem's disinvestment of part of its business was a strategic move that had a substantial negative effect on the revenue model of the joint venture with EuroPower.

Second, certain aspects of the relationship between the partners may change. Most importantly, the alliance itself may become a success or a failure. When an alliance is highly successful, as with the KLM–Northwest relationship, a more extensive alliance design may be necessary.[5] A less successful alliance may require less oversight or may be disbanded altogether. When partners get to know each other, the level of trust grows, information and knowledge sharing may increase, and, consequently, the partners may identify new areas of collaboration. This change may require a new alliance structure and, sometimes, new control elements to keep track of a variety of alliance-related initiatives. In contrast, increasing trust may also mean loosening control when partners deem it no longer necessary to review each particular action in the alliance. The Novartis–Orion case illustrates this situation.

Some alliance types are more susceptible to change than others. For alliances with a broader scope, a less clear division of labor, higher relevance for the partners, and a significant opportunity to broaden its scope, the chances increase that they will undergo one or more redesigns during their lifespan.[6] In addition, some tension is inherent in alliances that, if not managed, may undermine alliance stability. The sources of such tension include:[7]

- Competition versus cooperation. Most alliance partners experience the simultaneous necessity of collaboration and competing for revenues. When partners are direct competitors in some areas as in the HP–Cisco alliance, this tension becomes very explicit. In non-competitive relationships, this tension also exists because each partner competes for a share of the benefits.

- Horizontal versus vertical. Each partner has its own vertical and often rigid structures that need to be adhered to, whether accounting guidelines, corporate policies, or cultural routines. These vertical structures can weigh down an alliance and make it either too complex or too inflexible. When sufficient counterweights are lacking, the alliance will become unstable. The HP–Cisco alliance was able to tackle this issue by giving alliance managers a prominent place in the collaboration process and by ensuring CEO support. In the Senseo alliance, Philips dealt with this tension by putting a business unit manager in charge who also had sufficient mandate to steer the alliance.

- Short versus long term. Partners often have different time horizons and, therefore, different views on what to invest. In the Novartis–Orion alliance, for Orion the development of a smaller tablet for their Alzheimer drug was important, whereas Novartis came to another conclusion. When partners believe that an alliance will be around for a long time, entirely different possibilities exist than when they believe its lifespan will be short. Companies will usually have different views on the lifespan.

- Dependence versus independence. The success of an alliance depends on the autonomy of the partners and their collaboration. Because the partners are independent, they bring different capabilities to the table, which are a precondition for the alliance to create value. Simultaneously, the partners' independence needs to be reined in to bridge the gap between them and to make collaboration possible. The Senseo alliance managed this situation well by defining the interfaces between the partners, but left them to be autonomous in their own specializations. In contrast, SkyTeam, Star Alliance, and oneworld created a central office to promote the interests of the alliance in each partner.

The third category of causes of dynamics is external changes. Social, political, legal, economic, and technological changes are continuous. A legal change was at the basis of the restructuring of the Americhem–EuroPower alliance after the liberalization of the European energy market. New technologies forced HP and Cisco to change their individual strategies, which affected their alliance. The Prominent alliance found its reason for existence in the decline in demand in Germany for Dutch tomatoes.

The core point of internal, relational, and external change is that they may occur anytime and anywhere. Therefore, managers need to spot the need for change and must understand the techniques to manage change. The next sections look at dealing with incremental change and, subsequently, discuss spotting the need for radical change and how to go about such change. Finally, elements are discussed that can be built into an alliance from day one to manage change.

Incremental change

Many of the changes that alliances experience can be addressed on a daily basis without major restructuring or contract revisions. A key element to understand regarding alliances is that, no matter how good their design, they always require:

- Mutual adaptation: the ability of partners to accommodate each other's wishes and align them with the business environment;

- Continuous negotiation: the process through which partners give and take to deal with the dynamics of the alliance.

A formal alliance design is of very little value if the partners are not prepared to mutually adapt and adjust their original agreement. Mutual adaptation and continuous negotiations bring an alliance to life and help it manage change. No structural elements exist to ensure that these two elements occur. Instead, they require an alliance-friendly attitude and an understanding of what really makes or breaks alliances. The twin processes of mutual adaptation and continuous negotiations are realized through various influencing tactics that companies employ to get their partner to go along with a proposed change. Such tactics include rational persuasion, making an inspirational appeal, consultation of individuals, ingratiation, exchanging favors, making a personal appeal, coalition building, emphasizing the legitimacy of a request, and putting pressure on a person.[8] Applying them in the right dose at the right time is a management skill that an alliance manager must possess.

The core task of many alliance managers can be described as influencing without power, which requires diplomatic skills to be effective. The application of various influencing tactics in the right way can greatly extend an alliance manager's reach in his own organization and in that of his or her partner. Correct use of influencing makes an alliance manager effective in dealing with incremental change.

Radical change

In the majority of alliances, a time comes when incremental changes to the structure are no longer sufficient to remain successful and the tactics for managing incremental change no longer suffice. Sometimes the signs that radical change is needed are easy to recognize, such as the following:

- The financial results for the alliance or the partners become negative. In the Americhem–EuroPower relationship, the changes in market conditions made the initial agreement on the cost/benefit sharing obsolete, which initiated the discussions on changing the deal.

- The alliance enters a different phase of the lifecycle. The Novartis–Orion case is exemplary for many pharmaceutical alliances. It follows a cycle from development to marketing to winding down after patent expiration. When lifecycle changes are as clear as that, the alliance also clearly needs to restructure to meet the requirements of each phase.

- Sudden external changes either undermine the alliance or present it with new opportunities. The anti-trust authorities' change in attitude toward airline alliances opened up new avenues for the KLM–Northwest alliance.

- Companies that execute a regular alliance health check will notice a decline in their scores, alerting them to the fact that something needs to change.

When the case for change is less clear, the questions in Table 8.1 may help indicate whether a structural change is necessary. When too many questions are answered with yes, a more thorough inquiry into why is necessary. This inquiry may give rise to a complete alliance redesign that calls for revisiting all elements of the Alliance Design Framework.

As the case studies in this book show, such a redesign is a perfectly normal process in alliances because they need to adapt to changing circumstances. The starting point for the redesign should always be a diagnosis of the existing situation through an alliance health check.[9] Joint discussion of the results will clarify the real issues. After clarifying the issues, the partners need to discuss the way forward. Of course, a core question is whether the alliance's value proposition is still strong enough and, if not, whether it can be changed in such a way to make the value proposition attractive again for clients and for the alliance partners. This discussion may lead to the following outcomes:

- The value proposition may still be strong, but additional investments may be needed to realize it, the alliance design is flawed, or the alliance staff are not capable of realizing the goals.

- The value proposition has to be renewed; consequently, the alliance design needs to be reviewed as well.

- The value proposition may be weaker than originally thought. This situation may require decreasing investments or disbandment. The assets may be

TABLE 8.1: Thirty questions that may indicate the necessity of alliance redesign

Strategic imperatives
- Has the alliance stopped meeting its targets?
- Does the alliance experience mission creep (in other words, the goals slowly changed, new goals were added, or people lost sight of the goals)?
- Has the scope of the alliance become broader or narrower than stipulated in the contract?
- Have changes in the market made the alliance value proposition less attractive for clients?

Formal structure
- Has the number of escalated issues increased substantially in the past year?
- Has decision making slowed down?
- Have decisions deteriorated in quality?
- Does the alliance experience team creep (in other words, an increasing number of teams and working groups have emerged)?
- Has the balance in the risk sharing shifted between the partners?
- Are progress reports late or incomplete, or do they contain irrelevant information?
- Is there disagreement over planning in the alliance?
- Are there complaints about being left out of the decision-making process?
- Have initiatives from working groups dried up?
- Has it become unclear who is allowed to decide what in the alliance?
- Has attendance at governance meetings fallen?

Informal structure
- Has informal communication on one of the levels of the alliance decreased substantially in the past year?
- Have formal elements received greater emphasis at the neglect of informal elements?
- Have incidents of miscommunication increased?
- Have people started to talk about the partner in a negative manner?
- Have key alliance staff members changed without onboarding them properly?
- Has "us versus them" thinking increased?
- Does one of the partners believe that the other holds back information?
- Do minor issues get too much attention?
- Have people started to refer to the contract more than they used to?
- Is the code of conduct no longer followed?

Internal alignment
- Has the importance of the alliance for one of the partners changed?
- Has executive sponsorship in the alliance partners become invisible?
- Does one of the partners experience difficulty in getting support for the alliance in its business units?
- Has one of the partners become more internally oriented?
- Has one of the partners changed its incentive system for those working in the alliance?

shared by the partners or acquired by one of them depending on the exit agreements developed at the alliance's initiation.

In the first two cases, an alliance redesign is called for. All elements from Chapter 2 need to be reviewed to develop a new design. A good tactic is to bring new faces into the alliance when redesigning it. New faces bring new ideas and are less prone to alliance fatigue, and the simple presence of new people may be a nice infusion for group dynamics. After completing the redesign, a relaunch will help bring onboard all relevant staff.

Organizing for dynamics

Regardless of whether change is radical or incremental, anticipating it and being proactive is always better than being reactive. The cases highlight some elements that organizations may incorporate into their alliance design to ensure that change runs smoothly when it needs to happen. Table 8.2 presents these mechanisms. Clear decision-making structures are a first element. In the ProRail alliances, changes in the scope are expected. The process for initiating and getting such changes approved are made clear from the outset to facilitate change.

A redesign process usually needs to involve senior management because it tends to require strategic input and the mandate to change contracts and reassign resources. In the latest evolution of the Delta–Air France/KLM–Alitalia alliance, the relationship to top management is explicitly embedded in the structure because the alliance and its operating environment are dynamic. Because the chance is high that important changes have to be made, CEO involvement was ensured. The next mechanism that facilitates change, the role of joint evaluation to signal the need for change, was already discussed previously, as was the role of behavioral elements such as a spirit of mutual adjustment.[10] If one of the partners believes that contracts are set in stone for the entire lifetime of an alliance, change is unlikely to go smoothly.

In some cases, anticipating dynamics may be possible. For example, when the phases of an alliance lifecycle are predictable, partners may already agree in the beginning of the alliance to a redesign when certain milestones are passed

TABLE 8.2: Mechanisms for guiding alliance change

- Clear decision-making structure to approve radical change
- Involvement/access to senior management to drive radical change
- Use joint evaluation to discuss radical change on a regular basis
- Develop a spirit of mutual adjustment
- Develop a structural development model
- Ensure the right alliance manager role

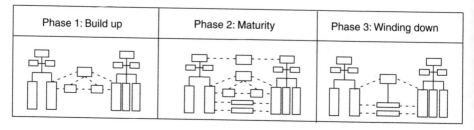

FIGURE 8.2: Structural development model (indicative)

or targets are met. This situation clearly applied in the Novartis–Orion alliance. The natural lifecycle of a drug dictates changes in the alliance design over time.

One method for anticipating dynamics is to develop a structural development model that shows how the alliance structure will change over time. Figure 8.2 provides a simple example. In the early phases of the partnership depicted in the model, a governance committee of middle managers oversees the work of two working groups that lay the foundation for the alliance. In the maturity phase, CEO-level contact and operational teams are added to the structure. In the final phase of termination, the governance committee directly oversees the work of some operational teams. For each phase, companies can agree on the indicators that signal that the alliance needs to transition to the next phase.

Figure 8.2 is a rather crude and high-level representation of a structural development model, but even such a high-level model is valuable. It directs the partners' attention to one of the main challenges of managing alliances: dealing with dynamics. Having such a model in place also facilitates discussions about changes in the alliance. Such a model signals to all involved that change is necessary and bound to happen. It lowers the barriers to discussing change. Even when the structures envisioned are not the precise structures that are implemented later, discussing the evolution beforehand is still valuable.

Finally, alliance managers play a crucial role in changing alliances. They may fulfill one or more of the following roles in an alliance change management process:

- Signal/initiate change: Alliance managers identify the need for change and develop proposals to change an alliance.

- Renegotiate/redesign: Alliance managers take the lead in renegotiating the alliance and developing the alliance design.

- Implement change: Alliance managers ensure that the changes to which the partners agree are implemented.

- Support change: Alliance managers prepare meetings, ensure that they are organized, and lend a helping hand where necessary.

In practice, different combinations of these roles exist. In the Novartis–Orion alliance, the alliance managers have broad and encompassing roles. They also lead the alliance change process. Before the new governance structure was implemented in the HP–Cisco alliance, the alliance manager's role primarily revolved around implementing and managing the alliance on a daily basis. In that case, other people picked up the remaining roles previously mentioned. In Air France/KLM and SkyTeam, the alliance manager has a support role, making his role in a change process primarily that of a facilitator. Each of these models has its benefits and challenges, as listed in Table 8.3. Based on the cases, a distinction is made between three different levels of roles for the alliance manager: broad (the alliance manager fulfills all roles), medium (the alliance manager fulfills two or three roles, but not the renegotiate/redesign role), and narrow (the alliance manager fulfills only the support role). The most effective combination depends on how the alliance manager's role is embedded in the overall alliance design. The support role is extremely useful in the Air France/KLM alliance, but would have been insufficient in the ProRail or the Senseo alliance. Alliance size also plays a role. Larger alliances may require splitting the roles across various functions because one individual cannot fulfill all of them. Creating the right roles is important in dealing with change.

Mutual adjustment and continuous negotiation

More important than getting the alliance design correct at the start is the ability to adapt it to changing circumstances. Because changes affect partners differently, no guarantee exists that change will be realized. This chapter identified mechanisms to help lower the risk that a redesign fails. In connection, the cases showed two of the most important characteristics of alliances: mutual adjustment and continuous negotiation. Mutual adjustment is the willingness of all partners in an alliance to adapt to another partner's needs, which requires:

- an understanding of the fact that alliances are inherently dynamic,

- that these dynamics cannot be captured in the contract,

- that, therefore, contracts are incomplete,

TABLE 8.3: Different roles for alliance managers in the change process

Level of involvement of alliance manager	Advantage	Disadvantage	Example
Broad: alliance manager leads the entire change	Planning and execution in one place Decisions are made by persons most knowledgeable about the alliance: meets the subsidiarity principle	Alliance manager may not be objective about the alliance: no fresh pair of eyes Higher risk that alliance manager gets damaged in the change process, making collaboration at a later stage more difficult	Novartis–Orion All alliances in which the alliance manager has contract management and/or business responsibility Small alliances in which splitting roles does not make sense
Medium: alliance manager fulfills all roles in the change process but does not lead in the renegotiate/redesign role	Alliance manager has more neutrality but is well positioned to influence the outcome Lower risk that alliance manager is damaged in the change process	Alliance manager's knowledge of practice may not be sufficiently used Alliance manager has to implement what others decided	HP–Cisco All alliances in which an alliance manager is primarily an influencer and implementer
Narrow: alliance manager has a support role	Alliance manager can represent the interest of the alliance; is relatively neutral Alliance manager can act as a go-between; diplomat Alliance manager can signal the need to change because he is a relative outsider	Alliance manager has no mandate, thus negotiations need to go through the hierarchy	KLM–NWA All alliances in which an alliance manager has a support role Large alliances in which one individual cannot do all the work required

- and that, consequently, partners need to give and take to make an alliance a success.

The process of giving and taking is not a one-time event; instead, it occurs regularly during the lifetime of an alliance. Each incident of giving and taking forms a negotiation process. Sometimes that process is very formal and involves lawyers and CEOs. At other times, the negotiation process may involve informal problem solving and subtle influencing. In every alliance, mutual adjustment and continuous negotiation are key mechanisms to keeping the alliance alive.

Notes

1   Reuer, J.J., M. Zollo and H. Singh. 2002. Post-formation dynamics in strategic alliances, *Strategic Management Journal*, 23, 135–151.
2   Ariño, A. and J. De la Torre. 1998. Learning from failure: towards an evolutionary model of collaborative ventures, *Organization Science*, 9, 3, 306–325.
3   Gulati, R. 1995. Social structure and alliance formation patterns: a longitudinal analysis, *Administrative Science Quarterly*, 40, 619; Inkpen, A.C. and S.C. Currall. 2004. The coevolution of trust, control, and learning in joint ventures, *Organization Science*, 15, 5, 586–599.
4   Hagedoorn, J. and B. Sadowski. 1999. The transition from strategic technology alliances to mergers and acquisitions: an exploratory study, *Journal of Management Studies*, 36, 1, 87–107.
5   Bamford, J., B. Gomes-Casseres and M.S. Robinson. 2003. *Mastering Alliance Strategy*, San Francisco, Jossey-Bass.
6   Reuer, J. and M. Zollo. 2000. Managing governance adaptations in strategic alliances, *European Management Journal*, 18, 2, 164–172.
7   The next discussion is partly based on Das, T.K. and B.S. Teng. 2000. Instabilities of strategic alliances: an internal tensions perspective, *Organization Science*, 11, 1, 77–101 and De Rond, M. and H. Bouchikhi. 2004. On the dialectics of strategic alliances, *Organization Science*, 15, 1, 56–69.
8   Yukl, G. and J.B. Tracey. 1992. Consequences of influence tactics used with subordinates, peers, and the boss, *Journal of Applied Psychology*, 77, 4, 525–535.
9   De Man, A.P., M. Nevin and N. Roijakkers. 2011. Turning experience into alliance capability: alliance evaluation in Rolls Royce, in: T.K. Das (ed.), *Strategic Alliances in a Globalizing World*, Charlotte (NC), Information Age Publishing, 117–138; Futrell, D., M. Slugay and C.H. Stephens. 2001. Becoming a premier partner: measuring, managing and changing partner capabilities at Eli Lilly and company, *Journal of Commercial Biotechnology*, 8, 1, 5–13.
10 Mintzberg, H. 1983. *Structure in Fives*, Englewood Cliffs, NJ, Prentice Hall.

CHAPTER **9**

Designing and implementing strategic alliances: Art, science, and craft

Developing a solid alliance design is an art, a science, and a craft. It is an art because it requires creativity and because each alliance is a unique creation: no two alliances are the same. It is a science because getting it right requires knowledge about proven recipes. It is a craft because organizations get better at combining art and science when their experience with alliances increases. Alliances are multi-faceted organizational structures and their design is not a matter of following clearly specified rules that – when applied correctly – lead to a robust design. The process requires creativity, knowledge, and judgment. This chapter outlines some guidelines for designing alliances by describing seven steps in the design process (see Figure 9.1). In practice, these steps are not always taken consecutively because insights gained in a later step may lead organizations to reconsider earlier steps. However, the guideline presented ensures that all elements that should be covered in the design process are addressed.

Strategic background

Before the actual design of the alliance can start, the strategic background should be as clear as possible (see Chapter 2). Because strategy forms the point

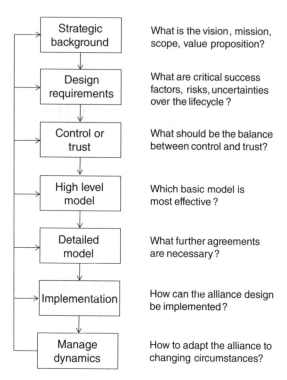

FIGURE 9.1: The alliance design process

of departure for the entire design process, it merits quite some attention. If one step is to be done correctly, it is clarifying the strategic imperatives. The mission, vision, value proposition, and scope of the alliance should be addressed. Summarizing them on a one pager and having that at hand during the rest of the design process is useful to help keep the focus on the why of the alliance and to prevent organizations from getting lost in the details.

The main thrust of the strategic background may be easy to agree on. However, clarifying all of the issues is difficult and may be time consuming. In the remainder of the design process, questions will arise that provide further details on the strategic imperatives. For example, during the process, scope may need to be defined more narrowly or broadly. Therefore, revisiting the strategic background on a regular basis is useful.

In this step, describing the partner contributions and benefits is also helpful. The division of labor in the alliance defines who executes what activities and who brings in what resources. Finally, the benefits each partner seeks need to be defined. Discussing these topics early on clarifies the relevant business processes of the alliance and keeps the focus on concrete issues.

Design requirements

Once the strategic background is clear, the prospective partners need to clarify the key elements that the design needs to address. Because many elements may require attention, the task is to identify the most important ones for the design to address. Three questions need to be answered to develop a set of design requirements that help to realize the aims of alliance design as defined in Figure 2.1:

- What critical success factors need to be filled in to ensure value creation? The alliance design must facilitate that these factors are met. Any obstacles to realizing the critical success factors must be identified to enable the design to consider them.

- What are the most important risks and uncertainties that require attention to protect partners' interest? Three broad areas of risk require specific attention. The first area is any existing financial risk. Revenue, cost, investments, and liabilities may be affected by internal and external events, some of which may be manageable by designing the right structure; others may be addressed by agreeing on a procedure to solve them once they manifest. Second, partner-related risks pertain to a partner's intentions and behavior. For example, if the partner is also a competitor, the question of where and where not to collaborate becomes pertinent. Third, business risks need to be identified. If the business is stable, the alliance design may reflect such stability. If the business is risky, the design must be flexible enough to go with the flow. All these risks may exist on an alliance level, but also on the level of the individual partner. Partner-specific risks must be identified.

- How do the previous elements change over the lifecycle of the alliance? This question is relevant to get a view on where and how change must be facilitated. Studying critical success factors, risks, and uncertainties during the starting phase of the alliance is insufficient. Discussing their implications across the alliance lifecycle makes the alliance design more robust.

The answers to these three questions generate a list of issues. To get an overview it may be helpful to gather them in a table per phase of the alliance lifecycle. A crucial step is to narrow that list down to the relevant issues, which help to

TABLE 9.1: Examples of design requirements in the cases

Alliance	Design requirements	Final design
ProRail	Incentivize contractor to contribute improvements	Alliance fund with 50/50 share
Novartis–Orion	Ensure consistency in marketing to meet regulations	Create marketing working group
KLM–Northwest	Enhance revenue generation	50/50 profit sharing; sales people count sales of partner tickets toward their target
Future Store Initiative	Ensure knowledge exchange between the partners	Co-locate staff
Cisco–HP	Avoid disagreement over customers	Rules of engagements are defined
Obvion	Ensure independence of Obvion from Rabobank	Rabobank board member on Obvion Supervisory Board; separate shareholder role from Supervisory Board role
SkyTeam	Ensure consistency of procedures among members	Create a separate entity to oversee implementation of guidelines in partners

formulate the design requirements. The final design needs to ensure that the critical success factors are realized and that the risks are managed across the alliance lifecycle. The design requirements need to be defined clearly and precisely. A good design criterion is specific (not: the design must realize the strategy; instead: the design must be able to scale up in one year), relates to the needs of the alliance and its partners, and does not provide a solution but a demand (not: a separate organization must exist; instead: economies of scale must be reaped). Table 9.1 lists some examples of design requirements and how the design addressed them based on some of the cases discussed in the previous chapters.

Control or trust

At this point it is a good idea to take a step back from the process and reflect on the level of control and trust needed. The required level of control tends to be higher when the following are true:[1]

- **The financial stakes are higher.** Greater financial controls are necessary when investments that flow into the alliance are substantial or when expected revenues are high. Revenues in the KLM–Northwest alliance were substantial, running into the billions of dollars, and necessitating a detailed definition and measurement of revenues and costs. More control mechanisms are required as the probability increases that an alliance can cause substantial financial damage to the partners.

- **Partner risk increases.** When a partner is a competitor or a first-time partner, or operates in another industry, companies are more uncertain about their behavior. Therefore, the need for control increases. When partners are trusted, such as in the Future Store Initiative in which most partners already knew each other well, trust-based governance may be a better way forward. The trust model is only feasible when partners already know one another and/or are fully confident about one another's behavior.[2]

- High business risk. When business risk is high because of volatility in demand, high technological turbulence, or uncertainty over governmental regulations, the control approach is difficult to maintain. The moment that the ink dries on an extensive contract, reality will have overtaken its terms. Therefore, high business risk forces companies to build more on the trust approach. In a stable environment, it is more important to exploit possibilities for optimization. Efficiency driven alliances have a higher degree of formalization.[3] The control approach is better suited in that case. The business environment co-determines the optimal alliance structure.[4]

As these three elements make evident, they are not necessarily aligned around control and trust. Low partner risk and low business risk, in conjunction with high financial risk, may imply that some control procedures still need to be implemented. Even though the pure models of control-based alliances and trust-based alliances exist (see, for example, the early phase of the KLM–Northwest alliance and the Future Store Initiative, respectively), most alliances are likely to have a mix of control and trust elements. The right question for them to ask is what to control and what not to control. The debate on control and trust is also valuable when discussing the detailed alliance design. A tendency exists for organizations to continue to raise issues and increase the level of contractual detail. This tendency is fine when a control-based alliance is needed. When a trust-based alliance is required, a reference to the control–trust discussion will help limit discussions on minutiae.

Some people have an instinctive preference for either control or trust. As the previous analysis showed, instinct is not the best way to go because both control and trust have their positive and negative aspects. The positive side of control is that it provides structure and clarity and helps the alliance stay on course. The downside to control is that it reduces initiative and values following rules over creativity. The positive element to trust is that it lowers the governance cost of an alliance and opens opportunities for growth and innovation. The downside to trust is that it provides little concrete guidance in difficult situations, and risks that the alliance is carried away with its own enthusiasm.

High-level design

The previous steps reviewed what is necessary for a particular alliance to work. The better such discussions, the faster the actual design process will run. A mutual understanding about the alliance exists, limiting the chance that ambiguities slow down the ensuing discussions. In this step, the high-level design of the alliance is defined. The high-level design usually describes the following elements:

- Main form of the alliance. Previous chapters described the following forms: supply chain alliance, contractual alliance, virtual joint venture, and joint venture. Multi-partner alliances include the lead partner model, general assembly, and alliance support office.

- Financial model (see Chapter 2 and Appendix). The choices are between revenue-driven, cost-driven, and profit-driven models. Next, the high-level model describes whether pooling takes place. Finally, the main financial flows in the alliance are analyzed.

- A rough sketch of the committee structure in terms of governance committees, working groups, and alliance management roles.

Making the choice between a contractual alliance and a joint venture is often difficult. Table 9.2 lists the benefits and challenges of the two, also compared with the standalone option (in other words, instead of the other options, the organization attempts to achieve its goals on its own) and the merger or acquisition (M&A) option. The supply chain collaboration is not mentioned because it is usually clear when this is the best option: when the main part of the relationship is of a client–supplier nature. In most respects but one, the virtual joint venture follows the regular joint venture. In a "real" joint venture, the benefits of separating the activities in the joint venture from the mother organizations are significant. In the virtual joint venture, creating a separate business is not possible or profitable because the alliance can benefit from a strong tie with the businesses of the mother organizations or the resources need to be deployed in both the alliance and the mother company. For example, in the KLM–Northwest case, giving the alliance its own resources was not meaningful because the

TABLE 9.2: The choice of form[5]

	Go it alone	Contractual alliance	Joint venture	M&A
When applicable	Core competence needs to be developed Time, money, and resources are available in the organization Stable markets (long-term commitments make sense)	To gain access to one or a limited number of complementary competences To meet temporary needs, usually in volatile markets To increase innovation through learning When collaboration on the interfaces between organizations is sufficient to realize the goals (compared with full-fledged integration in a new business)	To realize economies of scale To create a new business that supports core activities or that may become a core activity To combine similar assets coming from diverse businesses When long-term commitments and integration under one management team are necessary to realize the goals	To achieve economies of scale in core competences To acquire a new core competence To increase market power
Advantage	Limited integration problems of the new activity in the organization Complete control and independence Easier to maintain focus on the activity	Can be set up quickly Flexible: contracts are relatively easy to change Fewer cultural integration problems than mergers and acquisitions Sharing of costs and risks	Compared with contractual alliances: single management Sharing of risks and costs More possibilities for optimization than in a contractual alliance	Complete control Ability to reap cost savings Creates critical mass

(Continued)

TABLE 9.2: (Continued)

	Go it alone	Contractual alliance	Joint venture	M&A
Disadvantage	Time and resource consuming Limited flexibility because resources cannot be redeployed easily	Control must be shared; coordination may be a challenge Absence of a single manager makes optimization more difficult Increased chance of ending up stuck in the middle when partners cannot agree on a clear goal Sharing of revenues Chance of a partner behaving opportunistically	Shared control with a partner Shared revenues When companies combine existing businesses: integration problems More difficult to dissolve than a contractual alliance High setup costs	Significant integration problems divert attention from customers and innovation Indigestibility: a merger partner often has businesses that are not interesting and need to be sold Long lead times before the merger is effectuated Capital intensive Cultural integration problems Difficult to keep core people in; exit of talented staff

optimal use of aircraft required them to be available to the partners' businesses. Moreover, the alliance could also benefit from the use of both partners' sales forces. Separating the alliance in a joint venture causes a loss of the benefits of having a large fleet and access to a large sales force.

The Senseo alliance quite closely follows the table. The companies needed access to each other's competences (manufacturing machines and creating coffee blends) and innovation needed to be stimulated. To achieve this, it was sufficient to define the interfaces between the companies in the area of technical specifications for the pods and marketing. The Americhem–EuroPower joint venture rested on creating scale to generate steam and electricity at a low cost. For Americhem, these activities are "near core" in the sense that they are necessary to maintain the core, but they do not deliver a competitive advantage as such. The investments required a long-term commitment because the turbines needed a substantial capital investment and had a long payback period. Hence, a joint venture made sense. The Obvion joint venture was core to Rabobank's portfolio and supported the core of ABP. Increased scale was achieved by combining the existing businesses of ABP and Rabobank in the new organization. Hence, a long-term commitment in a joint venture was the right option.

In the process of designing an alliance, developing more than one possible high-level design works well, such as one joint venture and one or two contractual alliance models, for example based on the sub-models of specialization, joint teams or peer-to-peer design discussed in Chapter 4. Doing so provides insight into different feasible design options and helps clarify relevant issues and questions that need to be addressed. Then, each of the concept designs can be compared with the design requirements. A useful exercise may be to score each design against each design requirement. The primary goal of scoring is not to determine mathematically the right model. The value lies in discussing all of the pros and cons and clarifying everyone's perspective. When one person puts down a low score for a certain design on one design requirement whereas another person gives a high mark, such differences may result in fruitful discussions. Has one of them overlooked a problem or an opportunity? Is there a different vision of the alliance behind the score (if so, go back to step 1)? Scores can be weighted to reflect the greater importance of some requirements over others, but doing so may create the impression that the exercise is more precise than it really is. The value lies in the discussions among those tasked with designing the alliance.

Detailed design

Once the high level design is determined, the next step is to develop a detailed design for the alliance. This step requires a review of all of the elements of the Alliance Design Framework mentioned in Chapter 2. The partners need to judge which of these elements are relevant and, if they are, the extent to which they need to be filled in. A further scoring exercise against the design requirement will show whether the design satisfactorily matches the requirements.

Following the steps of the design process leads to an ideal design. In reality, of course, a gap may exist between what is ideal and what is possible. Important limits to an alliance design may lie in tax, legal, and anti-trust considerations. Some governments demand that a foreign company enter their country through a joint venture with a local partner. In that case, the entire exercise of designing an alliance structure will look quite different because the high-level structure is automatically known. In cases in which no clear legal limits exist beforehand, the best option is to design the alliance as if no legal barriers exist. Once the ideal design is known, how the alliance can fit into the legal constraints needs to be studied. Developing the optimal business solution first and then dealing with the constraints is better than listing all of the constraints and attempting to find a way to do business within those boundaries. The latter approach stifles creativity. Naturally, when an ideal design is tweaked to meet legal requirements, care must be taken to avoid undermining the ratio of the alliance. The fit of the result with the strategic background needs to be checked.

A similar approach should be taken with respect to cultural differences. An alliance may ask for a trust-based design, but if the corporate cultures of the partners involved are focused on control, the question is whether a trust-based design will be effective. Control elements may be implemented, but if these elements prohibit the alliance from meeting its goals, questioning whether it should get the go-ahead at all is legitimate. Likewise, country cultures may differ vastly. The examples given in Chapter 1 of the TNK–BP and Danone–Wahaha joint ventures are cases in point. Whether a good design can manage these differences and overcome them is debatable. The point is that they should not be taken for granted. The decision to create such joint ventures needs to either consider country differences or be based on a calculated risk that the partners are willing to take.

When judging the detailed design, the partners should at least have a clear view on:

- The consistency of all design elements. Alliance designs are configurations of many different elements that need to fit together.[6] In ProRail's alliances, the focus on margin instead of revenue led to the alliance fund. A behavioral change was also recognized as necessary and, therefore, was addressed. In the HP–Cisco case, the partners needed time to realize that the alignment of the internal organization with the alliance posed some challenges. Once this situation became clear, the governance structure was strengthened and both partners increased their investment in alliance management.

- The synergy between the elements. In the Future Store Initiative, co-location, time pressure, a fun vision, and the possibility of reputation damage worked together to create a unique innovative culture. The individual elements strengthened each other.

- The trade-offs in the alliance. In the Air France/KLM–Delta–Alitalia alliance, some things were left open in the contract. To manage these incomplete parts, introducing a regular CEO meeting was necessary. The alternative would have been to create an even more detailed contract. The trade-off between CEO involvement versus a very detailed contract was clear to everybody. Importantly, those involved in an alliance must understand the trade-offs made.

Implementation

Once the design is finalized, it needs to be implemented. The implementation process will go considerably faster when future alliance managers and other key alliance staff are involved in the design process. By involving in the design process those who need to execute the alliance, commitment to the alliance and its premises is ensured. When an alliance design is created without involving the key players, various negative effects will occur.

First, time is lost because the principles behind the alliance need to be transferred from the design team to the alliance team. Before the alliance team understands all of the details, significant time has elapsed. Second, knowledge is always lost when alliances transition from one team to the next. The rationale of the alliance and of the decisions made in designing it are never transferred completely to the next team, increasing the chance that the alliance team makes misinterpretations and unwarranted assumptions. Finally, the chance is much lower that the alliance design is robust. By involving the people who need to execute the alliance, many practical issues come to the fore that are not revealed when an alliance is designed by a team that does not have eventual daily responsibility for its operations.

The first implementation question is: who has to be in place and when? If not already selected, the alliance team needs to be formed and brought on board. Finding the right people with the right alliance mindset, mandate, time availability, and credibility in the partner organizations is imperative. Next, the alliance team will organize the other necessary resources. A large-scale launch event involving all relevant players of the partner organizations is an excellent first step to communicating the alliance internally and to "onboard" new people. Working groups must create their own team charters describing their tasks, roles, and responsibilities.

Manage dynamics

The previous chapter discussed at length the dynamics of alliance management. Although much of the dynamics are unexpected and unpredictable, some are predictable. Most alliances will go through a lifecycle that can be foreseen. For example, in the Novartis–Orion alliance, it was clear beforehand that the alliance would first emphasize development, next require greater investment in marketing and sales, and finally scale back because of patent expiration. The importance of such dynamics demands that the focus should not be on only finding the initial design throughout the design process, but also on the evolution of the design.

Run-through time of the process

No guidelines exist for how long a design process should take. Such timing depends on the alliance and on the time constraints of the partners involved. The Future Store Initiative accelerated alliance formation by setting an aggressive deadline for the store opening. This trick is useful in many alliances. A guideline does exist regarding the amount of time companies should devote in relative terms to each of the six steps. Most organizations devote too little time on the first strategic step because they believe that agreeing on the overall aims of the alliance is easy. During later steps, many disagreements and differences in perspective may emerge that are related to the fact that the strategic points of departure were not sufficiently addressed. In many cases, too much time is devoted to the nitty-gritty detail of working toward a contract. If companies want to invest in those details, they need to ask themselves whether that pays off given the fact that, in most industries, the dynamics are such that reality will have overtaken the contract within a year. Of course a contract should be solid but designing a governance structure that can handle change may make more sense than writing an ironclad contract.

Implications for the public sector and not-for-profits

With the exception of ProRail, all cases in the book are examples from the private sector and of for-profit companies. Alliances are not limited to private industry and have become increasingly common in the public sector. Over the past years public–private partnerships received special attention as a way to implement governmental policy. In other sectors such health care, the past years have also seen a proliferation of partnering initiatives. Collaboration has the potential to greatly improve patients' quality of life. Intriguingly, little transfer of alliance management knowledge takes place between private sector and public sector organizations.

A number of differences exist between private and public sector alliances. First, the strategic imperatives behind them are different. Value propositions in the public sector are often difficult to define and make tangible, partly because of the nature of the problems faced. For example, governmental policy includes broader societal goals that are not always easy to translate to particular alliances. In contrast, the public sector may complicate partnerships by attempting to realize too many different goals through a single alliance.

A further difference lies in partner selection. The relationship between partners is important for alliance design and the choice of partner influences the level of control and trust in an alliance. Private companies can choose a variety of partners and may select the one they believe is easiest to work with. In contrast, public sector organizations tend to have monopolies in their field. If a building contractor wants to be active in railroad construction in the Netherlands, ProRail is the only choice for a partner. Such a monopoly position influences the design choices that can be made if only because the balance of power in such an alliance is uneven.

In addition, public sector companies face many regulations regarding budgeting and control processes that tend to be less flexible than those in the private sector. Meeting those requirements can add complexity to an alliance. The public sector tends to operate more in a control mode because of them. Some of these differences are very fundamental. An often-heard complaint of businesses is that governments are not reliable. After an election, if the politicians change, policies tend to follow and partnerships may be negatively affected. Therefore, public–private partnerships may be affected by the election cycle, and getting high-level politicians or civil servants to serve on an alliance governance committee may be easier when the topic of the alliance is in the public eye. When interest subsides, their attention may divert elsewhere, weakening the alliance's governance.

Still, the implications of these differences for alliance design should not be overestimated. The vast majority of the design principles laid down in this book apply in the public sector as well. Goals, incentives, decision making, and relationship building are not exclusive to the private sector. The design of an alliance may become somewhat more complex but the fundamental principles remain unchanged. For example, the ProRail alliances show extensive control but also recognized the importance of relationships and trust. Although some elements of alliance design may be more important than others for public and not-for-profit organizations, the processes, checklists, and examples presented in this book remain relevant.

Notes

1   The relation between risk and alliance design was established by Das, T.K. and B.S. Teng. 1998. Between trust and control: developing confidence in partner cooperation in alliances, *Academy of Management Review*, 23, 3, 491–512. Also see: De Man, A.P. and N. Roijakkers. 2009. Alliance governance: balancing control and trust in dealing with risk, *Long Range Planning*, 42, 75–95.

2   Krishnan, R., X. Martin and N.G. Noorderhaven. 2006. When does trust matter to alliance performance?, *Academy of Management Journal*, 49, 5, 894–917.

3   Albers, S. 2010. Configurations of alliance governance systems, *Schmalenbach Business Review*, 62, July, 204–233.

4   Rowley, T., D. Behrens and D. Krackhardt. 2000. Redundant governance structures: an analysis of structural and relational embeddedness in the steel and semiconductor industries, *Strategic Management Journal*, 21, 369–386.

5   This table is based on the cases and on the next publications: De Man, A.P. and. G.M. Duysters. 2005. Collaboration and innovation: a review of the effects of mergers, acquisitions and alliances on innovation, *Technovation*, 25, 12, 1377–1387; Duysters, G.M. 2001. *Partner or Perish*, inaugural address, 22 June, Eindhoven, Eindhoven University; Dyer, J.H., P. Kale and H. Singh. 2004. When to ally & when to acquire, *Harvard Business Review*, July–August, 82, 7/8, 108–115; Garette, B. and P. Dussauge. 2000. Alliances versus acquisitions: choosing the right option, *European Management Journal*, 18, 1, 63–69; Hagedoorn, J. and G.M. Duysters. 2002. External appropriation of innovative capabilities: the choice between strategic partnering and mergers and acquisitions, *Journal of Management Studies*, 39, 2, 167–188; Hennart, J.F. and S. Reddy. 1997. The choice between mergers/acquisitions and joint ventures: the case of Japanese investors in the United States, *Strategic Management Journal*, 18, 1–12.

6   Albers, S. 2010. Configurations of alliance governance systems, *Schmalenbach Business Review*, 62, July, 204–233.

CHAPTER **10**

Open alliances: Towards the third generation of collaboration

Over time, new alliance forms have emerged. New structures and governance processes were designed and continue to be invented. As the previous chapters have shown, approximately three eras of alliance development were identified:

- The first generation: the joint venture era until the 1990s. In this era, the use of joint ventures was predominant and primarily for internationalization purposes, to create economies of scale or to obtain benefits related to organizations' non-core activities. The overall number of alliances was limited.

- The second generation: the contractual era from the early 1990s until 2010. In this era, contractual alliances became more important than joint ventures. Alliance purposes were aimed at innovation, flexibility, and dealing with dynamics in the business environment. Alliances also came closer to the core business as exemplified by the Air France/KLM/Delta/Alitalia alliance. During this period, the number of alliances grew rapidly and alliances became a normal way of organizing economic activity. The vast majority of alliances were bilateral.

- The third generation of alliances, open alliances, is an emerging model that centers on multi-partner alliances, open innovation, and the creation of shared value.[1] The Future Store Initiative goes a long way toward this model of open alliances.

Obviously, this development is not linear: multi-partner alliances existed before the 1990s and joint ventures will not disappear altogether. However, as a generalization, the characterization previously given broadly appears to support the developments in practice. This development ties in with changes in the business environment. The reduction of barriers to trade enables large constellations of partners to form. The internationalization of knowledge development also demands companies to tap into knowledge sources across the globe via partners. In addition companies have now mastered the skill of managing bilateral alliances and are ready to move to the next level of complexity.

The end of "vertical horizontalism"

The new business environment requires the development of new alliance structures. The environment demands increasingly sophisticated alliances, and the growth in alliance maturity enables companies to develop and manage more complex alliance forms. Still, the cases in the chapters devoted to the different alliance forms showed an interesting paradox. Alliances are normally considered non-hierarchical forms of organizing because no higher authority exists above the (usually two) partners that enter into an alliance. However, even a superficial glance at the structures of the Senseo alliance, the ProRail alliance model, the HP–Cisco alliance or any of the other cases discussed shows that hierarchy is inherent in these alliances through and through. Most companies imposed the traditional hierarchical notions of organization to alliances by creating an alliance executive board consisting of top management, an alliance management team consisting of middle management, and working groups representing the operational level. What is nonhierarchical about that structure? This structure is traditional in that any nineteenth century railroad or steel magnate would recognize it instantly.

To be fair, three important differences exist between these alliance structures and traditional hierarchies. First, an emphasis exists on horizontal over vertical coordination; second, they take place across organizational boundaries and not within the firm; and third, most initiatives are driven from the bottom up rather than from the top down. Still, vertical, hierarchical logics are used to address problems of horizontal coordination. The use of this "vertical horizontalism" signals that further steps away from the hierarchical model can be taken.

TABLE 10.1: Characteristics of open alliances[2]

	Second generation alliances	Open alliances
Ownership	Proprietary	Open
Partnering	Bilateral, invitation only, stable membership	Multilateral, open for any partner, in- and outflow
Partner heterogeneity	Low to medium	Medium to high
Agreement type	Detailed contract with some open ends	Framework with guidelines, highly open ended
Phasing	Define projects first, next launch the alliance	Launch the alliance, next use a bottom-up approach to define projects
Design	Blueprint	Emerging structures

The emerging model of open alliances dispenses with vertical horizontalism and takes an important step towards truly horizontal alliances. Hierarchy will never disappear altogether, but the new species of alliances will be more democratic, more bottom-up, and more horizontal than in the previous two alliance generations. Open alliances have a number of characteristics that distinguish them from the second generation of alliances (see Table 10.1). The model is open in a number of ways.

First, the ownership of knowledge is not exclusive to the partners that participate in the alliance, but is also shared with the outside world. In the previous alliance generation, the partners owned and protected the knowledge developed in the alliance. Second, open alliances are open to any partner that wants to join, leading to multilateral alliances. Second generation alliances operated on an invitation only basis and were bilateral. In open alliances, partners may also flow in and out over time, whereas in traditional alliances membership is stable. In addition, partners from many different backgrounds may join open alliances, following the fact that technologies integrate and that new technologies affect a wide variety of sectors. A fourth difference is that agreements in open innovation alliances tend to be more like frameworks that delineate general principles instead of detailed contracts. They take the fact that a contract is open-ended as a starting point, whereas second generation alliances see open ends as a problem that needs to be managed via the hierarchy. Another open element in open alliances is that not all alliance projects are defined upfront but are instead proposed during the alliance runtime in a bottom-up manner. Last but not least, the design of open alliances is not detailed in a blueprint upfront. Partners in open alliances allow the structure of the alliance to emerge over time. The METRO Future Store Initiative meets many of these characteristics. The design elements of open alliances are analyzed in greater detail below using the Alliance Design Framework.

Strategic imperative

The strategic imperative behind open alliances is the creation of shared value. The word "shared" in shared value refers not only to value that is shared by all partners in the alliance. It also implies that the alliance aims to have a broader benefit to society. For example, IBM's focus on creating smarter cities not only aims to generate profits but also attempts to do so by reducing energy consumption, inner city congestion, and pollution. IBM has to partner with many different organizations to achieve this aim. The benefits for these partners may be substantial, but if everything goes according to the vision of IBM, society will benefit as well. Transcelerate, an alliance of 10 leading pharmaceutical companies, aims to improve the process of clinical studies that need to be conducted before a drug can be introduced to the market. The partners of the alliance will benefit from their joint efforts. A safer and better clinical trial process will also benefit patients. The aim of open alliances is not only to generate a profitable business but also to generate broader benefits that may not always be clear at the start.

What IBM's smarter cities program and Transcelerate have in common is their aim to create profitable businesses by solving societal problems. To achieve that aim, they need to establish multi-partner alliances. Society faces many challenges that can be addressed by similar initiatives: orphan drugs, internet security, and systemic innovations such as smart cars, smart electricity grids, and others. The one-sided emphasis on shareholder value is replaced by creating shareholder value through creating value for others. Organizations are already embedded in networks of alliances. The shared value strategy will make them think more consciously about how to employ these networks to the fullest extent by, for example, creating more links between their partners. This will result in the discovery of new opportunities, not envisioned at the alliance launch.

Formal processes

The overall legal structure of the next generation of alliances will rest on memoranda of understanding (MOU), letters of intent, or short contracts. Partners in open alliances do not enter into detailed contractual arrangements that make it difficult to flexibly add new alliance projects. A multi-party memorandum of understanding may be supplemented by contracts on a per project basis, although the general guidelines of an MOU may very well suffice. Rather than seeing the open-ended nature of alliance contracts as a drawback of alliances that needs to be managed through steering committees, open alliances exploit this open-ended nature to the fullest extent. In this way they enable alliance partners to adapt swiftly to changing opportunities.

Open alliances further rest on brokered governance; that is, an alliance support office will ensure coordination between the partners or another neutral third party will be asked to lead the alliance. A number of reasons exist for choosing the brokered governance model. Strict neutrality is required from a control perspective: each partner's interest has to be protected and a neutral partner will feel freer to address free-riding by one of the partners. In addition, the coordination load of open alliances is high. Projects and partners are added and dropped, which results in handling around legal issues and around (dis-)integration of partners in the alliance. A neutral third party or alliance support office will ensure consistency in dealing with these dynamics. Finally, with high numbers of partners, hierarchical coordination becomes impossible. Other coordination mechanisms than vertical horizontalism are necessary. A neutral third party can provide true horizontal coordination.

Informal processes

The informal processes in open alliances are all the more important because the formal processes are limited in scope. The partners will need to behave more as democratic citizens able to manage simultaneous perspectives on the same issue. Partners must engage in non-dominant behavior rather than alpha male management. The alliance support office's diplomatic skills in dealing with multiple partners need to be well developed.

This description may create the impression that open alliances have the fun atmosphere and high performance culture of the Future Store Initiative. Such a statement is unlikely to be true and even the Future Store Initiative had its share of conflicts and difficulties. In the end, organizations participate in alliances based on enlightened self-interest. The definitions of "enlightened" and "self-interest" will change over time. Consequently, open alliances are not immune to opportunism, short termism, and infighting. Hence the necessity of brokered governance that should make open alliances better positioned to manage this dark side of alliances. A neutral party will address opportunistic behavior. The open nature of the alliance also makes it easier for partners to leave without harming the overall alliance once they believe that their interest is no longer adequately met.

Dynamics

In open alliances of this nature, dynamics occur at three levels. First, significant dynamism exists at the project level as new projects emerge and existing projects are dissolved. Second, partner entry and exit are common because strategic reorientation occurs in the partners. Partner entry and exit are enhanced by the following characteristics of open alliances:

- Project-based work, which makes it easier for partners to phase into and phase out of various projects at various times. They do not have to make an overall irreversible investment on the alliance level.

- A simple legal MOU structure creates low costs of entry and exit because of the simplicity of processes that are laid down in the MOU.

- Integration capability. In open alliances, partners are accustomed to new partners entering and are able to integrate them quickly.

- Equality, giving newcomers equal standing as long-term partners. Everybody becomes a member on the same terms.

The third level of dynamics concerns changes in the alliance itself. Dynamics in the alliance at the project and membership levels do not imply dynamics of the alliance in terms of revising the vision and scope. A larger number of parties involved means that restructuring an alliance will be more difficult. Restructuring of open alliances implies opening up the discussion about the vision behind the alliance. With so many companies involved, it is unlikely that a new vision can be established that satisfies all or even a majority of the partners' needs. Open alliances may be agile at the operational level, adding and dropping projects, but their strategic agility may be limited, which may not necessarily be a negative thing. Old structures need to make room for new ones once they become obsolete. Subsets of partners from a dissolved alliance may start a new one in a related territory.

One risk of open alliances is strategic drift. Because projects may start up rapidly, the alliance may take on too many projects or, even worse, initiate projects that are only marginally related to its vision. If the latter happens, over time partners will identify less and less with the alliance. Such a process undermines its existence. Combining an open scope with a strong vision is difficult; therefore, discussions about alliance boundaries will be frequent. The main challenge of open alliances is to maintain focus and ensure that diverse partners stay aligned and committed.

Internal alignment

Open alliances may seem unlikely to ever become a dominant form of organizing. If they become so, they will pose enormous challenges to existing organizational paradigms. Such alliances are difficult to fit into internal operating procedures of the individual partners. How does an organization budget for open alliances when it is unclear how many projects it will join in these alliances? If a company joins several open alliances that represent an important part of its business, how can these alliances be incorporated into the planning and control cycle? If much business is done outside the organization and in a bottom-up manner, to what extent can top management still be held accountable for their company's results? How can company staff that contribute to these alliances be rewarded?

Laws, rules, and shareholders demand answers to these questions. They increasingly force companies to focus on operational risks and being in control of every project. The point of open alliances is to manage strategic risk by controlling the elements that create a competitive advantage in a dynamic environment. This form of strategic control is often undermined by a focus on operational control that aims to ensure each alliance follows company control and audit procedures. Much more important than operational control in a specific alliance project is that alliance projects and all alliances together as an evolving portfolio give a company strategic control over its destiny. Operational risk and control on the one hand and strategic risk and control on the other hand often have different demands. Too often, operational control leads to risk avoidance, short termism, and bureaucracy. Strategic control demands the opposite. The current institutional frameworks focus on the first and, therefore, are at odds with the demands of open alliances. Business requires dynamism, whereas institutions demand stability. Therefore, to implement open alliances, alliance managers should act as change agents in their organizations, helping them to break away from a short-term control orientation and finding new ways to integrate open alliances into company procedures.

On the positive side, alliance maturity is growing and organizations have built their alliance management capabilities. Table 10.2 shows the substantial increase in investments in alliance management during the first decade of the 21st century. Almost all alliance management tools, processes, and functions were used twice or three times as frequently in 2011 as in 2002. This situation vastly expanded organizations' ability to manage more complex alliances. Although most companies still have some way to go in terms of mindset and culture,[3] the progress to date lays the foundation for the third generation of alliances.

TABLE 10.2: Percentage of companies that invested in alliance management practices[4]

Alliance management practices	2002	2011
Alliance best practices (based on experience, companies formulate best practices for alliance management)	32%	93%
Alliance database (database tracking information on the alliances of a company)	70%	79%
Alliance metrics (specific measures for alliance success are defined, for example, in an alliance scorecard)	39%	88%
Cross-alliance evaluation (companies compare individual alliances with each other to identify lessons)	20%	81%
Culture program (programs aimed at bridging the cultural differences between partners)	15%	66%
External alliance training (managers are taught by external alliance experts)	30%	75%
In-house alliance training (companies develop their own alliance training programs)	21%	73%
Individual evaluation (companies review their alliances based on their contribution to the organization)	65%	89%
Intranet (specific alliance resources are available on the company intranet)	48%	81%
Joint business planning (standardized approach for developing an alliance business plan together with a partner)	54%	96%
Joint evaluation (evaluation of alliances takes place together with the partner)	42%	92%
Standard partner selection approach (a fixed process for selecting alliance partners exists involving process steps and selection criteria)	52%	87%
Alliance department (a centralized department supports alliance managers in operations)	45%	81%
Alliance managers (persons responsible for one or more alliances)	50%	93%
Alliance specialist (expert who supports alliance managers with their day-to-day job)	72%	81%
Vice-president of alliances or chief alliance officer (recognized senior executive responsible for alliance management)	42%	63%
Alliance managers from different units/divisions formally exchange their experience	23%	83%

The investments shown in Table 10.2 make it easier for companies to function in the complex world of alliances. It helps them overcome the internal hurdles to collaboration and to be better aligned with alliance goals. When organizations become more capable in managing alliances they are more likely to accelerate the development toward open alliances. However, the management skills for bilateral alliances cannot be directly translated to open alliances. A new round of learning must take place to understand the specific requirements of open alliances. The next section gives some insight into where this learning should take place.

Open alliances and the alliance lifecycle

The alliance lifecycle discussed in Chapter 1 is the standard for second-generation alliances. For open alliances, some modifications to the lifecycle are necessary. The view of the lifecycle as a one-directional process could already be challenged for second-generation alliances. Reality is messier than the process suggests. However, the lifecycle was a very good rule of thumb for many second-generation alliances. The difference between the traditional lifecycle and the open alliance lifecycle can be summarized in two words: parallel and continuous.

Open alliances run continuously through the lifecycle. For example, take partner selection. As partners enter and leave open alliances with some regularity, partner selection is a continuous process. The consequence is that activities in the lifecycle may run in parallel. An open alliance may be evaluated and, simultaneously, negotiations with a new prospective partner may be conducted. Similarly, implementation of new alliance projects will take place in parallel with activities during the management phase, such as policing the maintenance of rules.

A more detailed look suggests that the first steps of the lifecycle remain unchanged. They deal with the strategies of the individual partners and remain unaffected by open alliances. However, in the partner selection phase, some new issues arise. First, because the alliance is open, partner selection may not be the right phrase. An open alliance sets general criteria that a partner must meet to become a member. Once a partner meets those criteria, it is automatically allowed in. The word selection does not appropriately reflect this process. Other alliances may be "half open" and may require partners to meet stricter criteria, such as fit with the other partners, and are likely to more closely follow the traditional lifecycle.

Regarding the phase of alliance design, designing the overall alliance may be quite simple, as a detailed blueprint is not necessary. However, once the overall framework is agreed, the work is not done. Alliance managers must be able to manage the evolving structure of the open alliance. Sometimes this means they must synthesize and formalize what emerges in practice. At other times it may require breaking through routines to allow alliance renewal. Open alliances are not only implemented at their start, but face implementation issues over their entire lifespan. The continuous flow of alliance projects also poses challenges. Ensuring partner alignment and avoiding that new projects overlap or compete with existing initiatives is important. In addition, when a new partner enters, the alliance has to address the implementation issue of including this partner in its processes. Implementation is not a one-time event but a continuous activity. As a consequence, the alliance support office must pay special attention to maintaining focus, alignment, and commitment. High demands are placed on the diplomatic skills of the people populating the office.

Alliances and progress

Nobel laureate Kenneth Arrow once stated that "among man's innovations, the use of organization to accomplish his ends is among both his greatest and his earliest."[5] Since organization was first discovered, it has developed into many different forms. The discovery of the multidivisional form defined the organization in the 20th century.[6] The latest evolution of organization is the alliance. New forms of alliances continue to emerge, which has a considerable effect on organizations, management, and the economy, thus making the process of designing them relevant for managers and the organizations they lead.

Knowledge about alliance design is indispensable to optimize existing alliances and to design new ones. The creation of new alliance models will help solve societal issues that have yet to be tackled to date. Similar to the multi-divisional form that enabled people to make great progress in many different areas, alliances are doing the same today. Therefore, alliance design should be on the agenda of top managers and policymakers. Creating the right collaboration structures can generate value for both shareholders and society at large.

Notes

1 Chesbrough, H. 2006. *Open Innovation*, Cambridge, MA, Harvard Business Press; Porter, M.E. and M.A. Kramer. 2011. Creating shared value, *Harvard Business Review*, January/February, 62–77.

2 This table builds heavily on Wilks, C. and C. Prothmann. 2012. Open innovation alliances, *Strategic Alliance Magazine*, 4, 42–45/50.

3 De Man, A.P. and D. Luvison. 2010. *Alliance culture: it's in the DNA!*, white paper, Association of Strategic Alliance Professionals.

4 This table is an excerpt from Duysters, G., A.P. de Man, D. Luvison and A. Krijnen. 2012. *The State of Alliance Management: Past, Present, Future*, Canton, MA, The Association of Strategic Alliance Professionals.

5 Arrow, K. 1971. *Essays in the Theory of Risk-Bearing*, Amsterdam, North Holland, p. 224.

6 Chandler, A.D. 1962. *Strategy and Structure*, Cambridge, MA, The MIT Press.

Appendix: Financial models behind alliances

1. To pool or not to pool?

After establishing whether the alliance is cost, revenue, or profit oriented, the next step in developing the financial model is to ask whether pooling costs, revenues, or profits is best for the alliance to achieve its goals, or whether a different model is needed. Whether pooling makes sense depends on:

- The potential economies of scale and scope to be gained. Economies of scale and scope usually require pooling because they usually can only be reaped when companies combine their capacity;

- Learning benefits. In particular, when products or service delivery processes have a steep learning curve, pooling makes sense. Having separate teams going through the same learning curve is inefficient;

- Benefits from increased market power. For example, if the bargaining power toward clients and suppliers can be increased, allowing for a better price to be negotiated, partners need to determine whether pooling part of their businesses is necessary or whether they can achieve that goal through a joint sales or joint purchasing agreement;

- Improved alignment of incentives in the alliances. Pooling may help align the partners' incentives better than when they are separate;

- Improved customer benefits. Last but not least, customer benefits may require pooling. If a client can only be served well when products or services are seamlessly integrated, pooling may make sense.

The answer may be different for each alliance. For example, in the Philips–Sara Lee/DE alliance, each partner brought a completely different competence.

Pooling would not create any of the benefits previously mentioned. In contrast, in the Air France/KLM–Delta case, customer benefits from selling each other's tickets were substantial. In addition, a profit share makes aligning the targets of the people involved in the alliance easier because everybody is working to increase joint profits. Hence, profit pooling makes sense. This case also shows that pooling does not necessarily involve the creation of a joint venture. However, all joint ventures involve pooling.

A cost pool occurs when two car companies decide to build a factory to produce cars. In that case, for them to put together their investments to build the factory is more beneficial. In this way, they will be able to benefit from economies of scale. Next, each partner may produce its own car brand in the factory and reap its own revenues. This model is often used in agricultural cooperatives as well. In the Prominent cooperative of tomato growers, 20 growers pooled the cost of experimenting with new growing techniques. Each individual member had the responsibility to decide whether the lessons learned from those experiments would be implemented in its organization. A revenue pool occurs when two IT companies jointly sell a solution to a client and split the revenue. Each company still has its own costs.

2. Sharing arrangements around pooling models

When pooling takes place, the question of how to share the pooled profits, revenues, or costs arises. This sharing normally occurs based on a pre-established criterion, and a handful of mechanisms exist for such sharing, including the following:

- Sharing is based on the number of partners: with two partners, each takes 50 percent. Such sharing occurred in the original KLM–Northwest Airline alliance in which both partners pooled their profits and the net profit or loss was then divided 50/50. This model works best when the partners are approximately equal in size related to the scope of the alliance.

- With pay per use, costs are shared in relation to the degree to which companies use the services of the alliance, or revenues are shared in relation to the degree to which they sell through the alliance. In an example of a car factory that is a joint venture between two car manufacturers, the partner that produces the highest volume of cars in a plant or that uses the highest number of hours in the factory pays more of the cost.

- Based on company size, sharing occurs based on the number of employees or the revenue of the organizations involved. This situation works better when companies are of different size relative to the scope of the alliance, and requires that the partners' activities in the alliance are related to their size; otherwise, an imbalance may occur.

- Sharing is based on initial investment. For example, in joint ventures sharing may occur based on the shares that each partner holds in the joint venture (although the shareholding agreement may stipulate differently). The dividend policy of a joint venture may be used to share profits between the partners.

- Sharing is based on retained earnings (in joint ventures only). In joint ventures, earnings can be retained for reinvestment. In this way, the joint venture can invest in new production capacity or innovation, which may increase the value of the joint venture when its sale is contemplated.

3. Non-pooling arrangements

When companies do not pool their finances, different arrangements for sharing must be agreed to. The two main models are "to each his own," in which each company has its own costs and revenues related to the alliance, and "performance-based" mechanisms, in which any financial arrangement depends directly on the volume of business the partners do.

The "to each his own" model occurs frequently and makes sense when:

- Two partners have diverse competencies, indicating that little in terms of learning, economies of scale, or market power can be generated; and/or

- The partners are able to integrate their products by defining only the interfaces instead of having to combine them altogether.

This basic model was behind the Philips–Sara Lee/DE alliance in which one company develops coffee machines and the other develops coffee pods. The combination makes for a strong coffee concept in the market and generates higher sales than if each partner went its own way. The METRO Future Store Initiative also follows this main model: each organization carries its own costs and must compete to obtain its own share of the pie. The combination of the partners' knowledge ensures that the pie grows.

In the performance-based model, the financial model is based on elements related to the performance of a partner in the alliance. Examples include the use of commissions, royalties, or license fees based on goods sold or produced. For example, when companies cross-sell each other's products, they may earn a percentage of each sale or a fee for each item sold. The Novartis–Orion alliance operates according to this model. Targets connected to bonuses are another example of performance-based models. Performance-based models are most frequent in vertical relationships, such as sales alliances in which one partner sells the products or solutions of the other. Alliances between pharma companies and contract research organizations or biotech companies tend to be based on milestones (see below).

4. Variations

The basic models previously described are usually insufficient for developing a complete financial model. For that reason, a number of variations to these basic models exist, including the following:

- Thresholds and caps. When a certain threshold is crossed, a new mechanism for dividing revenues and costs becomes operative. ProRail's mechanism for sharing a deficit in the alliance fund is an example here. A special case of this mechanism occurs when a maximum or minimum payment is defined. In the Future Store Initiative alliance, all partners carried their own costs and revenues. However, to become a member, a partner contributed an initial fee to a common fund. Out of this fund, the alliance paid for marketing events that promoted its activities. A maximum payment may be relevant when the possibility exists that payments become very high, for example when a small company collaborates with a large one. In principle, the companies may agree to equally share costs, but the larger company can carry more of the costs when they become higher than a certain level to avoid the situation in which the smaller partner faces prohibitive costs.

- Penalties/bonuses and milestones. These incentive mechanisms are regularly applied in alliances. When a partner does not meet a certain target, it may be penalized; when a partner meets a target, it may receive an extra payment. Bonuses are often defined as milestone payments. In that case payments are made to a partner when it achieves a certain predefined intermediate goal (the milestone). Such rewards are common in pharmaceutical collaboration. For example, when one party researches whether chemical compounds of another party may be suitable for further drug development, the researching party may be paid after looking into a number of compounds or after finding a certain number of interesting compounds.

- Transfer pricing. If a partner delivers a product or service to its alliance partners or to their joint venture, the question is what price the other partners or the joint venture pays for such product or service. A full commercial price paid may be a source of profits for the partner delivering the product. In contrast, a price close to the cost price is a source of profit for the other partners. Similarly, a joint venture may charge its partners. The joint venture between the two insurance companies ING and Fortis delivered certain services to its parents. All of these services were delivered at cost price. Therefore, the joint venture did not operate at a profit (or loss), but the benefits immediately accrued to the parent companies. This setup made sense because the joint venture was exclusively created to save money through economies of scale.

- Prioritization. One partner takes priority over another in sharing the costs or revenues. An example is when one partner faces greater risk from participating in a joint venture because, for example, it has invested a larger amount. Therefore, that partner is the first to receive dividends.

- Special compensating payments. In the Senseo alliance, Philips sells its coffee machine at a relatively low price and does not earn a good margin. To compensate for the low margins, Philips receives a percentage of the revenue of coffee pods sold by Sara Lee/DE.

- Temporary provisions. For example, the prioritization previously mentioned may be limited to a certain period, such as five years, or until a certain amount has been paid to the partner with priority.

- Alliance fund. For example, organizations create a fund that pays for cost overruns. Any remaining money is split according to one of the rules previously mentioned or may be reinvested in the alliance. A fund may also contain portions of the revenues or profits, or may pay for marketing, innovation, or unexpected risks. ProRail's alliance fund shows how central such a fund can be to an alliance.

- Lump sums. Lump sums are one-time payments from one partner to the other to compensate for a special contribution to the alliance or to address financial imbalances that emerge over time between the partners. For example, when two partners create a joint venture in which one partner contributes its existing machines and both contribute equally in cash, the partner contributing the machines may receive a direct lump-sum payment from the other partner as compensation.

5. Definitions

With sharing costs and revenues, much may depend on the exact definition of revenue or cost. Imagine an alliance between one airline that has a modern, fuel-efficient fleet of aircraft and another airline that operates old, inefficient planes. Assume that the airlines are of equal size. When these two partners share costs, obviously the latter airline benefits from its partner's modern fleet. As compensation, the two airlines may agree that the alliance's fuel costs are 100 percent of the efficient airline's fuel costs and 90 percent of the inefficient airline's fuel costs. Now, imagine that one of the airlines is bureaucratic and has 10 full-time staff members involved in managing the alliance, whereas the other one has only two people doing the same job. The first question is: are these management costs part of the alliance's costs? The second question is: if they are, then how should the differences in internal efficiency be addressed? Differences in accounting practices matter as well. Companies may have different depreciation terms or revenue recognition rules.

As an increasing number of alliances are looking at the real margins the partners make, all of these questions regarding what counts as a cost and what counts as revenue become highly relevant. To answer these questions, open book accounting is necessary. Partners that open their books to each other will find out the revenue and cost structures of their partners. Not all companies are sufficiently advanced to allow open book accounting to occur (barring regulatory issues such as anti-trust legislation that may restrict companies from sharing information), but it is becoming more common within the alliance world.

6. Property rights

Because alliances are created by independent organizations, the question of who owns what has profound implications for the performance of the partners involved. Naturally, ownership of tangible assets brought into or created in the alliance must be clarified.

The intangible assets also pose interesting challenges. Intellectual property rights (IPR) include patents, copyrights, trademarks, databases, designs, growing rights, and the like. A distinction is usually made between background IPR (which partners already own and then contribute to the alliance) and foreground IPR (created new in the alliance). For each element, the ownership and rights of use need to be defined. IPR licensing agreements may further underpin the alliance by giving one partner a license on the IPR of the other. Runtime of the license, pricing, the area in which the IPR can be used (in all geographies? for all products?) need to be defined.[1] Various models for sharing IPR exist and range from individual ownership to joint ownership to making it available to the public at large. The optimal sharing model depends on whether the IP will become a core competence for the firms, whether other companies may block its use if not properly protected, and on the specific institutional context faced by the alliance partners.[2]

IPR agreements may be very simple or very complex. The agreement for the Future Store Initiative initiated by METRO Group was simple. All background IPR contributed to the Initiative remained with the partners. All foreground IPR was to be made publicly available, which made sense because the foreground IPR created was to develop a technology standard. By openly sharing the foreground IPR, the chances increase dramatically that the standard is taken up in the market.

Rights of use can be defined for both tangible and intangible assets. Rights of use delineate how partners are allowed to use a certain asset. For example, a jointly owned brand may be used only for the product produced or service delivered in the alliance and not for anything else. Alternatively, a patent may be used only for products delivered in the USA but not for products delivered in Asia.

Some assets may be owned by only one of the partners. For example, company A owns patent 1 and company B owns patent 2. By combining the patents, they are able to deliver an innovative product. If company A decides that it no longer wants to be active in the alliance because the market it serves is no longer a strategic priority, it may sell patent 1. Such a sale may harm company B if, for example, the patent ends up at B's competitor. As part of the alliance agreement, B may negotiate a right of first refusal to buy the patent, meaning that A has to first offer the patent to B before selling it to someone else.

Assets may also be transferred as part of an alliance. Existing machines may be brought into a new joint venture or partners may sell patents or trademarks to each other. The valuation of these contributions is often grounds for discussion. If assets change ownership, companies are advised to agree on the valuation procedure early on to avoid future related conflicts.

7. Intangible value

Finally, some alliances have elements that cannot be expressed in direct monetary terms but still raise the stock market value of one of the partners through enhanced innovativeness, a strengthened brand image, new business creation, and the like. This type of value is often difficult to determine and is mostly ignored. However, sometimes this type of value is considerable and companies may attempt to compensate for it. Such compensation may be done through various mechanisms. A minority stake by a big pharma company in a small biotech company that is its alliance partner is a source of capital for the biotech company. The minority stake also enables the big pharma company to capture some of the increased value of the biotech company that resulted from the alliance. Similarly, lump-sum payments or other special payments may also be compensation. However, the amount is very subjective.

Notes

1   Slowinski, G. and M.W. Sagal. 2006. Allocating patent rights in collaborative research agreements, *Research Technology Management*, January/February, 49, 1, 51–59.
2   Teng, B.S. 2007. Managing intellectual property in R&D alliances, *International Journal Technology Management*, 38, 1/2, 160–177.

Index

4PL (fourth-party logistics) 54–5
9/11 attacks 112
50/50 joint ventures 134–5
51 percent fever mistake 14–15

Abbott–Reata behavioral principles 40–1
ABP 128–33, 189
accounting, open book 212
Air France/KLM–Delta Airlines–Alitalia
  alliance 1, 26, 27, 103, 104, 114–17,
  169, 175, 177
airline alliances
  alliance support office model 157–60
  costs/revenues 212
  cultural differences 43
  design of alliances 24–5
  reasons for 103–4
  see also Air France . . .;
    KLM–Northwest Airlines alliance
Alitalia 1, 26, 27, 103, 104, 114–17, 169,
  175, 177
Alliance Design Framework 21–50
  formal building blocks 27–39
  informal building blocks 39–46
  internal alignment 46–8
  strategic rationale 24–7
  trust and control 48
  see also design of alliances
alliance funds 59–65, 211
  deficit sharing 62–3
alliance support office model 147,
  157–60, 163, 164
alliances
  definition 3
  lifecycles 5

norms and values 40
numbers 4
tensions 170–1
Amepco joint venture 136–42
  arbitration process 139
  collaboration 139–40
  conflict of interests 138–9
  control elements 140
  governance structure 137
América Móvil 125
Americhem–Europower joint
  venture 136–42, 188–9
arbitration 139
Australia 57, 58
autonomy of partners 171

banking sector 128–33
Bayer–Millennium alliance 30
biopharma see pharma sector
bonus schemes 47, 210
  see also incentives
BP 2

car industry 15, 18–19, 122
case studies
  Future Store Initiative 12, 27–8,
    151–7, 169, 209, 210
  Holst Centre joint venture 160–2
  HP–Cisco alliance 75, 89–97, 169, 177
  KLM–Northwest Airlines
    alliance 102–19, 122, 173
  METRO Group 12, 27–8, 151–7, 169,
    209, 210
  Novartis–Orion alliance 74–5, 80–9,
    97, 169, 173, 177

Obvion joint venture 128–33, 189
Prominent cooperative 147–51
ProRail alliances 59–67, 168
Rolls–Royce alliance 54–6
Senseo alliance 8, 17, 26, 27, 74,
 75–80, 97, 168, 209
SkyTeam alliance 157–60, 169,
 177
CEVA Logistics 54, 55–6
change management *see* dynamics of
 alliances
charters 35, 45
China 2
CHP (combined heat and power)
 136
Cisco *see* HP–Cisco alliance
client-supplier alliances *see* suppliers
co-opetition 43, 96
codes of conduct 40–1
coffee market 26, 75–80, 97
combined heat and power (CHP)
 136
committees 18, 33, 34, 35
communication 15, 42, 45–6
competition 4, 37–8, 145, 170
Comtan (drug) 81, 82
conflicts 33, 170–1
continuous negotiations 172, 177–9
contractors 59–60, 61, 62–4
contractual alliances 3–4, 16, 71–99
 advantages 72, 187
 control elements 10
 cultural differences 31
 disadvantages 188
 exit clauses 38
 goals 73
 HP–Cisco alliance 75, 89–97
 IT partnerships 89–97
 joint team model 74, 80–9
 knowledge-sharing 73
 lone ranger model 73, 89–97
 long-term relationships 72–3
 management of 73–4
 mirror structure 73, 77–8
 multiple points of contact model 73,
  74
 Novartis–Orion alliance 74–5, 80–9,
  97
 open-ended contracts 7
 peer-to-peer model 74, 89–97
 purposes 73
 relevance of model 97–8
 scope 97

Senseo alliance 74, 75–80, 97
 single point of contact model 73
 specialization model 74
 speed 98
 uses 97–8, 187
control-based alliances 3, 6–10, 12–13,
 22–3, 67
cooperatives 44, 147–51
costs 18–19, 29, 212
creative industries 7–8
cultural differences 31, 43, 79, 190

Danone 2
DE *see* Sara Lee/DE alliance
decision making process 31–3
Delta Airlines 26, 27, 103, 104, 114–17,
 169, 175, 177
democracy model 147–51, 163,
 164
design of alliances 21–50,
 181–94
 aims 21–2
 building blocks 22–4, 27–46
 challenges 6–13
 competition clauses 37–8
 control 6–13, 36–7, 184–6
 cost-cutting 18–19
 cultural differences 190
 decision making 31–3
 dynamics management 192
 exit agreements 38–9
 financial models 27–30, 207–14
 internal alignment 46–8
 joint ventures 139–40
 legal agreements 30–1
 lifecycle of alliances 183
 management short-sightedness
  19
 mistakes 13–19
 not-for-profits sector 192–4
 objectives 21–2
 organizational structure 34–6
 overview ix
 planning 36–7
 problems 13–19
 processes 173–5, 182
 public sector 192–4
 redesign process 173–5
 relevance 3–4
 requirements 21–2, 183–4
 risk identification 183
 run-through time 192
 scoring 189

strategy   24–7, 181–3
trust   6–13, 184–6
diagnostics   37
Disney–Siemens alliance   25
drug sector   30, 40, 44–5, 80–9, 82, 145, 198
dynamics of alliances   6–7, 17–18, 22, 167–79
  changes   171, 172–5
  continuous negotiations   172, 177–9
  design of alliances   192
  mutual adaptation   172, 177–9
  open alliances   200–1
  organizing for   175–7
  sources   169–71
  structural development model   176

electricity industry   136–42
Eli Lilly   44–5
energy companies   136–42
engineering sector   7–8
equity alliances   3, 17, 71–2, 121–44
  competitors   125
  financing needs   122–3
  goal alignment   125–6
  information asymmetry   123
  ownership structures   133–6
  reasons for   122–6
  shareholdings   133–6
  types   121
  value capture   124–5
escalation model   78, 86
European Union (EU)   61
EuroPower   136–42
evolution of alliances   195–6
exclusivity   37–8, 94, 155, 161
executive committees   34, 35
exit agreements   8, 38–9, 142
expertise   17, 32
external changes   171

financial models   27–30, 207–14
  intangible value   214
  non-pooling arrangements   209–10
  performance-based models   210
  pooling models   207–9
  property rights   212–13
fourth-party logistics (4PL)   54–5
Freemove alliance   145
freight industry   106

Future Store Initiative   12, 27–8, 151–7, 169, 209, 210

Gazprom   2
general assembly model   147–51, 163, 164
General Motors (GM)   15, 124–5
Germany, METRO Group   1, 2–3, 12, 27–8, 151–7, 169, 209, 210
Global Physical Logistics (GPL)
  alliance   54–6
GM (General Motors)   15, 124–5
go it alone   187–8
governance structures
  Amepco joint venture   137
  change management   167–9
  HP–Cisco alliance   92–4, 95, 96
  joint ventures   126–8
  KLM–Northwest Airlines
    alliance   106–7, 109–11, 118–19
  Novartis–Orion alliance   84–6, 88–9
  Obvion joint venture   129–30, 133
  overview ix
  Senseo alliance   77
  SkyTeam alliance   158–9
  vertical structures   170–1
GPL alliance   54–6

hierarchies   6, 196
history of alliances   195–6
Holst Centre joint venture   160–2
horticultural sector   44, 147–51
HP–Cisco alliance   75, 89–97, 169, 177
  business planning   92
  co-opetition   96
  conflicts   94
  metrics   92
  teams   92, 95–6

IBM   45, 198
implementation   191
incentives   36, 47, 53, 111–12, 210–11
independence of partners   171
information asymmetry   123
intangible value   214
Intel   123, 151
intellectual property (IP)   38, 161
intellectual property rights (IPR)   212–13
internal alignment   46, 201
internships   42

IT industry
  alliance lifetimes 7–8
  contractual alliance model 97
  go-to-market approaches 90–1
  HP–Cisco alliance 75, 89–97
  metrics 91
  multi-partner alliances 145

Japan 54
joint team model 74, 80–9
joint ventures (JV) 2, 121–44
  50/50 agreements 134–5
  advantages 187
  Amepco 136–42
  board members 141
  contracts 38
  dangers of 16–17
  disadvantages 188
  equity alliances 71–2
  exit clauses 142
  governance structure 126–8
  Holst Centre 160–2
  independent company
    comparison 126–8
  internationalization 72
  multi-partner alliances 147, 160–2,
    163, 164
  Obvion 128–33
  ownership structures 133–6
  Philips' use of 123
  shareholdings 133–6
  uses 121, 126, 142–3, 187
  virtual joint ventures 101–19, 122
joint vision 11
JV see joint ventures

KLM–Northwest Airlines alliance
    102–19, 122, 173
  decision making 110
  Enhanced Alliance Agreement
    108–13
  financial incentives 111–12
  governance structure 106–7, 109–11,
    118–19
  knowledge sharing 112–13
  mergers effect 114–17
  Open Skies Treaty 106
  personnel roles 112
  tensions 107–8
  timeline 105
  working groups 110–11
  see also Air France/KLM . . .
Kuehne + Nagel Ltd (KN) 54, 55

lead partner model 32–3, 147, 151–7,
    163, 164
leadership 41–2
legal agreements 30–1
letters of intent (LOIs) 30–1
Liberty alliance 145
lifecycle of alliances 5, 183, 203–4
lifetime of alliances 7–8
linking-pins 35–6
logistics suppliers 54–6
LOIs see letters of intent
lone ranger model 73, 89–97
lump sums 211

M&A see mergers and acquisitions
McCain 25
management/managers 6, 34, 176–7,
    178, 202–3
  leadership 41–2
  short-sightedness of 19
  see also governance structures
memoranda of understanding (MOU) 31,
    198, 199
mergers and acquisitions (M&A) 40,
    187, 188
METRO Group 1, 2–3, 12, 27–8, 151–7,
    169, 209, 210
Microsoft 145, 153
Millennium 30
mirror structure, contractual
    alliances 73, 77–8
mission statements 25
mistakes, design of alliances 13–19
mortgage business 128–33
MOU see memoranda of understanding
multi-partner alliances 145–65
  alliance support office model 147,
    157–60
  challenges 146–7
  decision making 146–7
  democracy model 147–51
  features of 162–3
  Future Store Initiative 151–7
  general assembly model 147–51
  Holst Centre joint venture 160–2
  joint ventures 147, 160–2, 163,
    164
  lead partner model 147, 151–7
  METRO Group 151–7
  opportunistic behavior 146
  Prominent cooperative 147–51
  SkyTeam alliance 157–60
  uses 145–6, 162–4

multiple points of contact model   73, 74
mutual adaptation   172, 177–9

NDAs *see* non-disclosure agreements
Netherlands
    Obvion joint venture   128–33
    Prominent cooperative   44, 147–51
    ProRail alliances   59–67
Nissan   122
non-disclosure agreements (NDAs) 30
norms and values   39–40
North Yorkshire Fire Service   25
Northwest Airlines (NWA) *see* KLM–Northwest Airlines alliance
not-for-profits sector   192–4
Novartis–Orion alliance   74–5, 80–9, 97, 169, 173, 177
    cost sharing   83
    governance structure   84–6, 88–9
    relationship building   86–7
    supply relationship   82–3
    teams   85
number of alliances   4
NUMMI joint venture   124–5
NWA *see* KLM–Northwest Airlines alliance

Obvion joint venture   128–33, 189
    control elements   133
    funding   130, 131
    governance structure   129–30, 133
    shareholder meeting   130
    shareholdings   129, 133
    supervisory board   130, 132
oil industry   2, 134
oneworld alliance   157, 159–60
open alliances   195–205
    characteristics   197
    control/risk   201
    dynamics of organizations   200–1
    internal alignment   201–3
    lifestyle of open alliances   203–4
    management practices   202–3
    strategic imperative   198
    vertical horizontalism   196–8
open book accounting   212
open-ended contracts   7

operational control   201
opportunism   9–10
Oracle   153
Orion *see* Novartis–Orion alliance
outsourcing contracts   52
overview ix

partner selection phase   5, 6
partnership surveys   83
patents, drugs   88
peer-to-peer mapping   35
peer-to-peer model   74, 89–97
penalties   210
pensions business   128
performance-based models   210
personnel exchanges   42
pharma sector   30, 40, 44–5, 80–9, 145, 198
Philips Electronics
    joint ventures   123–4
    Sara Lee/DE alliance   8, 17, 26, 27, 74, 75–80, 97, 168, 209
planning and control   36–7
pooling models   28, 207–9
power systems sector   54–6
procurement   51, 57
profit focus   28
project alliances   57–67
    alliance funds   59–65
    control elements   67
    dos and don'ts   58
    ProRail case study   59–67
    risk management   59–65, 68
    staffing   57, 58
    time pressures   57–8
    trust-building   65–6
project teams   34–5
Prominent cooperative   147–51
property rights   162, 212–13
ProRail alliances   59–67, 168
public sector   192–4
purchasing   52, 57

Rabobank   128–33, 189
RACI schemes   33
redesign of alliances   173–5
Renault–Nissan alliance/merger   122
reputation   44–5
    Business Partner Charter IBM   45
reseller relationships   91
reward systems   47, 210
    see also incentives
rights of use   213

risks
business risk 185
identification 183
management of 59–65, 68, 201
partner risk 185
Rolls–Royce alliance 54–6
Rosneft 2
Russia 2

Samsung 123
sanctions 36
SAP 153
Sara Lee/DE alliance 8, 17, 26, 27, 74, 75–80, 97, 168, 209
scope 26–7, 97
scorecards 36
securitization 130
sell-through model 90
sell-to model 90
sell-with model 90
Senseo alliance 8, 17, 26, 27, 74, 75–80, 97, 168, 209
cultural differences 79
governance structure 77
mirror structure 77–8
trust elements 80
shareholdings 133–6, 142
sharing arrangements 208–9
Siemens 25, 124
single point of contact model 73
SkyTeam alliance 157–60, 169, 177
social capital 10–12
social media 35
specialization model
contractual alliances 74
Senseo alliance 75–80
Stalevo (drug) 81, 82, 88
Star Alliance 35, 157, 160
steering committees 18, 33
strategic alliances
control-trust dilemma 1–20
design of 24–7, 181–94
open alliances 198
strategic imperatives
scope 26–7, 97
value proposition 26
vision, mission 24–5
structural development model 176
structure of alliances 6
subsidiarity principle 33
supermarket sector 1, 12, 27–8, 151–7, 169, 209, 210

suppliers 51–69
incentives 53
knowledge role 53, 67–8
long-term partnerships 52–7
margins focus 56, 68
Novartis–Orion alliance 82–3
project alliances 57–67
ProRail alliances 59–67
purchasing mindset 52
relationship duration 67
Rolls-Royce alliance 54–6
timing of alliances 67–8
Toyota alliances 53–4
types of alliances 52
when to form alliances 67–8

takeovers 124
targets
aligning 17–18, 46–7
defining 9–10
teams 34–5, 42
technological development 4
telecommunications sector 125
Telefonica 125
Telekom Austria 125
television business 123
temporary provisions 211
thresholds and caps 210
TNK-BP 2
"to each his own" model 209
tomato production 147–51
Toyota alliances 15, 18–19, 53–4, 124–5
TPV 123
Transcelerate alliance 198
transfer pricing 211
trust-based alliances 6–9, 12–13, 23, 43–4, 48
design of alliances 184–6
Future Store Initiative 156
limitations 13
Novartis–Orion alliance 80–9
project alliances 65–6
social capital building 10–12
trust-building, ProRail guidelines 66
TSMC 123
types of alliances ix

value creation 11
value propositions 26
values and norms 39–41
vertical horizontalism 196–8
vertical structures 170–1

virtual joint ventures 101–19
  Air France/KLM–Delta Airlines–Alitalia
    alliance 103, 114–17
  benefits 102
  financial transparency 102
  KLM–Northwest Airlines
    alliance 102–19, 122
  uses 119

vision and mission
  24–5
voting rights 32

Wahaha 2
Whirlpool 123
working groups 18,
  34–5

Index compiled by Indexing Specialists (UK) Ltd